Tranforming Government

General Editor: **R.A.W. Rhodes**, Professor of Political Science, Research School of Social Sciences, Australian National University.

The Economic and Social Research Council mounted the Whitehall Programme on 'The Changing Nature of Central Government in Britain' between 1994 and 1999. The Programme sought to repair gaps in our knowledge about the workings of British central government and to explain how and why British government changed in the post-war period. Also, because we cannot understand the effects of these changes by focusing only on Britain, the Programme analysed the experience of the advanced industrial democracies of Europe and the Commonwealth. Initially the 'Transforming Government' series reported the results of that five-year research programme, publishing ten books. Now, the series publishes any research consistent with its long-standing objectives:

- **Develop theory** – to develop new theoretical perspectives to explain why British government changed and why it differs from other countries.

- **Understand change** – to describe and explain what has changed in British government since 1945.

- **Compare advanced industrial democracies** – to compare change in Britain with other EU member and other states with a 'Westminster' system of government, especially the Old Commonwealth.

- **Build bridges** – to create a common understanding between academics and practitioners and to make academic research accessible to a varied audience covering 6th-formers and senior policy makers.

The series encompasses any theoretical approach to the study of government and governance. We welcome books on such notions as hollowing-out, governance, postmodernism, core executives, new institutionalism and cultural theory alongside the more traditional topics of the civil service, prime ministers and government departments. All books should meet the conventional criteria of theoretical and empirical rigour, but also seek to address topics of broad current interest that open the field of study to new ideas and areas of investigation.

Titles include:

Simon Bulmer, Martin Burch, Caitríona Carter, Patricia Hogwood and Andrew Scott
BRITISH DEVOLUTION AND EUROPEAN POLICY-MAKING
Transforming Britain to Multi-Level Governance

Nicholas Deakin and Richard Parry
THE TREASURY AND SOCIAL POLICY
The Contest for Control of Welfare Strategy

Neil C.M Elder and Edward C. Page
ACCOUNTABILITY AND CONTROL IN NEXT STEPS AGENCIES

Oliver James
THE EXECUTIVE AGENCY REVOLUTION IN WHITEHALL
Public Interest Versus Bureau-Shaping Perspectives

David Marsh, David Richards and Martin J. Smith
CHANGING PATTERNS OF GOVERNANCE IN THE UNITED KINGDOM
Reinventing Whitehall

Iain McLean
THE FISCAL CRISIS OF THE UNITED KINGDOM

Hugh Pemberton
POLICY LEARNING AND BRITISH GOVERNANCE IN THE 1960s

B. Guy Peters, R.A.W. Rhodes and Vincent Wright (*editors*)
ADMINISTERING THE SUMMIT
Administration of the Core Executive in Developed Countries

R.A.W. Rhodes (*editor*)
TRANSFORMING BRITISH GOVERNMENT
Volume One: Changing Institutions
Volume Two: Changing Roles and Relationships

Martin J. Smith
THE CORE EXECUTIVE IN BRITAIN

Kevin Theakston
LEADERSHIP IN WHITEHALL

Kevin Theakston (*editor*)
BUREAUCRATS AND LEADERSHIP

Patrick Weller, Herman Bakvis and R.A.W. Rhodes (*editors*)
THE HOLLOW CROWN
Countervailing Trends in Core Executives

Transforming Government
Series Standing Order ISBN 0–333–71580–2
(*outside North America only*)

You can receive future titles in this series as they are published by placing a standing order. Please contact your bookseller or, in case of difficulty, write to us at the address below with your name and address, the title of the series and the ISBN quoted above.

Customer Services Department, Macmillan Distribution Ltd, Houndmills, Basingstoke, Hampshire RG21 6XS, England

The Fiscal Crisis of the United Kingdom

Iain McLean
Professor of Politics, Oxford University
Official Fellow in Politics, Nuffield College

First published 2005 by
PALGRAVE MACMILLAN
Houndmills, Basingstoke, Hampshire RG21 6XS and
175 Fifth Avenue, New York, N. Y. 10010
Companies and representatives throughout the world

PALGRAVE MACMILLAN is the global academic imprint of the Palgrave
Macmillan division of St. Martin's Press, LLC and of Palgrave Macmillan Ltd.
Macmillan® is a registered trademark in the United States, United Kingdom
and other countries. Palgrave is a registered trademark in the European
Union and other countries.

ISBN 1–4039–0366–2

This book is printed on paper suitable for recycling and made from fully
managed and sustained forest sources.

A catalogue record for this book is available from the British Library.

Library of Congress Cataloging-in-Publication Data
McLean, Iain.
The fiscal crisis of the United Kingdom / Iain McLean.
      p. cm. – (Transforming government)
   Includes bibliographical references and index.
   ISBN 1–4039–0366–2 (cloth)
      1. Finance, Public–Great Britain–History. 2. Intergovernmental fiscal
relations–Great Britain–History. 3. Government spending policy–Great
Britain–History. 4. Regionalism–Great Britain–History. 5. Great
Britain–Politics and government. I. Title. II. Transforming government
(Palgrave Macmillan (Firm))

HJ1011.M355 2005
336.41–dc22   2004060143

10   9   8   7   6   5   4   3   2   1
14   13   12   11   10   09   08   07   06   05

Printed and bound in Great Britain by
Antony Rowe Ltd, Chippenham and Eastbourne

Contents

List of Tables

List of Figures

Preface

The United Kingdom is in a fiscal crisis because the centre taxes and the localities spend; and the centre's mechanisms for distributing money for the localities to spend are broken.

Almost all (96%) of UK tax revenue comes from taxes that are levied and collected by the central government. The devolved governments of Scotland, Wales, and Northern Ireland levy none independently. Only Scotland even has the power to levy taxes. But in 1997 Labour leader (soon to become Prime Minister) Tony Blair announced, even as he was proposing the tax power, that a Labour administration in Edinburgh would not use it. To date it has not. British local authorities possess only one tax base, namely domestic real estate. The main tax that they levy (Council Tax) raises only 4 per cent of total UK tax revenue and covers less than a quarter of their spending. Local government lost its penultimate tax base at the start of the Poll Tax fiasco, when the collection and distribution of business rates was centralised. Rising political protests against Council Tax increases led the UK Government to set up a Balance of Funding Review in summer 2003. This review, led by the English local government department the Office of the Deputy Prime Minister (ODPM), was wound up inconclusively in June 2004. The Treasury also took a hand. In autumn 2003 Chancellor of the Exchequer Gordon Brown commissioned a report from the business economist Kate Barker on the stickiness of the UK housing market. Her two reports in 2004 also put alternatives for local taxation on to the agenda. Her proposals are examined below, as are ideas that her analysis implies but that she did not propose.

Back in 1976, the Layfield Committee into local government finance (Cmnd 6453/1976) clearly stated the dilemma. In its view, there was a local option, in which government restored both tax bases and policy autonomy to the localities, and a central option, in which government retained all its tax bases, but stopped pretending that local spending bodies had any autonomy. Since 1976, central control of local spending has actually increased, but all governments since then have failed to take up Layfield's centralist option honestly. The fiction of local autonomy is maintained. The Labour government elected in 1997 started to speak enthusiastically about 'New Localism' in its second term. However, in June 2004, Home Secretary David Blunkett went to court to override the decision of Humberside Police Authority not to suspend or dismiss their Chief Constable. This book explores both honest centralism and honest localism.

The geography of taxing and spending is the same in any democracy. Rich areas yield more tax revenue per head, but have fewer needs for public spending per head. Poor areas are the opposite on both counts. Therefore any tax system needs to have a redistributive mechanism. In most countries, these are of two kinds – vertical and horizontal distribution. Vertical distribution concerns the grants that the centre gives to the localities in order to deliver local public services. Horizontal distribution concerns the mechanism for transferring some of the tax receipts of the rich localities to the poor ones. Because the centre has almost all the power to tax in the UK, it also does all the horizontal distribution. Vertical distribution is governed by three sets of formulae, only one of which works. The result is what Lord Barnett, who has given his name to the best-known formula, calls 'terrible unfairness'. He used to be proud of his formula's fame, but now disowns it.

This book explains how the UK got into this mess, and how it might get out. The history goes back to the dawn of public finance. It starts with the vertical distribution clauses of the Act of Union 1707 ('the Scottish Equivalent'), but speeds up in the Victorian age, when governments started serious spending on private goods other than bribes. From mid-Victorian times onwards, governments had to solve the vertical and horizontal problems. Mr Gladstone's attempt to solve them in the Irish Home Rule Bill of 1886 failed. The succeeding Unionist government laid the matter to rest, for a time, with the 'Goschen formula', or 'proportion', which dates to 1888. It returned to high politics in 1977, retreated under the Conservatives, and returned with full force with the devolution programme of the Labour government elected in 1997. By 2004, both the Barnett Formula, which governs transfers to the three devolved territories of the UK, and the mechanisms for distributing local government grant around England, were plainly broken, and the problem of vertical distribution will not be solved until they are fixed. This book offers a solution.

Chapter 1, *The setting of the problem,* introduces central concepts from the politics of public finance: vertical and horizontal distribution; incrementalism; centralism and localism; credible threats. It shows how poorly the UK performs in international comparison, especially with two Anglophone federations that might be the models for reform of the UK arrangements, namely Canada and Australia. It introduces some data to show why Joel (Lord) Barnett calls the outcome of his formula 'terribly unfair'. The problem is most acute along the Anglo-Scottish border, where each citizen of Berwickshire (Scotland) benefits from up to 40 per cent more public spending than each citizen of Berwick-on-Tweed (England).

Chapter 2. *Public Finance in the UK before 1888* looks at the politics of distribution before the Home Rule crisis of 1886. Starting with the Acts of Union of 1707 (between England and Scotland) and 1800–01 (between Great Britain and Ireland), governments in the newly United kingdom mostly allocated public goods such as foreign policy and a state religion (two, actually). A public good is anything whose benefits are indivisible and non-excludable; a private good is anything else. Governments have always spent money on private goods such as the expenses of the court and bribes to politicians. However, extensive spending on private goods for citizens dates to the 19th century with landmarks including the Municipal Corporations Act 1835 and various education acts from 1872 onwards.

Chapter 3, *Gladstone, Chamberlain, Goschen and the Webbs* deals with the acute crisis in public finance that broke out with W.E. Gladstone's Government of Ireland Bill of 1886. Gladstone's bill went down to defeat for many reasons, one of which was Joseph Chamberlain's objection to the financial clauses. Gladstone did not have a viable solution to the problem of finance. George Goschen, Chancellor of the Exchequer in the Unionist government of 1886–92, produced the first viable solution at a time when the Unionists were 'killing Home Rule with Kindness' – i.e. making very substantial fiscal transfers from Great Britain to Ireland. However, the Goschen proportion did not solve the chronic problems, even in Ireland or Scotland. And it did not determine the distribution of expenditure in England or Wales.

The hyper-energetic Fabians Sidney and Beatrice Webb set the agenda for distributive politics after the National Insurance Act 1911. They argued for a 'national minimum ... below which the individual, whether he likes it or not, cannot ... ever be allowed to fall'. After 1911, governments of all three parties edged towards that principle. None got there, nor did any solve the problems of horizontal or vertical equity. Various failures since 1911 in central-local relations, and in implementing unemployment insurance, illustrate this.

Chapter 4, *The origins of Barnett*, explains how the Goschen Formula, or Proportion, continued in a quiet backwater until the 1970s. It mattered hugely to a few people in Scotland, Ireland (later Northern Ireland), and the Treasury, but was politically unseen. But in 1974, the incoming Labour government responded to the challenge of Scottish nationalism by proposing devolution to Scotland (and to Wales for consistency's sake). This awakened an English backlash and brought the issue of relative public spending per head out into the open. The Labour government's devolution plan was destroyed in a backbench revolt spearheaded by MPs from the north-east of England in 1977. The government response was not only to arrange for Jimmy Carter to visit Newcastle upon Tyne, but also...(Chapter 5, *Barnett and devolution*)... the Barnett Formula and the Needs Assessment, explained in this chapter.

Barnett had two functions – as an anti-rounding-up device and as a convergence formula. It succeeded in the first role, but failed in the second until 1999, when it started to succeed. The Barnett Formula was written into the Scottish and Welsh devolution settlements of 1998, but it is fundamentally flawed. It operates against the interests of Wales and Northern Ireland, and soon will operate against those of Scotland as well. It ties the UK government and the devolved administrations (DAs) into an unhealthy embrace, with bizarre consequences in both directions. For instance, each year the DAs get an increase in their block grant which is entirely a function of decisions taken about spending in England, over which the DAs have no control. Conversely, they can manipulate their capital and current spending from within that grant in ways which knock on to expenditure on England – and the UK government, which doubles up unsatisfactorily as the government of England, has no control over that.

Chapter 6. *Health – getting it right*, examines the history of NHS health spending by formula since 1976, and explains why it has been relatively successful, while Chapter 7, *Local government – getting it wrong*, examines the least successful form of vertical distribution, viz., the distribution of funds for local authorities in England – by a formula called Standard Spending Assessment. In December 2001, then-Secretary of State Stephen Byers surprisingly announced that the critics of SSA had been right all along, and promised to abolish it. But, as with Railtrack earlier in the year, he did not explain what would come along next. Quite a number of trains (the Balance of Funding Express, the Barker Limited) have passed by, but none has stopped to deliver a reformed tax system.

Chapter 8, *The whys and wherefores of fiscal flows*, examines the fiscal flows both from the UK government to the devolved territories, and around England. One would expect public spending per head to have a fairly close inverse relationship with both social security spending per head and GDP per head. In fact, the relationship is extremely weak (especially by international standards). This chapter starts to outline a solution. It could apply either to four territories (England, Scotland, Wales, and Northern Ireland) or to 12 (Scotland, Wales, Northern Ireland, and each of the nine standard regions of England, assuming that they have elected regional assemblies). In the localist solution, the grant distributing body, the Territorial Grants Commission, is a strictly independent body, not an arm of the UK government, nor of any (or all) of the subnational governments. The proposed solution has two main components: an intergovernmental meeting (joint ministerial council) deciding on distribution of grant by a unanimity rule, and a publicly known default which would apply if the joint ministerial council failed to agree on a distribution. The publicly known default would be 'inverse GDP'. This means that new grant to each territory in the next time period would have an inverse relationship to that territory's GDP per head relative to the other territories of the UK.

The centralist solution maintains much of the same machinery, but treats England as a whole instead of giving any role to the nine English regions. However, honest centralism would involve dropping the pretence that the territories can have substantial policy autonomy except in cheap symbolic policies.

Both the localist and the centralist solution require better numbers and more openness than at present. Until 2004, statistics on regional public spending (especially within England) were unreliable and brittle. Recent work on improving the data is discussed.

Chapter 9, *The Australian* model and Chapter 10, *The Canadian model* compare UK practice with that in those two countries, with particular attention to the (Australian) Commonwealth Grants Commission (CGC), which might be a model for a future UK Territorial Grants Commission.

Chapter 11, *Honest localism and honest centralism*, returns finally to Layfield's dilemma. Honest localism would involve the devolution of tax bases, and of policy, to localities. Honest centralism would involve ceasing to pretend that localities had policy independence. I revisit the Territorial Grants Commission in the light of the evidence from Australia and Canada and ask whether it could be made politician-proof.

It is a pleasure to acknowledge the many debts I incurred while writing this book. It arises from the Leverhulme Trust programme 'Nations and regions in the UK', and from policy work with the Office of the Deputy Prime Minister (ODPM) and HM Treasury. My Research

Officer on the Leverhulme project, Alistair McMillan, had a substantial role in data collection and analysis for this book. Although he modestly declined my invitation to co-author this book, it would not have been possible without his work. It also benefits from the generous help of colleagues in other projects in the Leverhulme programme (based at the Constitution Unit, University College, London), and in the contemporaneous ESRC Devolution Programme, comprising multiple research projects around the UK. I likewise acknowledge the help I received from the tiny community of UK fiscal federalism academics, especially David Bell and David Heald. Dan Corry, Bob Elliott, Christopher Foster, Will Paxton, Tony Vickers and Dave Wetzel commented helpfully on draft chapters. I have been talking fiscal federalism for four years to Stewart Wood, who has put up with it very patiently. David Penny worked very efficiently on checking and sourcing data for the tables and on layout and preparation. To all of these my grateful thanks.

In 2002 and 2003 I led a research contract for the ODPM, with co-funding and support from the Treasury and the Department for Environment, Food, and Rural Affairs (DEFRA), to 'identify the flow of domestic and European expenditure into the English regions'. We reported in September 2003, and our report has led to substantial changes in the reported data and in how they are collected. Compiling the report took us into the heart of UK public finance. We are extremely grateful to officials in HM Treasury and the reporting departments for the access to their raw data which, as far as we know, no analyst outside government had ever previously seen. Our Advisory Committee, containing representatives of the three sponsoring departments, of the Office for National Statistics, and of users of regional statistics, made many helpful suggestions that found their way into our report and therefore into this book. So have officials in HM Treasury, the ODPM itself, and the devolved administrations, whom it is conventional not to name. I think that is a pity, because they have been uniformly helpful. Needless to say, neither the Leverhulme Trust nor any government department should be held responsible for any opinions expressed in this book.

I incurred further debts during highly informative research trips to Australia (autumn 2002) and Canada (summer 2003). Grateful thanks to Geoffrey Brennan, for arranging a Visitorship in the Social and Political Theory Programme, Research School of Social Sciences, Australian National University; to Michael L'Estrange (Australian High Commissioner to the UK), Malcolm Nicholas (Assistant Secretary,

Commonwealth Grants Commission) and their staff for arranging visits in Australia; to George Anderson (formerly Privy Council Office, later Natural Resources Canada), Bill Lawton (Canadian High Commission, London), and staff of the Québec Government Office in London for arranging visits in Canada; and to the many Australian and Canadian public servants, at federal and state (provincial) levels, and academics who answered my idiot questions about their public finance.

Earlier versions of some of this material have appeared in *Fiscal Studies*, *Public Administration*, and *Political Quarterly*. I am grateful to the editors of all of these, and to my co-authors Gavin Cameron, Chris Wlezien and Alistair McMillan for permission to re-use this material. Some of it will be offered in 2005 as evidence to the Lyons Inquiry into local taxation.

Glossary

ACA	Area Cost Adjustment
ACT	Australian Capital Territory
Alta	Alberta
AME	Annually Managed Expenditure: a UK Treasury public expenditure control total
ATSIC	Aboriginal and Torres Strait Islander Council
AUD	Australian dollars
Barnett Formula	The formula used since 1978 to allocate block grant to Scotland, Wales, and Northern Ireland. The three territories entered the Formula at different times, but it has been used in them all since the early 1980s.
Barnett squeeze	The convergence property of the Barnett Formula: in the long run it tends to bring spending per head in each territory to which it applies to an equal per capita level with England
BC	British Columbia
BMA	British Medical Association (trade union and professional association of UK doctors)
BNA Act	British North America Act 1867 (known in Canada as Constitution Act 1867)
BQ	Bloc Québécois
CA	Canadian Alliance
CGC	Commonwealth Grants Commission (Australia)
CGT	capital gains tax (UK)
CHST	Canada Health & Social Transfer
CIPFA	Chartered Institute of Public Finance and Accountancy
CPA	comprehensive performance assessment
DA	devolved administration (i.e. any of Scotland, Wales, or Northern Ireland)
DEFRA	Department for Environment, Food, and Rural Affairs
DEL	Departmental Expenditure Limit: a UK Treasury public expenditure control total
DfES	Department for Education and Skills

DHSS	Department of Health and Social Security
Dreadnought	a class of British battleships inaugurated in 1906 with better armour-plating and with big guns of one calibre. An engine of the pre-1914 UK-German arms race
DTI	Department of Trade and Industry
DTLR	Department of Transport, Local Government, and the Regions. In 2002 a separate Department for Transport was created, and the remainder of DTLR became ODPM, *q.v.*
DWP	Department for Work and Pensions
ecological fallacy	the fallacy of making inferences at the wrong level of aggregation, e.g. of making inference about individuals from aggregate-level data. Example: areas with a high prevalence of non-white voters swung disproportionately to the Conservatives in the 1960s and 1970s. It is incorrect to infer from this that non-white voters are disproportionately Conservative.
eminent domain	term in (mostly US) law denoting the power of the state to appropriate private property for public use, especially for constructing utilities such as railroads, highways, or power lines.
EPC	equal per capita [expenditure]
EU	European Union
GOI Bill	Government of Ireland Bill: First (1886); Second (1893); or Third (1912, enacted 1914 but operation suspended till 1920; in 1920 superseded by Government of Ireland Act 1920 and by Anglo–Irish Treaty 1921)
golden rule	UK public expenditure rule introduced by Chancellor Gordon Brown in 1997. It states that, on average over the economic cycle, the Government will borrow only to invest and not to fund current expenditure
Goschen formula (also Goschen proportion)	The ratio 80:11:9, in which Chancellor G.J. Goschen split some assigned revenues to England (with Wales); Scotland; and Ireland. After Irish independence in 1921, the Goschen proportion of 80:11 continued to govern some assignments of public spending between England & Wales and Scotland

GDP	gross domestic product
GO	Government Office (for an English region)
GP	general practitioner
GSP	gross State product (Australia)
GST	goods and services tax (=VAT)
hereditament	a parcel of real property
HFE	horizontal fiscal equalisation
IHT	inheritance tax (UK)
inverse GDP rule	proposal that incremental grant to each territory should be inversely proportional to its GDP per head
LABGI	Local Authority Business Growth Incentive scheme, see http://www.local.odpm.gov.uk/finance/labgi.htm.
LCA	labour cost adjustment, the principal component of ACA, *q.v.*
LGFFGD	Local Government Finance Formula Grant Distribution. Successor to SSA, *q.v.*. See http://www.local.dtlr.gov.uk/review/consult/index.htm.
Lib	Liberal
LIT	local income tax
LVT	land value tax
Man, MB	Manitoba
Median voter	voter at the median of the main issue dimension (i.e. with exactly as many voters to her left as to her right). *Median voter theorem*: if political issues can be shown on a single dimension, then the median voter's optimum is unbeatable under any well-behaved voting procedure.
moral hazard	The risk that the presence of a contract will alter the behaviour of one or more parties. Especially in insurance, where coverage against a loss increases the likelihood of risk-taking behaviour by the insured
NB	New Brunswick
NDP	New Democratic Party
NHS	National Health Service (UK)
NNDR	National Non-Domestic Rate. The GB tax on non-domestic real estate. Since 1990 the rateable value of businesses is set by an independent

	government agency (the Valuation Service). The rate in the £ is set by central government. The proceeds are collected by local authorities, but remitted to central government, which redistributes them back on an EPC basis to local authorities, so that in effect they form part of the transfer from central to local government.
Nfld, NL	Newfoundland & Labrador
NS	Nova Scotia
NSW	New South Wales
NT	Northern Territory (Australia)
NUTSx	Nomenclature of Units for Territorial Statistics (NUTS), a European Union hierarchy that provides a single uniform breakdown for the production of regional statistics for the European Union. The three upper levels of NUTS in the UK are: NUTS1: nine Government Office Regions in England plus Scotland, Wales and Northern Ireland; NUTS2: 37 areas – sometimes referred to as sub-regions;·NUTS3: 133 areas – generally groups of unitary authorities or districts
NWT	North West Territory (Canada)
ODPM	Office of the Deputy Prime Minister (since 2002 the name of the UK government department that deals with English local government and English regions. Previously DTLR, *q.v.*)
ONS	Office for National Statistics (UK)
Ont	Ontario
Pareto-superior	having the property that no player is made worse off, and at least one player is made better off
PAYE	Pay as you Earn: the UK system for deducting income tax from payroll income at source.
PC	Progressive Conservative
PCO	Privy Council Office (Canada: functional equivalent of Cabinet Office in UK)
PEI	Prince Edward Island
PESA	*Public Expenditure Statistical Analyses*: an annual publication from HM Treasury
Personal property, personalty	all assets other than land and buildings
PPP	purchasing power parity

Precept (n. and v.)	a demand from one authority to another that the second should collect local tax on behalf of the first; to issue such a demand.
probate duty	UK tax upon the gross value of the personal (as opposed to real) property of a deceased person. In 1894 it was merged with tax on real property as *estate duty* (now inheritance tax).
Prog. Con.	Progressive Conservative
PSA	public service agreement
PSS	personal social services
RAWP	Resource Allocation Working Party
RDA	regional development agency
Real property, realty	land and buildings
riding	parliamentary constituency (Canada).
Qld	Queensland
Que, QC	Québec
S&P	Standard & Poors
SA	South Australia
Sask, SK	Saskatchewan
Sewel motion	Motion in the Scottish Parliament, inviting the UK Parliament to legislate on a matter even though it is devolved to Scotland. Named after a junior minister at the time of the Scotland Act 1998, who introduced the power in a Lords amendment
SDLP	Social Democratic & Labour Party (Northern Ireland)
SNP	Scottish National Party
SPP	special purpose payments (from the Commonwealth of Australia to States)
SR200x	(Comprehensive) Spending Review: published by the UK Chancellor of the Exchequer every even-numbered year since 1998. Announces departments' spending limits (DELs, *q.v.*) for an overlapping 3-year period beginning on 1 April in the year after the review
SSA	Standard Spending Assessment: the basis for English local government finance from 1990 until 2002
St Andrews House	Government office block in Edinburgh opened 1939: principal site of Scottish administration since then

Stormont	suburb in east of Belfast: site of Northern Ireland government and administration since 1922
Sustainable investment rule	UK public expenditure rule introduced by Chancellor Gordon Brown in 1997. It states that public sector net debt must not exceed a set proportion of GDP (currently fixed at 40 per cent)
Tas	Tasmania
TES	Total Expenditure on Services: a public expenditure control total defined by the UK Treasury as 'spending within Total Managed Expenditure [*q.v.*] that can be allocated by function'
TME	Total Managed Expenditure: a UK Treasury public expenditure control total
Transport House	former headquarters office of the Labour Party, shared with the Transport & General Workers' Union.
UBR	Uniform Business Rate: strictly, the rate in the pound at which NNDR, *q.v.*, is levied; in practice, used as an alternative acronym for NNDR
VAT	value added tax
VFI	vertical fiscal imbalance
Vic	Victoria
virement	the process of transferring public expenditure from one expenditure category to another
WA	Western Australia

1
The Setting of the Problem

Like any modern state, the UK has to solve the problem of fiscal federalism. Essentially, the centre taxes, but the localities spend. In 2001, the centre raised 96 per cent of UK tax revenue; local authorities only 4 per cent (Travers 2001, p. 135). So the centre must allocate grant to the localities. The sums of money involved are huge, as they cover a large part of public spending, both current and capital. Therefore, the most minute adjustment of the formulae can have huge distributional consequences. Three quite different formulae are used: one, the notorious 'Barnett Formula', to allocate block grant to Scotland, Wales, and Northern Ireland for devolved services; the second, to allocate grant to English local authorities; the third, to allocate grant to English health authorities. The combined consequence of the three procedures is an allocation that is very hard to justify, politically, socially, or economically. Some regions of the country seem to do conspicuously better than others.

- Politically, the 'losing' regions ask why they are doing so badly; while the 'gaining' territories complain that they are in a 'Barnett squeeze' (see Glossary).
- It is hard to see what social ends are advanced by such apparently arbitrary inequalities in public spending per head as Table 1.1 shows. It suggests severe problems of inter-territory equity.
- Neither the Barnett nor the English local government grant system gives the territories an incentive to become economically efficient.

Table 1.1 introduces the problem.

The first column of Table 1.1 shows the spending per head on what corresponded, as closely as the source permits, to those domestic

1

Table 1.1 Public spending per head, regions of the UK, 2001, £

Region	Public expenditure/head on 'devolved' service	GDP/head	Social security spending/head	Covered by Barnett formula?	With representative government?
South-east	2,550	15,098	1,450	n	n
East	2,624	15,094	1,518	n	n
Greater London	3,431	16,859	1,636	n	y
South West	2,654	11,782	1,658	n	n
West Midlands	2,736	11,900	1,755	n	n
East Midlands	2,632	12,146	1,648	n	n
Yorkshire and Humberside	2,905	11,404	1,764	n	n
North West	2,928	11,273	1,960	n	n
North East	3,022	10,024	2,126	n	n
Wales	3,289	10,449	2,013	y	y
Scotland	3,638	12,512	1,920	y	y
Northern Ireland	4,347	10,050	2,077	y	y

Sources: HM Treasury, *Public Spending Statistical Analysis 2002–3*, derived from Tables 8.6b and 8.12b. Column 1 reports (for the Barnett territories) 'Identifiable total managed expenditure per head 2000–2001, and (for the non-Barnett territories) 'Identifiable general government expenditure per head, by region and function, 2000–2001'. In each case the total for Social Security, which is a non-devolved function, are deducted from total regional spending and reported separately in column 3. Office for National Statistics, *Regional GDP 1999*, summary table. All sources Crown copyright.

services that are devolved functions in Scotland, Wales, and Northern Ireland, the three 'Barnett' territories. In descending order cf size, the big three such services were *Health and personal social services; Education;* and *Law, order, and protective services.*[1] In Scotland, Wales, and Northern Ireland, the allocation of spending within and among devolved headings is entirely the responsibility of the devolved administrations. Although they receive block grant which is a function of the amount spent in England on health, education, and so on, they are under no obligation to split their spending on these programmes in the same proportions as in England. The UK government can also exercise no control over any alterations in their balance of capital and revenue spending.

In England, the UK government can and does exercise tight control over spending in the regions. The system discourages or forbids virement (see Glossary) between one service and another, and encourages spending bodies (local authorities and health authorities) to stick very closely to UK government priorities.

Social security spending is excluded from column 1 and reported separately in column 3 of Table 1.1. There are two reasons for this:

1. Social security is not a devolved programme. Terms and conditions are identical throughout the UK.
2. It is an entitlement programme. The number of people who qualify for, and claim, each entitlement wholly drives spending on it.

The higher the social security spending per region, the higher the prevalence of poverty, and therefore, *prima facie*, the greater need for government to spend on other programmes. Another *prima facie* indicator of regional needs is GDP per head. Official figures for this are in Table 1.1, column 2. Until the mid-1990s these data seriously underestimated the disparity between the south-east (regions South East, East, and Greater London) and the rest of the country (Cameron and Muellbauer 2000). This may cast its shadow forward because past grant is a very powerful predictor of present grant.

Almost all governments, when they distribute the proceeds of centrally raised taxes for the localities to spend, do so under some sort of equalisation arrangement, so that poor areas get more per head and rich areas get less. The equalisation arrangements in two mature federal systems, Canada and Australia, are described later in this book. There are good reasons both of efficiency and of equity for equalisation, and it is supposed to be built in to the arrangements for transfers within

England. The equity reasons are self-evident. As to efficiency, it is reasonable to suppose that a pound spent improving infrastructure, health, or human capital where they are low is more effective than one spent where they are high. Therefore, there should be a strong positive correlation between social security spend per head and other public spending per head, and a strong inverse correlation between GDP per head and non-social-security spending per head.

Table 1.2 shows that, in the years shown, the correlation between GDP and public expenditure per head was only slightly negative at –0.265. Figure 1.1 graphs the relationship between them. It shows that the relationship would be reasonably well-behaved if three outliers, namely Scotland, Northern Ireland, and London, were not there. If we remove these three cases from the analysis, the correlation between PUBEXP and GDP becomes –0.769.

Table 1.2   Correlations among GDP, public expenditure per head and social security expenditure per head for the 12 UK regions in 2001

		GDP	SOCSEC
PUBEXP	Pearson Correlation	–.265	.683
GDP	Pearson Correlation		–.770

GDP: GDP per head
PUBEXP: public expenditure per head
SOCSEC: social security expenditure per head
Sources for Table 1.2: as Table 1.1.

These tables and figures provide the setting for our enquiry. UK governments have professed for a very long time to believe in redistribution to poor people and poor areas. Redistribution of tax revenue from England to Scotland goes back to 1707, when the 'Scottish Equivalent' was carried to Edinburgh in carts guarded by dragoons. Two of the UK's leading banks – the Bank of Scotland and Royal Bank of Scotland – both did their first business on Anglo-Scottish fiscal transfers. Similar redistribution from Britain to Ireland goes back implicitly to 1801 (because Britain undertook to defend Ireland without taxing Ireland to pay for it) and explicitly to the 1880s. Redistribution from rich areas of England and Wales to poor areas dates to the first formal transfer programme in 1888, and was accentuated by the first programmes for social security (state pensions in 1909; National Insurance against sickness and unemployment in 1911). If 300 years of redistribution is factored into the geography of public spending, one would expect

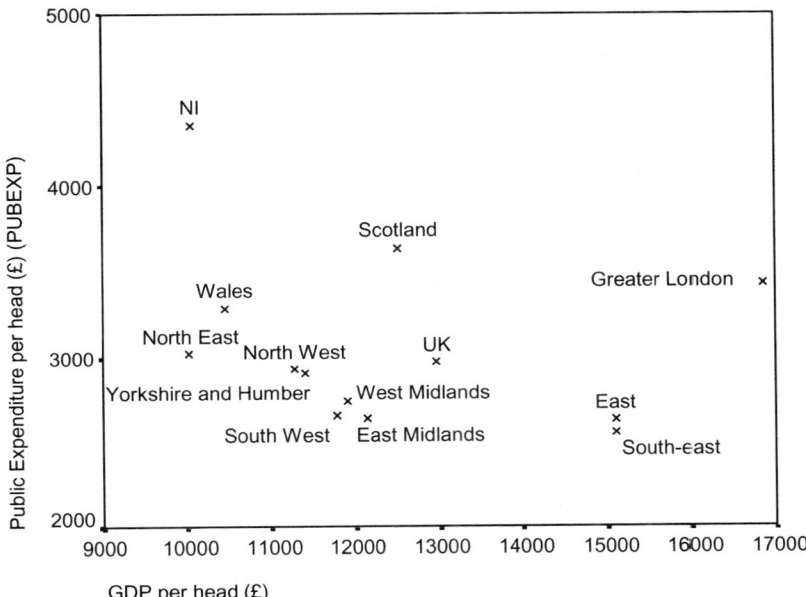

Figure 1.1 Scatter-plot of per capita public expenditure and GDP, for UK regions and territories
Source: As Table 1.1.

the correlation between public spending and GDP to be strongly negative. Yet it is almost zero. That is the fundamental puzzle this book addresses.

Public economics, public finance and public choice

To address it I rely on the tools of economics and political science. From public finance, a branch of public economics, I take some concepts and some measurement tools. However, I believe that public choice has more to tell us than does public finance about the distribution of public expenditure around the UK. Public choice started as a branch of economics, but is now mostly (and correctly) regarded as an approach to political science.

Here are some data first. Table 1.3 shows the changing composition of the UK tax base since 1707.

In 1707, when England and Scotland united to form Great Britain, the largest tax base was land, followed by excise duties (on commodities such as alcohol and tobacco) and customs duties (tariffs). Two of

Table 1.3   UK governmental receipts at current prices, selected years since 1707

Year	Total, £m	Central government receipts, Of which, %							Local government receipts Total, £m	Local government receipts Of which, %		
		Customs	Excise	Stamp duties	Post office	Land taxes	Property and income tax	Other		(Poor) rates [g]	County & police rates	Trading income
Note a			b	c	d			e	f			
1707	5.47	24.97	31.90	1.59	1.04	37.18		3.33	n/a			
1801 [h]	39.10	22.51	29.67	8.18	3.32	11.76	14.83	9.72	5.63	94.92	5.08	
1821	61.60	20.62	48.54	11.04	3.25	13.47		3.08	8.38	92.66	7.34	
1851	56.30	39.43	27.35	11.55	4.26	6.75	9.59	1.07	7.36	89.00	11.00	
1885	89.60	22.10	28.46	12.95	11.05	3.24	16.96	5.25	34.50	84.06		15.94
1914	226.70	17.07	18.66	15.88	13.10	1.15	26.16	7.98	127.10	62.16		37.84
1922	914.00	13.46	18.56	8.65	5.83	0.31	41.47	11.73	298.00	63.52		36.48
1939	1006.20	22.49	14.89	9.78	8.64	0.00	41.77	2.43	470.10	45.48		54.52
1965	7727.00	25.98	17.50	4.87	0.72	0.00	47.81	3.11	1919.00	63.99		36.01

Table 1.3 UK governmental receipts at current prices, selected years since 1707 – *continued*

Year	Total, £m	Central government receipts, Of which, %							Local government receipts, Total, £m	Local government receipts, Of which, %		
		Customs	Excise	Stamp duties	Post office	Land taxes	Property and income tax	Other		(Poor) rates [g]	County & police rates	Trading income
Note a			b	c	d		e		f			
1979	50321.00		38.12	2.09	0.00	0.00	56.98	2.81	10669.00	61.17		38.78
2003 [i]	392600.00		30.82	2.55	0.00	0.00	55.43	11.21	25600.00	69.14		30.86

Notes:

a The end of the accounting year varied. The numbers given are for the accounting year into which most of the given calendar year fell.

b Includes motor vehicle duty from 1939.

c Includes death duties from 1885.

d Includes telegraph from 1885 and telephone from 1914. NB these are gross takings, not net proceeds to central government. 1965: includes only broadcast receiving licences.

e Not given in source: calculated by subtraction.

f England & Wales only to 1851; GB excluding Ireland thereafter.

g County and police rates not separately reported after 1884. All local government own revenue (excluding loans, and transfers from central government) is from rates and charges from this point onward.

h Local government data for 1802.

i With tax credits netted off against property and income tax.

Sources: Mitchell, Abstract of British Historical Statistics and Mitchell and Jones, 2nd Abstract of Historical Statistics (Cambridge 1962/1971); HM Treasury, Budget 2004, C4; HM Treasury, National Accounts (HMT publications Crown copyright).

the great radicals of the 18th century, Robert Burns and Tom Paine, were both excisemen (although Burns wrote the song *The deil's awa, the deil's awa, He's danced awa wi'th'exciseman*). Adam Smith became a commissioner of customs for Scotland, although his *Wealth of Nations* shows that customs duties are a bad tax. By 1801, when Ireland joined the Union, land taxes had dropped away, although stamp duty should perhaps be regarded as a surrogate land tax, levied on transactions in land rather than ownership of land. Property and income appear as a tax base for the first time. Prime Minister William Pitt the Younger introduced income tax to help pay for the Napoleonic Wars in 1799. It was abolished at the end of those wars, but Prime Minister Sir Robert Peel reintroduced in it 1842 and it has remained ever since.

By 1885, when a 'hung' General Election forced Irish Home Rule on to the political agenda, customs revenue had dropped because of the Repeal of the Corn Laws in 1846 and the subsequent UK move to uni-lateral free trade. Property and income had grown as a tax base, but excise was the largest, and stamp duty and customs remained substan-tial. Not until 1922, the year most of Ireland left the Union, does prop-erty and income (mostly income) assume its modern predominance as the largest tax base. In 2002–03, the latest year for which data are avail-able, the top five taxes were, in descending order, income tax, social security payments (really another form of income tax), VAT, corpora-tion tax, and fuel duties. Income tax accounted for 29 per cent of tax receipts; social security payments, 17 per cent; VAT, a further 17 per cent; corporation tax 8 per cent, and fuel duties 6 per cent.

The tax base for local government in the UK has always been prop-erty. Property taxes are traditionally known as 'rates', and are levied on either the capital value or the annual rental value of premises. Table 1.3 shows that rates have never been one of the largest sources of tax revenue. In the nineteenth century rates for special purposes were gradually added as the scope of local government increased, but these were later consolidated into just one rate payment. Rates on domestic property were abolished in 1987–8 in favour of the poll tax (except in Northern Ireland). The poll tax was in turn abolished in 1990 in favour of Council Tax, which is a form of rate based on a coarse banding of house values in 1991. Rates on businesses were transferred from local government to central government in 1988. The impact of these changes is discussed in later chapters.

Table 1.4 attempts to chart the make-up of public expenditure over the same period. This is a harder task, because the data are more elusive and definitions change over time. But some trends are clear.

Table 1.4 UK general government expenditure at current prices, selected years since 1707

| Year | Total, £m | Of which, % | | | | | | | | |
| | a | Debt charges | Civil Government – Education | Civil Government – Health | Civil Government – Social Security and Personal Social Services | Civil Government – Total | Military | Cost of collection | Special votes | Other |
Note								b	c	d
1707	8.747	21.10				7.45	65.99			5.45
1801	65.5	30.38				8.55	57.25	3.66		0.15
1821	58.4	54.62				9.59	28.60	7.36		-0.17
1851	54	52.22				12.78	25.37	9.07		0.56
1885	92.2	25.49				20.82	32.21	10.85		10.63
1914	559.5	3.88				10.72	14.39	5.49	63.81	1.72
1922	812.5	39.88				37.23	12.50	7.53		2.86
1939	1401	16.32				31.49	44.71	6.69		0.79
1965	8871	12.81				56.16	23.18	1.15		6.70
1980	111,800	8.20	11.52	11.06	22.56	69.09	10.02	0.85		11.84
2003	458,997	4.54	12.97	16.47	32.64	88.42	6.09	0.83		0.12

Notes:

a The end of the accounting year varied. The numbers given are for the accounting year into which most of the given calendar year fell.

b But this column includes running costs of post office (and telegraph). In modern accounting procedures this would be netted off against receipts. The finances of the Post Office were separated from the Exchequer from 1st April 1961 following the Post Office Act 1961 and are thus excluded from this date onwards.

c Presumably for war, so should be counted with 'Military'.

d Not given in source: calculated by subtraction. Negative number for 1821 indicates error in data.

Sources: Mitchell, Abstract of British Historical Statistics and Mitchell and Jones, 2nd Abstract of Historical Statistics (Cambridge 1962/1971); HM Treasury, Budget 2004; HM Treasury, National Accounts (HMT publications Crown copyright); I am grateful to Christopher Wlezien and his co-authors for the use of their standardised figures of spending on services for 1980.

Until 1885, public expenditure in the UK went almost entirely on two things: military costs and debt servicing. The proportion going on military spending dropped sharply after the Napoleonic wars ended in 1815. But those wars, like others before and since, were financed largely out of new government debt. Therefore the Victorians continued to pay for the cost of past wars in debt servicing, even though they were paying less on current wars than their predecessors. The share of debt charges in national expenditure had just reached a historic low in 1914, when Archduke Franz Ferdinand was assassinated in Sarajevo.

The whole of the rest of civil government remained small until 1885. We take 1885 as a data point because it marked the dawn of redistributive expenditure. Although Mr Gladstone's conversion to Irish Home Rule in that year failed to produce Home Rule, it did lead to a programme of increased public spending in the poorest parts of the UK, beginning with rural Ireland and extending to Britain as the Edwardian welfare state accelerated. Old age pensions and unemployment insurance redistributed income from taxpayers to recipients of benefit. This had spatial implications as the first were concentrated in some places and the second in others.

The late Victorian boom in the cities involved an increase in local public expenditure. In the 19th century, this was not redistributive, except within cities. Cities raised their own rates and spent them within their own boundaries. However, it became redistributive, starting in 1888 with the first formula funding of local authorities. Cities in poor areas could raise less in rates, and needed to spend more on services, than cities in rich areas. It was probably inevitable that the proportion of local expenditure that was met by grants from the centre rose steadily through the 20th century, although the biggest single spike was as recently as 1990. As the government became more and more desperate in the wake of the Poll Tax disaster, it halved the proportion of local expenditure that was financed from local taxation and flung central money at local services to keep down the rates of Poll Tax and its successor, Council Tax.

The year 1885 also marks the first General Election in which most male householders had the vote. Each extension of the franchise (in 1832, 1867, 1885, 1918 and 1928) extended the electorate down the social and economic scale. It added more poor people than rich people to the electorate. Therefore, the median voter was someone lower in the income distribution than previously. In public choice theory, the median voter is deservedly a famous figure. If all voters are arranged along some line such as income per head, the median voter is the person exactly in the middle of the queue. Marxists always argue that governments redistribute resources to the rich; conservatives that they redistribute resources to the poor. The theory of public choice says that they redistribute resources to the middle – more strictly, to the median. A very simple piece of maths, the *median voter theorem*, underlies this. Assume, first, that each voter is concerned with his or her own welfare. They do not have to be exclusively concerned. They may care about animals, national glory, or the Third World as well. It is only necessary to assume that they have *some* concern for their own welfare for the result to go through.

Assume, now, a two-party system. Another important result, *Duverger's Law*, states that *the simple-majority single-ballot system favours the two-party system* (Duverger 1954, p. 217). In the British (and Canadian, Indian and US) electoral system, it becomes common knowledge that only two parties have a chance of election in each constituency. Therefore third parties abandon the fight, or their supporters abandon it for them. The two remaining parties will both pitch their appeal at the median voter. One might expect the Rich People's Party to pitch its appeal to the rich and the Poor People's Party to pitch its appeal to the poor. The median voter theorem (MVT) contradicts this. Suppose the Rich People's Party goes anywhere other than to the median voter's favourite tax-and-spend combination. We can assume that the voter at, say, the 67th percentile of the income distribution, who is fairly rich, would prefer both lower taxation and lower public spending than the voter at the median point. But if the Rich People's Party writes a manifesto that perfectly satisfies voters at the 67th percentile of the distribution, the Poor People's Party need only write a manifesto that perfectly satisfies voters at the 66th percentile. Then the Poor People will win the next election by a majority of 66 per cent to 34 per cent.

Of course this model is oversimplified. It ignores the possibility of political activists, who will tend to pull the parties away from the median. It also ignores the possibility that the poorest and the richest will abstain in disgust, which will have the same effect. Nevertheless, the MVT embodies a powerful truth which we can expect to observe when we explore where governments spend the proceeds of taxes.

The second main concept we take from public choice is the *credible threat*. It is rational for political agents to threaten the government with unpleasant consequences if it does not do what they want, but only if the threat is credible. It is credible if the government has reasonable grounds for believing that it would be carried out if the government does not concede the threatener's request. Specifically, the peripheries of the UK have all posed a credible threat to England at different times in British history. Northern and western Wales posed one in the time of Edward I (late 13th century). That is why Caernarfon, Beaumaris, Conwy and Harlech Castles were built to contain it, successfully. Eastern Wales was less warlike but the English government still needed to license semi-independent marcher lords to contain the Welsh threat. That explains Ludlow, now the gastronomic capital of the Midlands. By 1707, when our story starts, Wales posed no credible threat.

The Scots repulsed Edward I and Edward II at Stirling (1297) and Bannockburn (1314). From about 1560, the Scottish Reformation took a more extreme form than the English. Scotland became Calvinist, England was Erastian. At the other religious extreme, Scotland also looked like an attractive route for Catholic dynasties to (re)gain control of Britain. From then until 1745, these two security threats remained credible. It is essential to grasp that the English needed the Union of 1707 more than the Scots did, to secure their northern frontier. Scotland posed a credible threat, and extracted important concessions in return for Union in 1707.

Ireland also contained both Calvinists and Catholics, but in opposite proportions. The Catholics were the larger, and entirely credible, threat to the Union. Enemy forces invaded the British Isles through Ireland in 1690, 1798, and 1916. Irish Catholic discontent had to be appeased for the Union to work. Hence the Union of 1801. But the British promise of Catholic emancipation for Ireland was broken as soon as the Union was complete. Therefore it was never legitimate in Irish Catholic eyes. The potential for armed rebellion was always there. The potential for electoral rebellion would be realised, and was, as soon as most Irishmen got the vote, in 1885. By 1912, the UK government seemed to be stuck in a zero-sum conflict. The majority Catholics of Ireland demanded Home Rule for the whole of Ireland. The minority Protestants, mostly in the north-east but also located in Dublin and the country estates of the Ascendancy, demanded that the whole of Ireland must stay in the Union. The results were independence for most of Ireland and a heavily-subsidised, predominantly Protestant, province in the north-east, which became Northern Ireland.

No English region since 1707 has posed a comparably credible threat to the centre. Only unusual circumstances, such as those that led to the defeat of the government's proposals for Scottish and Welsh devolution in 1977, would give any of the English regions a credible threat.

Unlike public choice, public finance begins by assuming politics away, but in sophisticated hands such as those of Adam Smith, the politics quickly come back in. Smith's analysis has stood the test of time. In Book V of the *Wealth of Nations* (Smith 1776/1976), Smith analyses, first public expenditure (section V.i) and then taxation (V.ii). For Smith, the proper functions of government were the defence of the realm, the administration of justice, and the

> erecting and maintaining the publick institutions and those publick works, which, though they may be in the highest degree advantageous to a great society, are, however, of such a nature, that the profit could never repay the expence to any individual or small number of individuals, and which it, therefore, cannot be expected that any individual or small number of individuals should erect or maintain (Smith 1776/1976, V.i.III, p. 723).

Smith, like his best friend David Hume, was one of the first to understand what we now call public goods. A public good is anything with the property that if anyone consumes it, everybody can. Usually public goods are characterised by two features: jointness of supply and the difficulty of exclusion. The goods supplied by the state in Smith's day were mostly public goods. If the British Navy defended anybody in London, they defended everybody in London. Naval services were supplied jointly to every Briton, and it was impossible to exclude any Briton from their benefits. To a greater or lesser extent, this applied to all Smith's 'publick institutions' (e.g. a legal system) and 'publick works' (e.g. a bridge).

However, as Smith and Hume knew, not all public goods were pure public goods. A bridge can be excludable if it is a toll bridge (but then the tolls needed to be fixed by Act of Parliament, a public institution). A legal system can pay for itself, up to a point, by charging its clients. But it must not charge per line of judgements delivered, or judgements will become verbose. Likewise, university education can pay for itself if students pay a fee per class (as Smith's own students in Glasgow did). If professors were wholly salaried, as in Oxford and Cambridge, the teacher's 'interest is ... set as directly in opposition to his duty as it is possible to set it.... In the university of Oxford, the greater part of the publick professors have, for these many years, given up altogether even the pretence of teaching' (pp. 760–1). Even bridges and universities, however, may have to be initially provided by the state even when their running costs can be met from charges. There remains a core of desirable activities which will not happen unless the state provides them, and where charging is impracticable or undesirable. National defence is an obvious example.

As to taxation, Smith sets down some rules for optimal taxation that economists have followed ever since. Taxes should be certain, cheap to collect, and non-distorting. Smith approves of land tax, the main tax in his day, although he thinks it should be levied on the rental value of land, not its capital value (V.ii.c). Anticipating Ricardo (Chapter 7 below), Smith argues that the ground rent of houses is a particularly suitable subject for taxation. Taxes on profits or wages are more likely to be distorting than those on land. As to consumption taxes, if levied on essentials they have the same impact as income tax. If levied on luxuries, they do not necessarily raise the price of labour, but they may reduce the consumption of the good taxed, so that maximising the yield of the tax and discouraging socially undesirable consumption, as of alcohol and tobacco, are opposed to one another.

Adam Smith was the founder both of public finance and of public choice. Most policy arguments, according to Smith, represent the self-interest of the parties arguing. Some famous *bons mots* from the *Wealth of Nations* make Smith's point:

> People of the same trade seldom meet together, even for merriment and diversion, but the conversation ends in a conspiracy against the publick, or in some contrivance to raise prices. (I.x.c, p. 145)

> There is no art which one government sooner learns of another than that of draining money from the pockets of the people. (V.ii.h, p. 861)

It is good policy therefore to finance public expenditure as economically as possible from minimally distorting taxation.

Most subsequent work in public finance is little more than footnotes to Smith. An important restatement of Smith's ideas on optimal taxation and the role of public expenditure by the current Chancellor of the Exchequer appeared recently (Brown 2003). The only point we need to consider for this book is the theory of fiscal federalism (especially Oates 1972; Foster, Jackman and Perlman 1980, pp. 30–34; Mueller 2003, chs 9–10). On the expenditure side, this theory argues that local government should provide local public goods and central government should both provide national public goods and redistribute. Parks, street lighting, and local planning are examples of local public goods. Defence and a legal system are examples of national public goods. Redistributive goods are goods supplied in cash or in kind to the poor out of taxes predominantly paid by the rich. Social security and personal social services are obvious examples. Health and education are examples of private goods with a public tinge, but also with a redistributive tinge. Each individual is the main beneficiary of health and education spending on that individual. So why should they not be provided entirely privately? One answer is that the state has an interest in the public good of a healthy and educated workforce. Furthermore, public health is a near-pure public good; so is scientific research.

Another answer, quite different in kind, is that the median voter prefers public provision to private. In the UK, almost everybody uses the National Health Service, and over 90 per cent of school children are educated in the public schools – i.e. not in the so-called Public Schools or other independent schools. In this perspective, whether the state *ought* or ought not to be providing health or education is a question only for ideologues. The fact is that it does, and will continue to. It provides schools and hospitals in particular places. Therefore public expenditure has a spatial component that is the subject of this book.

The term 'fiscal crisis of the state' was popularised by James O'Connor (1973). By that he meant that the state would in future be unable to collect sufficient revenue to pay for the public services that citizens demanded. O'Connor's Marxist prediction was echoed across the political spectrum by the libertarian conservative Samuel Brittan (1977). That crisis has not materialised. Instead, a crisis that has been much longer in the making is creeping up on UK policymakers. The chapters that follow aim to show that the arrangements for taxing and spending around the territories of the UK have never been defensible. As long as public spending was the small operation that it was before the Welfare State, this was the tolerable price of national unity. Now, it is more likely to lead to national fragmentation, as each part of the country becomes more aware, and more resentful, of what other parts get. Nobody expects the Barnett formula, which as explained below governs the allocation of block grant to Wales, Scotland, and Northern Ireland, to survive for long. Of the three recipients, only Scotland still supports it, and it is more and more resented in poorer parts of England (often for reasons based on a poor understanding of what it does). The allocation of grant around England has become a headache that led both to the creation and to the demise of the Balance of Funding Review. This was commissioned in 2003 by the Office of the Deputy Prime Minister to review the proportion of local government spending that should come from local government taxation. It worked against a background of sharp rises in Council Tax and a known forthcoming storm in 2007, when the next revaluation of houses for Council Tax liability is due. But the Review ended in 2004 with a non-committal report, which was immediately to be reviewed itself by a nominee of the Chancellor of the Exchequer (not of the Deputy Prime Minister). This book aims to boldly go where governments fear to tread.

2
Public Finance in the UK before 1888

The Scottish union

When Scotland and Ireland joined the UK, each was relatively poor. So their joining in itself implied some vertical redistribution. Government services had to be delivered to a larger number of people, while the tax base per head of population had gone down. However, until the mid-19th century, most of the goods provided by government were public goods. Not until government started providing private goods would the conflicts of vertical redistribution come into the open.

The Unions of 1707 and 1800–01 were driven by politics, not economics. On both occasions, a relatively rich nation gained little, economically, from union with a relatively small nation on its periphery. The English governments of the day needed Union for a variety of reasons, but the principal one was national security. In 1703 the Scots threatened to break up the 1603 Union of Crowns by appointing as their next monarch a different successor to Queen Anne to the Hanoverians already chosen by the English Act of Settlement of 1701. In 1705, the last Scots parliament passed the Duke of Hamilton's Resolve: 'Not to name the Successor till we have a previous Treaty with *England* for regulating our Commerce, and other Concerns with that Nation.' Thus weak Scotland forced strong England to the bargaining table.

The bargain was struck between Scots and English Commissioners who drafted Articles of Union in the summer of 1706. These Articles were then enacted by the Scots and English Parliaments, which both added safeguards for their respective established churches. Thus what we usually call the Act of Union of 1707 is actually a treaty (the Articles) and two Acts. The economic clauses of the Articles show that the Scots had a bargaining strength out of all proportion to their numbers or their wealth.

The economic clauses (Articles IV to XV) are given as an appendix to this chapter. Articles IV to VI created a UK customs union and free trade zone. As in any customs union, Article VI unified customs duties between the two uniting states. Each territory would lose the revenue (and, more important in 1707, the threat and counter-threat) that it could otherwise raise from tariffs against the other state. The theory of comparative advantage would in due course teach that internal free trade would bring benefits to both partners that would outweigh the tax forgone. But the theory of comparative advantage would not be formulated until 1817 (Ricardo 1817), and it was to be well into the 18th century before Scotland saw any economic advantages from Union. From a contemporary point of view, Article VI imposed a cost, not a benefit, on both sides. Articles VII, VIII and X to XIV represented concessions to Scotland, relieving the burden of excise, coal, salt, malt, stamp, and window taxes that would have been imposed if the English tax rate had immediately been imposed on Scotland.

Article IX is the central one for the public finance of union. Land tax was the principal source of public revenue in the 18th century (Table 1.1). Article IX of the Treaty set a ratio between the required yields in England and Scotland that was extraordinarily favourable to Scotland. That tax that was currently being collected in England at the rate of 4/- in the £ (i.e. 20 per cent of assessed value) was expected to yield, according to Article IX, the astonishingly precise sum of £1,997,763 8s. 41/2d. Scotland was to yield the sum of £48,000 in land tax 'and so proportionably for a greater or lesser Sum raised in *England* by any Tax on Land, and other Things usually charged together with the Land'. This represents a ratio of 42:1 between the required English and Scots receipts. But the population ratio of the two countries was more like 6:1 (Deane and Cole 1967, Table 2). Elsewhere (McLean 1995) I have examined and (I hope) disposed of the claim that Scotland was promised overrepresentation in the Parliament of the United Kingdom. In fact, in proportion to population, Scotland was somewhat under-represented by the 45 MPs and 16 peers agreed in 1706. But in proportion to tax receipts, that apportionment looks astonishingly generous. Each English man and woman was to be assessed for land tax at a rate 7 times heavier than each Scots man and woman.

Finally, Article XV dealt with the payment of the 'Equivalent', amounting to just under £400,000 sterling, to compensate Scotland for the higher taxation and adoption of the English and Welsh national debt. This highlights the fact that the treaty of Union was not simply based on the establishment of freedom of trade, but also included a number of measures protecting supposedly vulnerable areas of the Scottish economy. It also shows that the Westminster parliament was willing to accept significant concessions to Scottish trading interests.

The Articles were submitted first to the Scots Parliament, then to the English. It was during their passage through the Scots Parliament that most of the further concessions to Scotland embodied in the definitive version were added. Article IV, the basic free-trade provision, was passed with the largest majority of any Article: securing 154 supporting votes versus 19 against. It received support from the most consistent opponents of the Union programme.

But in 1707 free trade connoted access to markets, not removal of protection. In contrast to the smooth passage of Article IV, the Articles dealing with customs and duties (referred to as the 'explanations') were much more contentious in the Scots parliament, and led to significant amendments to the negotiated treaty, all adding elements of protection for particular aspects of Scottish trade and industry. Indeed, Article VIII, dealing with the Salt Tax, involved the executive's only defeat during the passage of the Act of Union (on an amendment demanding drawbacks on the export of salted beef and pork (Macinnes 1990: 17)). The English spy Daniel Defoe describes the debate over Article VIII and the Salt Taxes as the 'Grand Affair' (Whatley 2001: 72–77). The Scottish amendments agitated the English minister Godolphin who was worried that this could complicate the passage of the Act of Union through the Westminster parliament (Riley 1978: 291). In fact, the amended Articles passed the English parliament with ease. However, the passage of the 'explanations', and the success of the Scottish parliament in adding protectionist measures, show the limitations of a purely free trade explanation of the passage of the Act of Union. There was significant concern about the vulnerability of particular industries – and particular interests of Scottish members of parliament.

The payments under Article XV went mostly to compensate Scottish investors for their total losses on the Darien scheme. The Darien venture to establish a Scottish colony on the Panama isthmus in Central America had failed totally, victim to disease and the Spanish Empire. It squandered Scottish capital and exposed the crown's disinterest in Scottish affairs. William III had no motivation to pick a quarrel with Spain just because some Scots had invaded Spanish territory.

From 1702 compensation for these losses, totalling £153,631 – estimated to be one quarter of Scotland's entire capital stock – were made part of the Scottish negotiations over a possible incorporating union (Riley 1978: 35, 199). This compensation was linked to the payment of the 'Equivalent', the sum of money paid to Scotland upon Union in order to assuage the burden of the English national debt, which a unitary state would have to bear. Rather than defraying past or future tax payments across the Scottish nation, it was appropriated by a number of sectional interests who were seen to have been affected by Union: those who had lost out from the switch from Scottish to English coinage; the share-holders of the Company of Scotland; a subsidy to the Scottish woollen industry; and allowances to Commissioners who negotiated the Union.

> When at last the Equivalent did arrive, carried in carts, with an escort of dragoons, demonstrations took place. Crowds collected to see it brought in and stones were thrown at the wagon drivers (Riley 1964: 210–11).

The English exchequer could not afford to pay the Equivalent all in cash, so bills were issued; a situation that caused some consternation, although it helped establish the Bank of Scotland, founded in 1695, which was charged with overseeing the exchange (Scott 1911: 268). The compensation was directed at those with the clearest claim, and so subscribers to the Company of Scotland and the Union Commissioners received first charge. For more ambiguous recipients, such as the Woollen traders, the result was less satisfactory: they 'could not be paid because nobody had been named in the Act anent the Public Debts to receive it' (Riley 1964: 212). The rest of the Scottish population received nothing. Debates over the liabilities of creditors to the Scottish government prior to 1707 continued to 1724, and holders of 'Equivalent' debt ended up by creating a joint stock bank in the form of the Royal Bank of Scotland. Thus two of the UK's biggest bank groups both originate in the public finance of the Act of Union. The Bank of Scotland (1695) is now the core of HBOS, and the Royal Bank of Scotland (1727) of the RBS group.

The expansion of the English tax regime to Scotland was entrenched in the Acts of Union, although Brewer (1989: 22–23) notes that the entrenchment of taxation policy through the Union meant that the Scots were particularly reluctant to accept any variation in the levels at which tax was levied. However, the Union brought Scotland within the ambit of what was becoming an established and efficient tax gathering establishment. Saville observes that, 'Scotland had a per capita tax base inferior to that of England, and the collection procedures were later found by Parliamentary inquiries to be inadequate and open to corruption' (1996: 5). Further, the Union prevented tax avoidance by English subjects, either lawfully through trade and investment north of the border in preference to England, or unlawful tax evasion by imports through Scotland.

The Union thus absorbed the Scottish government system into an English tax and debt regime which had undergone radical transformation; what Dickson (1967) terms the 'Financial Revolution in England', which followed on the heels of the political revolution of 1688. Under the guidance of Godolphin, Lord Treasurer between 1703 and 1710, the tax-raising functions of the government were consolidated, and allied to a system of long-term loans which reduced uncertainty over the liquidity of government and the markets. The land tax, levied at four shillings in the pound, was the 'chief pillar of direct taxation', and underwrote approximately two-thirds of the government's long-term debt (Dickson 1967: 358).[1] The figures for England and Wales show an expansion in the share of national income appropriated as taxation (calculated in constant price values) from 6.7 per cent in 1690 to 9.2 per cent in 1710 (O'Brien 1988: 3, Table 2).[2]

The raising of public debt was facilitated by the success of the East India Companies, which provided finance for the Exchequer, and the creation of the Bank of England in 1694. This was consolidated by the close links between these companies and parliament. Interest rates on East India bonds fell from 6 per cent between 1688–September 1705, to 5 per cent between September 1705–September 1708 (Dickson 1967: 411, Table 67), and this was associated with a general lowering of interest rates on (English) government borrowing over the period in which the Union with Scotland was forged (Table 2.1).

Table 2.1   English (British) government long term borrowing (1704–8)

Date of royal assent to Loan Act	Sum raised (£)	Interest (%)
24 Feb 1704	1,382,976	6.6
16 Jan 1705	690,000	6.6
16 Feb 1706	2,855,762	6.4
27 Mar 1707	1,155,000	6.25
13 Feb 1708	640,000	6.25
11 March 1708	2,280,000	6.25

Source: Dickson 1967: Table 3: 60–61.

In Scotland, the Bank of Scotland and the Darien Companies were unable to provide a comparable basis for a government debt. The Scottish economy was, somewhat surprisingly, capable of financing the capital calls of both the Company and the Bank of Scotland, but such investment was unsustainable in the light of the lack of returns from both these issues, and by 1697 there was a credit crisis (Jones 2001: 38). The transformation of the credit culture in Scotland dates from the Bank of Scotland's financing of the 'Equivalent'.

The Articles of Union passed the English parliament smoothly, the only threat to them being the protection of the presbyterian Church of Scotland that the Scots had insisted on adding. This provoked an unsuccessful revolt by high Anglican Tories in the House of Commons. The economic clauses, with all the extra concessions to Scotland added in the Scots Parliament, passed unchallenged. Table 2.1 shows that there was no adverse market reaction to Union. This is particularly important in the light of the thesis of North and Weingast (1989) and the revisions to this theory presented by Stasavage (2003). North and Weingast argue that the constitutional limitations imposed on the crown as part of the Glorious Revolution of 1688 imposed a financial environment in which government was less liable to default on debt, and so enabled a system of national debt which enhanced the state's capacity to raise funds and function effectively. Stasavage adds that Parliamentary constraints on the crown were dependent on a competitive party system, and the political interplay between land-owning and financial interests.

North and Weingast and Stasavage do not consider the implications of the Union with Scotland for the British state. However, Wells and Wills (2000) argue that the presence of a viable Jacobite threat to the crown would have an effect on the financial institutions which had developed alongside the government of England and Wales: 'asset prices should have fallen in the face of events that threatened the future viability of institutions established after the Revolution; any events that strengthened these institutions, in contrast, should have had a positive impact on the value of financial assets' (Wells and Wills 2000: 429). Their study shows that the period of Union negotiations coincided with a strengthening stock price of both the Bank of England and the East India Company, suggesting that this period was characterised by a growing confidence in the constitutional environment and trading prospects for the companies (Wells and Wills 2000: 430: figure 1). An index of the London stock price index, developed by Neal (1990: 47, Figure 3.1), shows a general rise in market prices between November 1705 and 1708. Not only the market for government debt (Table 2.1), but the stock market, regarded Union as good economic news.

Scotland was, however, unquestionably the main gainer from Union. Traditionally, commentators have concentrated on the expansion of the UK free trade area and the consequential economic growth. But, as argued above, this Ricardian perspective is anachronistic. The theory of comparative advantage would not be produced for a century; and the growth effects of 1707 on Scotland were delayed by decades. The public finance effects, however, were immediate. As a grumpy English commentator said of the Equivalent, which wiped out Darien debts:

> the sayd [English Government] debts have been contracted by a long War entered into more particularly for the Preservation of England & the dominions thereunto belonging, yet that Scotland has tasted of the Benefits which have accrued to Great Brittain in general from the Opposition that has been made to the Growth and Power of France (q. Dickson 1967: 8).

Scotland had free-ridden on English wars. And it continued to take, no longer a free, but a cheap ride. If we refer again to Table 1.4, we note that public expenditure in 1707 was almost entirely for UK–wide public goods – debt interest (incurred mostly to pay the bills for past wars), and military expenditure. As defence is a public good, all citizens of the Union benefited from it to an equal extent. Yet, as noted above, the Scots were taxed far more lightly than the English to pay for the public goods produced by government. Although government in 1707 had not invented the modern concept of egalitarian fiscal transfers, the system of public finance created in 1707 involved a huge fiscal transfer from England to Scotland, which persisted throughout the life of the 1707 system. Some may wish to argue that the system lives to this day, and the fiscal transfer with it.

The Irish union

The Irish Union and income tax are both products of the Napoleonic War. Table 1.3 shows that taxes on income first appear in the table in 1801, the year that the Irish Union came into effect. 'Certain duties upon income' as outlined in an Act of 1799 were introduced as a tax to beat Napoleon. As the Inland Revenue's history pages on its website (http://www.inlandrevenue.gov.uk/history/taxhis1.htm) note, income tax was to be applied in Great Britain (but not Ireland) at a rate of 10 per cent on the total income of the taxpayer from all sources above £60, with reductions on income up to £200. Income tax was abolished at the end of the war in 1815, but revived by one of the three great figures of 19th-century public finance, Sir Robert Peel, in 1842.

However, the main effect of income tax comes later in our story. The Irish union was more immediate. Like the Scottish union, it was necessitated by security. Britain's loss of its American colonies coincided with (and was partly responsible for) a depression in the Irish economy. Between 1763 and 1773 the national debt almost doubled, approaching a million pounds (Beckett 1966: 206). The American rebels complained that they were suffering taxation without representation: well, so were the Irish. The prospect of increasing the tax revenue raised in Ireland mirrored the complaints of the anti-British revolutionaries in the United States, with a Dublin newspaper arguing, in January 1775, that: 'by the same authority which the British parliament assumes to tax America, it may also and with equal justice presume to tax Ireland without the consent or concurrence of the Irish parliament' (q. Beckett 1966: 206). The rise of the Irish Volunteer movement in the last quarter of the 18th century was a response to the military weakness of the Irish state, but also reflected a desire to consolidate the Irish fiscal situation in a way which would be based on a more assertive Dublin administration. In 1782, determined to prevent another American rebellion, the British government substantially increased the powers and independence of the Irish Parliament. Henry Grattan, its leader, hoped that the parliamentary system which was named after him would widen the popular basis of the Irish government, partly through the incorporation of the Catholic and Presbyterian middle classes. However, the legislature proved less willing to follow Grattan's reformist programme, and largely served to consolidate the political control of the 'ascendancy' and maintain the fiscal status quo.

Just as the American revolution precipitated a political and financial crisis, so did the war with France and the threat of rebellion: 'An internal drain of cash had already developed in Ireland, where political conditions were becoming more unsettled and invasion from France appeared imminent, in the course of 1796' (Cullen 1968: 180). The Irish national debt rose dramatically throughout the 1790s, as military and administrative costs imposed on the Dublin administration rocketed and revenues remained static (Table 2.2). The Bank of Ireland was weak, partly because Catholics and Quakers were debarred from its

Directorate. Table 2.3 shows that it was unable to fund the growing Irish debt at acceptable rates of interest. Irish debt therefore had to be funded from loan stock issued by the Bank of England.

Tables 2.2 and 2.3 show that Irish public finance was in chaos. The Irish financial system had proved incapable (and unwilling) to fund the growing Irish national debt. The basis of the Irish revenue reflected the monarchical basis of the Williamite succession in Ireland (rather than parliamentary basis, as in Scotland). The Irish administration was

Table 2.2   Irish national debt, 1794–1801

Year ending 25 March	£
1794	2,874,267
1795	4,002,452
1796	4,477,098
1797	6,537,467
1798	10,134,675
1799	15,806,824
1800	23,100,785
1801*	28,541,157

Note: * 9 months to 5 January.
Source: Hall 1949: 63.

Table 2.3   Public loans for Irish government, raised in Ireland and Britain, 1793–1801

Year	Ireland Amount of loan £	Interest rate	Britain Amount of loan	Interest rate
1793	184,615	5.0		
1793	138,462	5.0		
1794	950,446	5.55		
1795	1,469,231	5.63		
1796	590,769	5.71		
1797	300,000	8.04		
1797	369,277	7.93		
1797	461,538	7.75		
1798	184,690	8.2	1,500,000	6.34
1798	966,212	8.2		
1799	1,846,154	6.24	2,000,000	6.24
1800	2,307,692	5.77	3,000,000	5.25
1801			2,000,000	4.71

Source: Thomas 1986: Appendices 2–3, pp. 256–9.

largely funded through taxes and duties which flowed automatically to
the monarch:

> The Hereditary Revenue was composed of the Crown Rents, arising
> from confiscations during the reign of Henry VIII and following
> Tyrone's Rebellion; the Quit rents, from similar confiscations after
> the 1641 Rebellion; Hearth Money, a general tax on hearths first
> raised in the reign of Charles II; certain Customs and Excise duties;
> and finally licences for the sale of ale, beer and spirits. These formed
> a perpetual grant to the crown for specific purposes of government;
> as such they were outside the control of parliament (Johnston 1963:
> 96–97).

These resources were sufficient to cover most of the administrative
expenses of the Irish government up to around 1715. Costs not covered by the 'Hereditary' revenue were covered by the 'Additional', revenues raised with the assent of the Irish parliament. Throughout the
eighteenth century the importance of the 'Additional' element of the
revenue increased, as did Britain's dependence on the Irish parliament.

The crisis broke in 1798, when a French force linked up with Irish
rebels, forcing the British government to open up a second front in the
Napoleonic wars. This loophole must be closed, hence the Irish union.
Like the Scottish union, therefore, it involved a favourable tax and
expenditure treatment of Ireland. If favourable tax treatment was the
cost of peace, it was a cost that the government of William Pitt the
Younger felt worth paying. The British government needed to spend
money in Ireland on the defence of the kingdom. It could not raise
that from traditional Irish sources (too meagre), nor from Irish taxpayers (cries of taxation without representation), nor by issuing debt
(see Tables 2.2 and 2.3). Union was the only logical solution, with the
cost of the defence of the new United Kingdom – a national public
good – being met out of the undifferentiated tax receipts of the United
Kingdom.

The plan for Union drawn up by Pitt and Lord Grenville in 1798 was
intended to be generous to the Irish, restricting exposure to the British
national debt. After discussions in London, Lord Castlereagh, the Irish
Chief Secretary, wrote that 'the terms are considered as highly liberal,
the proportional arrangements of the expenses having completely
overset the argument on which the enemies of the measure had hith-
erto principally relied, viz., the extension of English debt and taxation
to Ireland' (q. McCavery 2000: 355). Although the provisions for trade

and the national debt were attacked by the opponents of the Union, and the demands for some protectionist measures for manufacturing conceded, the economic basis of the union was not a source of major division in either Ireland or Britain. It would appear that the concessions won for the cotton industry was the result of an initiative from Ulster manufacturers and not from politicians opposed to the Union. Again, in this debate, the opposition did not divide the Irish House on any clause. The leaders did not even attend (McCavery 2000: 361). Perhaps more significantly, the economic provisions of the Union did not arouse the hostility of any significant political interest in Britain. Although protests from Yorkshire woollen manufacturers led to a demand for amendment of the economic article in the Act of Union in the House of Commons – providing 'the only spark of excitement in England on the Union' – it was easily defeated (Bolton 1966: 201).

Public finance in the 19th century

Fiscally, therefore, Scotland and Ireland both got a good deal out of the Union. As government spending in 1801 was still almost entirely on public goods – defence and servicing of government debt – the people of Ireland and Scotland benefited as much as the people of England, but contributed less. Referring again to Table 1.4, if we treat 'Debt charges', 'Military', and 'Cost of collection' as all being expenditure in pursuit of public goods, the only public spending with distributive consequences is that shown as 'Civil government' in Table 1.4 – and by no means the whole of that. Therefore, with one qualification, a maximum of an eighth of public spending in 1851, and a fifth in 1885, raises distributional implications.

The necessary qualification is that even public-goods expenditure takes place *somewhere*. Payments to service the national debt went to debtholders, partly overseas but those in the UK being presumably located mainly in the rich parts of the country. Military payment went to bases, to soldiers and sailors, and to procurement. Beyond the obvious fact that naval expenditure would be concentrated where the Navy had bases, I know of no data on the spatial distribution of 19th-century public expenditure, and so cannot speculate further.

The period did see heavy infrastructure spending, on roads, canals, harbours, railways, water and sewage, and (later on) gas and tramways. However, not all infrastructure spending was public spending.

Turnpike roads, canals, and railways were all privately financed, although Parliament gave them compulsory purchase rights in return for regulating their charges. The most important form of local public expenditure was on public health, following the shocking discoveries of medical and social reporters in the 1830s and 1840s about the appalling hygiene and disease rates of towns. This was still public good expenditure in a classical sense. Communicable disease is a public bad as nobody, not even the rich, is immune. All three Brontë sisters, for instance, died between 1848 and 1856 of diseases caused by urban living conditions. But unlike national defence, public health is a *local* public good with some overspills. In 1665, the bubonic plague of London had reached Eyam in Derbyshire, its pathogens carried on a bolt of cloth. But the urban killers of the 19th century stayed put. Apart from travellers, the people of Devon did not directly benefit from improvements of sewage in London. So it was appropriate that local public goods should be financed out of local public expenditure, raised by local authorities.

This structure developed only slowly between 1707 and the 1880s. Throughout this period there were historic boroughs (burghs in Scotland) but none of them had any real powers until the Municipal Corporations Act 1835, which applied only to the larger towns of England. Outside the towns, there was no elected local government before 1888. Local public expenditure was the responsibility of Justices of the Peace, Poor Law Unions, and similar *ad hoc* bodies, which had the power to set local rates. Table 1.3 shows that the proceeds of local rates remained a small proportion of the total tax take. And there was no mechanism to equalise for the fact that poor areas had high needs and low resources, whereas rich areas had relatively low needs and high resources. Therefore poor relief was ineffective despite the attentions of the Benthamite reformers who wrote the New Poor Law of 1834. Any equalisation for differential needs and resources takes us straight into the territory of vertical imbalance and horizontal equity. But there was no serious thought in the UK about these issues until after the great shocks of the 1880s, which are the subject of the next chapter.

Appendix

Economic articles of the Treaty of Union incorporated into the Acts of Union 1706–7.

ARTICLE IV

Freedom of Trade, and of all other Rights, &c.

That all the Subjects of the united Kingdom of Great Britain shall, from and after the Union, have full Freedom and Intercourse of Trade and Navigation to and from any Port or Place within the said united Kingdom, and the Dominions and Plantations thereunto belonging; and that there be a Communication of all other Rights, Privileges, and Advantages, which do or may belong to the Subjects of either Kingdom; except where it is otherwise expresly agreed in these Articles.

ARTICLE V

Scots Ships to be British Ships.

That all Ships or Vessels belonging to her Majesty's Subjects of Scotland, at the Time of ratifying the Treaty of Union of the two Kingdoms in the Parliament of Scotland, though foreign built, be deemed, and pass as Ships of the Built of Great Britain; the Owner, or where there are more Owners, one or more of the Owners, within twelve Months after the first of May next, making Oath, That at the Time of ratifying the Treaty of Union in the Parliament of Scotland, the same did, in Whole or in Part, belong to him or them, or to some other Subject or Subjects in Scotland, to be particularly named, with the Place of their respective Abodes; and that the same doth then, at the Time of the said Deposition, wholly belong to him or them; and that no Foreigner directly or indirectly, hath any Share, Part, or Interest therein; which Oath shall be made before the chief Officer or Officers of the Customs, in the Port next to the Abode of the said Owner or Owners; and the said Officer or Officers shall be impowered to administer the said Oath; and the Oath being so administred shall be attested by the Officer or Officers, who administred the same; and being registred by the said Officer or Officers, shall be delivered to the Master of the Ship for Security of her Navigation; and a Duplicate thereof shall be transmitted by the said Officer or Officers, to the Chief Officer or Officers of the Customs in the Port of Edinburgh, to be there entred in a Register, and from thence to be sent to the Port of London to be there entred in the General Register of all trading Ships belonging to Great Britain.

ARTICLE VI

Trade. Scots Cattle. Importation of Victuals.

That all Parts of the united Kingdom for ever, from and after the Union, shall have the same Allowances, Encouragements, and Drawbacks, and be under the same Prohibitions, Restrictions and Regulations of Trade, and liable to the same Customs and Duties on Import and Export; and that the Allowances, Encouragements, and Drawbacks, Prohibitions, Restrictions and Regulations of Trade, and the Customs and Duties on Import and Export, settled in England when the Union commences, shall, from and after the Union, take Place throughout the whole united Kingdom; excepting and reserving the Duties upon Export and Import of such Particular Commodities, from which any Persons, the Subjects of either Kingdom, are specially liberated and exempted by their private Rights, which, after the Union, are to remain safe and entire to them in all Respects, as before the same. And that from and after the Union, no Scots Cattle carried into England, shall be liable to any other Duties, either on the publick or private Accounts, than those Duties to which the Cattle of England are or shall be liable within the said Kingdom. And seeing by the Laws of England, there are Rewards granted upon the Exportation of certain Kinds of Grain, wherein Oats grinded or ungrinded are not expressed, that from and after the Union when Oats shall be sold at fifteen Shillings Sterling per Quarter, or under, there shall be paid two Shillings and six Pence Sterling for every Quarter of the Oatmeal exported in the Terms of the Law, whereby, and so long as Rewards are granted for Exportation of other Grains, and that the Bear of Scotland have the same Rewards as Barley: And in Respect the Importation of Victual into Scotland from any Place beyond Sea, would prove a Discouragement to Tillage, therefore that the Prohibition as now in Force by the Law of Scotland, against Importation of Victuals from Ireland, or any other Place beyond Sea into Scotland, do, after the Union, remain in the same Force as now it is, until more proper and effectual Ways be provided by the Parliament of Great Britain, for discouraging the Importation of the said Victuals from beyond the Sea.

ARTICLE VII

Excises.

That all Parts of the united Kingdom be for ever, from and after the Union, liable to the same Excises upon all exciseable Liquors, excepting only that the thirty-four Gallons English Barrel of Beer or Ale, amounting to twelve Gallons Scots present Measure, sold in Scotland by the Brewer at nine Shillings six Pence Sterling, excluding all Duties, and retailed, including Duties and the Retailers Profit, at two Pence the Scots Pint, or eighth Part of the Scots Gallon, be not after the Union liable, on account of the present Excise upon exciseable Liquors in England, to any higher Imposition than two Shillings Sterling upon the aforesaid thirty-four Gallons, English Barrel, being twelve Gallons the present Scots Measure. And that the Excise settled in England on all other Liquors, when the Union commences, take place throughout the whole united Kingdom.

ARTICLE VIII

Foreign Salt. Scotch Salt. Home Salt. Flesh exported from Scotland. Curing of Herrings. Fish exported.

That from and after the Union, all foreign Salt which shall be imported into Scotland, shall be charged at the Importation there, with the same Duties as the like Salt is now charged with being imported into England, and to be levied and secured in the same Manner: But in regard the Duties of great Quantities of foreign Salt imported may be very heavy upon the Merchants Importers, that therefore all foreign Salt imported into Scotland, shall be cellared and locked up under the Custody of the Merchants Importers, and the Officers employed for levying the Duties upon Salt, and that the Merchant may have what Quantity thereof his Occasion may require, not under a Wey or forty Bushels at a Time, giving Security for the Duty of what Quantity he receives, payable in six Months. But Scotland shall, for the Space of seven Years from the said Union, be exempted from paying in Scotland, for Salt made there, the Duty or Excise now payable for Salt made in England; but from the Expiration of the said seven Years, shall be subject and liable to the same Duties for Salt made in Scotland as shall be then payable for Salt made in England, to be levied and secured in the same Manner, and with proportionable Drawbacks and Allowances as in England, with this Exception, That Scotland shall, after the said seven Years, remain exempted from the Duty of two Shillings four Pence a Bushel on Home Salt, imposed by an Act made in England in the Ninth and Tenth of King WILLIAM the Third of England; and if the Parliament of Great Britain shall, at or before the expiring of the said seven Years, substitute any other Fund in Place of the said two Shillings four Pence of Excise on the Bushel of Home Salt, Scotland shall, after the said seven Years, bear a Proportion of the said Fund, and have an Equivalent in the Terms of this Treaty; and that during the said seven Years, there shall be paid in England, for all Salt made in Scotland, and imported from thence into England, the same Duties upon the Importation, as shall be payable for Salt made in England, to be levied and secured in the same Manner as the Duties on foreign Salt are to be levied and secured in England; and that after the said seven Years, as long as the said Duty of two Shillings four Pence a Bushel upon Salt is continued in England, the said two Shillings and four Pence a Bushel shall be payable for all Salt made in Scotland, and imported into England, to be levied and secured in the same Manner; and that during the Continuance of the Duty of two Shillings four Pence a Bushel upon Salt made in England, no Salt whatsoever be brought from Scotland to England by Land in any Manner, under the Penalty of forfeiting the Salt, and the Cattle and Carriages made use of in bringing the same, and paying twenty Shillings for every Bushel of such Salt, and proportionably for a greater or lesser Quantity, for which the Carrier as well as the Owner shall be liable, jointly and severally, and the Persons bringing or carrying the same to be imprisoned by any one Justice of the Peace, by the Space of six Months without Bail, and until the Penalty be paid. And for establishing an Equality in Trade, that all Flesh exported from Scotland to England, and put on Board in Scotland to be exported to Parts beyond the Seas, and Provisions for Ships in Scotland, and for foreign Voyages, may be salted with Scots Salt, paying the same Duty for what Salt is so employed as the like Quantity of such Salt pays in England, and under the same Penalties, Forfeitures, and Provisions for preventing of Frauds as are mentioned in the Laws of England; and that from and after the Union, the Laws and Acts of Parliament in Scotland, for pining, curing, and packing of Herrings, white Fish and Salmon for Exportation with foreign Salt only, without any Mixture of British or Irish Salt, and for preventing of Frauds in curing and packing of Fish, be continued in Force in Scotland, subject to such Alterations as shall be made by the Parliament of Great Britain; and that all Fish exported from Scotland to Parts beyond the Seas, which shall be cured with foreign Salt only, and without Mixture of British or Irish Salt, shall have the same Eases, Premiums, and Drawbacks, as are or shall be allowed to such Persons as export the like Fish from England; and that for Encouragement of the Herring Fishing, there shall be allowed and paid to the Subjects, Inhabitants of Great Britain, during the present Allowances for other Fish, ten Shillings five Pence Sterling for every Barrel of White Herrings which shall be exported from Scotland; and that there shall be allowed five Shillings Sterling for every Barrel of Beef or Pork salted with foreign Salt, without Mixture of British or Irish Salt, and exported for Sale from Scotland to Parts beyond Sea, alterable by the Parliament of Great Britain; and if any Matters of Fraud relating to the said Duties on Salt shall hereafter appear, which are not sufficiently provided against by this Article, the same shall be subject to such further Provisions as shall be thought fit by the Parliament of Great Britain.

ARTICLE IX

Land Tax. Quota of Scotland.

That whensoever the Sum of one million nine hundred ninety-seven thousand seven hundred and sixty-three Pounds eight Shillings and four Pence Halfpenny, shall be enacted by the Parliament of Great Britain to be raised in that Part of the united Kingdom now called England, on Land and other Things usually charged in Acts of Parliament there, for granting an Aid to the Crown by a Land Tax; that Part of the united Kingdom now called Scotland, shall be charged by the same Act, with a further Sum of forty-eight thousand Pounds, free of all Charges, as the Quota of Scotland, to such Tax, and so proportionably for a greater or lesser Sum raised in England by any Tax on Land, and other Things usually charged together with the Land; and that such Quota for Scotland, in the Cases aforesaid, be raised and collected in the same Manner as the Cess now is in Scotland; but subject to such Regulations in the Manner of collecting, as shall be made by the Parliament of Great Britain.

ARTICLE X

Stampt Vellum.

That during the Continuance of the respective Duties on stampt Paper, Vellum, and Parchment, by the several Acts now in Force in England, Scotland shall not be charged with the same respective Duties.

ARTICLE XI

Window Tax.

That during the Continuance of the Duties payable in England on Windows and Lights, which determine on the first Day of August one thousand seven hundred and ten, Scotland shall not be charged with the same Duties.

ARTICLE XII

Coals, Culm, and Cynders.

That during the Continuance of the Duties payable in England on Coals, Culm, and Cynders, which determine the thirtieth Day of September one thousand seven hundred and ten, Scotland shall not be charged therewith for Coals, Culm, and Cynders consumed there; but shall be charged with the same Duties as in England for all Coals, Culm, and Cynders not consumed in Scotland.

ARTICLE XIII

Malt.

That during the Continuance of the Duty payable in England upon Malt, which determines the twenty-fourth Day of June one thousand seven hundred and seven, Scotland shall not be charged with that Duty.

ARTICLE XIV

Scotland not chargeable with any other Duties before the Union, except these consented to. Proviso.

That the Kingdom of Scotland be not charged with any other Duties laid on by the Parliament of England before the Union, except these consented to in this Treaty; in regard it is agreed, That all necessary Provision shall be made by the Parliament of Scotland for the publick Charge and Service of that Kingdom, for the Year one thousand seven hundred and seven. Provided nevertheless, That if the Parliament of England shall think fit to lay any further Impositions by way of Customs, or such Excises, with which by virtue of this Treaty, Scotland is to be charged equally with England, in such Case Scotland shall be liable to the same Customs and Excises, and have an Equivalent to be settled by the Parliament of Great Britain; with this further Provision,

That any Malt to be made and consumed in that Part of the united Kingdom now called Scotland, shall not be charged with any Imposition on Malt, during this present War. And seeing it cannot be supposed that the Parliament of Great Britain will ever lay any sort of Burthens upon the united Kingdom, but what they shall find of Necessity at that Time for the Preservation and Good of the Whole, and with due regard to the Circumstances and Abilities of every Part of the united Kingdom; therefore it is agreed, That there be no further Exemption insisted upon for any Part of the united Kingdom, but that the Consideration of any Exemptions beyond what are already agreed on in this Treaty, shall be left to the Determination of the Parliament of Great Britain.

ARTICLE XV

Equivalent. Uses to which Equivalent Money is applied. Coin of Scotland. African Company. Publick Debts. Manufacture of coarse Wool. Fisheries. Commissioners for the Equivalent.

That whereas by the Terms of this Treaty, the Subjects of Scotland, for preserving an Equality of Trade throughout the united Kingdom, will be liable to several Customs and Excises now payable in England, which will be applicable towards Payment of the Debts of England, contracted before the Union; it is agreed, That Scotland shall have an Equivalent for what the Subjects thereof shall be so charged towards Payment of the said Debts of England, in all Particulars whatsoever, in Manner following, viz. That before the Union of the said Kingdoms, the Sum of three hundred ninety-eight thousand and eighty-five Pounds ten Shillings, be granted to her Majesty by the Parliament of England, for the Uses after mentioned, being the Equivalent to be answered to Scotland for such Parts of the said Customs and Excises upon all exciseable Liquors with which that Kingdom is to be charged upon the Union, as will be applicable to the Payment of the said Debts of England, according to the Proportions which the present Customs in Scotland, being thirty thousand Pounds per Annum, do bear to the Customs in England, computed at one million three hundred forty-one thousand five hundred and fifty-nine Pounds per Annum; and which the present Excises on exciseable Liquors in Scotland, being thirty-three thousand and five hundred Pounds per Annum, do bear to the Excises on exciseable Liquors in England, computed at nine hundred forty-seven thousand six hundred and two Pounds per Annum: Which Sum of three hundred ninety-eight thousand eighty-five Pounds ten

Shillings, shall be due and payable from the Time of the Union. And in regard that after the Union Scotland becoming liable to the same Customs and Duties payable on Import and Export, and to the same Excises on all exciseable Liquors as in England, as well upon that Account, as upon the Account of the Increase of Trade and People, (which will be the happy Consequence of the Union) the said Revenues will much improve beyond the before-mentioned annual Values thereof, of which no present Estimate can be made; yet nevertheless, for the Reasons aforesaid, there ought to be a proportionable Equivalent answered to Scotland; it is agreed, That after the Union there shall be an Account kept of the said Duties arising in Scotland, to the End it may appear what ought to be answered to Scotland as an Equivalent for such Proportion of the said Increase as shall be applicable to the Payment of the Debts of England. And for the further and more effectual answering the several Ends hereafter mentioned, it is agreed, That from and after the Union, the whole Increase of the Revenues of Customs, and Duties on Import and Export, and Excises upon exciseable Liquors in Scotland, over and above the annual Produce of the said respective Duties, as above stated, shall go and be applied, for the Term of seven Years, to the Uses hereafter mentioned; and that, upon the said Account there shall be answered to Scotland annually from the End of seven Years after the Union, an Equivalent in Proportion to such Part of the said Increase, as shall be applicable to the Debts of England; and generally, that an Equivalent shall be answered to Scotland for such Parts of the English Debts, as Scotland may hereafter become liable to pay by reason of the Union, other than such for which Appropriations have been made by Parliament in England, of the Customs, or other Duties on Export and Import, Excises on all exciseable Liquors, in respect of which Debts, Equivalents are herein before provided. And as for the Uses to which the said Sum of three hundred ninety-eight thousand eighty-five Pounds ten Shillings to be granted as aforesaid, and all other Monies which are to be answered or allowed to Scotland as aforesaid, are to be applied, it is agreed, That in the first Place, out of the aforesaid Sum, what Consideration shall be found necessary to be had for any Losses, which private Persons may sustain by reducing the Coin of Scotland to the Standard and Value of the Coin of England, may be made good; in the next Place, that the Capital Stock, or Fund of the African and Indian Company of Scotland advanced, together with Interest for the said Capital Stock, after the Rate of five per Centum per Annum, from the respective Times of the Payment thereof, shall be paid: Upon Payment of which Capital Stock and Interest, it is agreed, the said Company be dissolved and cease, and also, that from the Time of passing the Act of Parliament in England, for raising the said Sum of three hundred ninety-eight thousand eighty-five Pounds ten Shillings, the said Company shall neither trade nor grant Licence to trade; providing, that if the said Stock and Interest shall not be paid in twelve Months after the Commencement of the Union, that then the said Company may from thence forward trade, or give licence to trade, until the said whole Capital Stock and Interest shall be paid. And as to the Overplus of the said Sum of three hundred ninety-eight thousand eighty-five Pounds ten Shillings, after Payment of what Consideration shall be had for Losses in repairing the Coin, and paying the said Capital Stock and Interest, and also the whole Increase of the said Revenues of Customs, Duties and Excises, above the present Value, which shall arise in Scotland during the said Term of seven Years, together with the Equivalent which shall become due upon the Improvement thereof in Scotland after the said Term; and also, as to all other Sums, which, according to the Agreements aforesaid, may become payable to Scotland by way of Equivalent, for what that Kingdom shall hereafter become liable towards Payment of the Debts of England; it is agreed, That the same be applied in the Manner following, viz. That all the publick Debts of the Kingdom of Scotland, as shall be adjusted by this present Parliament, shall be paid: And that two thousand Pounds per Annum for the Space of seven Years, shall be applied towards encouraging and promoting the Manufacture of coarse Wool within those Shires which produce the Wool; and that the first two thousand Pounds Sterling be paid at Martinmas next, and so yearly at Martinmas, during the Space aforesaid; and afterwards, the same shall be wholly applied towards the encouraging and promoting the Fisheries, and such other Manufactures and Improvements in Scotland, as may most conduce to the general Good of the united Kingdom. And it is agreed, That her Majesty be impowered to appoint Commissioners, who shall be accountable to the Parliament of Great Britain, for disposing the said Sum of three hundred ninety-eight thousand and eighty-five Pounds ten Shillings, and all other Monies which shall arise to Scotland, upon the Agreements aforesaid, to the Purposes before-mentioned: Which Commissioners shall be impowered to call for, receive, and dispose of the said Monies, in Manner aforesaid, and to inspect the Books of the several Collectors of the said Revenues, and of all other Duties, from whence an Equivalent may arise: And that the Collectors and Managers of the said Revenues and Duties be obliged to give to the said Commissioners subscribed authentick Abbreviates of the Produce of such Revenues and Duties arising in their respective District: And that the said Commissioners shall have their Office within the Limits of Scotland, and shall in such Office keep Books containing Accounts of the Amount of the Equivalents, and how the same shall have been disposed of from time to time, which may be inspected by any of the Subjects, who shall desire the same.

ARTICLE XVI

Coin.

That from and after the Union, the Coin shall be of the same Standard and Value throughout the united Kingdom, as now in England, and a Mint shall be continued in Scotland, under the same Rules as the Mint in England, and the present Officers of the Mint continued, subject to such Regulations and Alterations as her Majesty, her Heirs or Successors, or the Parliament of Great Britain shall think fit.

ARTICLE XVII

Weights and Measures.

That from and after the Union, the same Weights and Measures shall be used throughout the united Kingdom, as are now established in England, and standards of Weights and Measures shall be kept by those Burghs in Scotland, to whom the keeping the Standards of Weights and Measures, now in Use there, does of special Right belong: All which Standards shall be sent down to such respective Burghs, from the Standards kept in the Exchequer at Westminster, subject nevertheless to such Regulations as the Parliament of Great Britain shall think fit.

Source: www.justis.com.

3
Gladstone, Goschen, Lloyd George and the Webbs

The GOM goes for Home Rule

'If the GOM [Grand Old Man – sarcastic nickname for Gladstone] goes for Home Rule', said the streetfighting Tory Lord Randolph Churchill in 1885, 'the Orange card will be the card to play. Pray God it will be the ace of trumps and not the two'. The GOM did go for Irish Home Rule in November of that year. His Government of Ireland Bill was defeated in June 1886. The Orange card was indeed one of those that the Unionists played to defeat it. The Home Rule proposal contained no opt-out for the Protestant Orangemen of Ulster. But the Bill had equally profound failings on representation and finance. This section explores why that Victorian Titan of public finance, W.E. Gladstone, labelled by one of his eminent successors 'the Chancellor who made the job' (Jenkins 1995, title of chapter 9), made such a poor job of the public finance of Home Rule.

Mr Gladstone opened a new volume of his diary on 8 September 1885 with three Greek epigraphs, two from Aeschylus and one from Homer, which translate as *Be not faint-hearted*; *What are you doing? Stand up, do not be overcome with weariness*; and *Endure now, heart* (Matthew 1990, 08.09.1885[1]). His second government had imploded earlier in the year; the Tories under the 3rd Marquess of Salisbury formed a minority government, which was about to call a General Election for November of the same year. The 75-year-old Gladstone led a fissile party. The right wing under Lord Hartington deplored the radicalism (including concessions to Ireland) of his 1880–5 administration; the left wing under Joseph Chamberlain and Sir Charles Dilke deplored its timidity. Gladstone described them as 'our two poles' (to Lord Derby, 14.09.85).

In that autumn of 1885, brooding at his estate in Hawarden and later, while fighting his constituency of Midlothian, at Lord Rosebery's estate at Dalmeny, Gladstone came to see more clearly than any of his contemporaries that devolution to Ireland was inescapable. Much harder was to see how it could be enacted, given that his own party was split and the governing Conservatives were unsympathetic. His diary and accompanying letters (Matthew 1990) form a unique primary record in which one may follow his daily twists and turns from that autumn to the following spring. To do so is simultaneously to be astonished by his grasp and infuriated by his bone-headed failure to deal with points that seem obvious to us. Gladstone on Ireland is like Thomas Jefferson on slavery. He saw further than anyone else, and failed to see things that lay under his nose.

Ahead of any other British politician, he saw that the franchise reform he had enacted in 1884 (the Third Reform Act) was likely to give the Irish Party a block of 'between eighty and ninety seats' and its ruthless leader, Charles Stewart Parnell, possible blocking power in the Commons. In consequence, and as a simple matter of public order, Ireland had become ungovernable as part of a unitary UK. Hence Home Rule was inevitable.

Parnell displayed his ruthlessness by issuing a 'vote Tory manifesto' to the Irish in Great Britain for the 1885 General Election. In the event, Parnell's party won 86 seats, and would hold the balance in a hung parliament as soon as it met in January 1886 (McLean 2001b Tables 4.1 and 4.3). Gladstone was not at all put out by Parnell's ingratitude. He recognised the manoeuvre as that of a rational politician seeking to maximise his party's leverage. Parnell was (as Gladstone must have suspected) negotiating for Home Rule from Salisbury's minority government. Indeed, at a secret meeting in August 1885 with Salisbury's Viceroy, Lord Carnarvon, Parnell came to an agreement with Carnarvon in favour of a home rule bill. Salisbury ignored and then repudiated the deal; Carnarvon resigned; Salisbury persuaded him to keep his resignation a secret. If that had leaked out, instead of what Gladstone's son Herbert was shortly to leak deliberately, history would have been very different.

At the same time, Parnell was sending signals to Gladstone, using his mistress, Katharine O'Shea, as an intermediary. One of those signals was a proposed Irish constitution, which Gladstone received on 03.11.85. Although 'I observe .... that finance is only touched at a single point and that no provision is offered for the Irish share in the National Debt, in Naval Defence, or in Royal Charges', nevertheless, 'This is only by the way' (draft, not sent, to Mrs O'Shea, 03.11.85). Gladstone was pleased with Parnell's draft because it was close to his own ideas (Jenkins 1995, p. 532; Matthew 1999, p. 479). He saw that he could do business with Parnell, although tactically he would rather not.

Gladstone and Parnell (at least the Parnell who sent the November draft) both saw Ireland as a local Canada. Gladstone signalled his thoughts by asking his Chief Whip to secure a copy of the British North America Act 1867, an act of the Westminster ('Imperial') Parliament which was the Canadian constitution. Gladstone told his diary, unusually,[2] on 19.09.85:

> I have long suspected the Union of 1800. There was a case for doing something: but this was like Pitt's Revolutionary war, a gigantic though excusable mistake.

Accordingly, he read voraciously, among others, the speeches of Henry Grattan (leader of the Irish Parliament of 1782 and opponent of the 1800 Union) and Edmund Burke (prophet of Catholic Emancipation and a more equal union). He closed his speech introducing the 1886 Bill with a peroration from Grattan: *The Channel forbids union; the ocean forbids separation (Hansard* 08.04.86, c. 1082). So: was Ireland like Canada across the ocean, or was it not? Neither Gladstone nor Parnell answered coherently.

Canada had never sent representatives to the Imperial Parliament. Since the incorporating Union of 1800, Ireland had. Gladstone denied that he simply wished to repeal the 1800 Union; but his 1886 proposal that Irish MPs should cease to sit at Westminster was tantamount to a repeal. Parnell was happy with that; most Liberals were happy with it (because they were sick of Irish obstruction in the Commons); but as Gladstone well knew and unconvincingly parried, it implied taxation without representation, the issue which had led the American colonies south of Canada to secession in 1776.

Canada did not suffer from taxation without representation because it was financially self-sufficient. What it spent, it raised (BNA Act 1867, ss. 102–126). Ireland was not. Gladstone originally proposed that Ireland should control the level of Customs and Excise duties levied there, but was defeated by his own Cabinet, so that the Bill as drafted allowed Ireland to keep the proceeds net of an Imperial Contribution, but Westminster to set the level (GOI Bill 1886 cl. 14; Great Britain, *Parliamentary Papers* 1886 II, 465–88).

Gladstone produced his first draft of a bill on 14.11.85 while staying at Dalmeny, but did not show it to his host, Lord Rosebery. He told various correspondents that he would rather the Tories legislated for Ireland than that his party should. His most cogent letters were one to Mrs O'Shea for Parnell (unfortunately not sent) and one to Salisbury's nephew and colleague A.J. Balfour (unfortunately delayed until events had made it out of date). To Mrs O'Shea he drafted the statement 'Mr Parnell and his allies ought to seek a settlement of this question from the party now in office.... I bear in mind the history of 1829, 1845, 1846, and 1867, as illustrating the respective capacity of the two parties to deal under certain circumstances with sharply controverted matters' (03.11.85). In these four years, Tory governments had done things one would have expected Liberal governments to do and Tory ones to resist.[3] Once Tory leaders had decided to do these things, their enraged followers had nowhere else to go. The tactic has been labelled the 'Nixon goes to China' gambit, where only a right-wing leader can enact a left-wing policy. Gladstone hoped that Salisbury would repeat what Wellington, Peel (twice) and Disraeli had done before him.

Gladstone then staged an 'accidental' meeting with Balfour at the Duke of Westminster's estate a few miles from Hawarden, but delayed for a week before sending Balfour a message for his uncle Salisbury confirming what he had said:

> I feel sure the question can only be dealt with by a Government, & I desire specially on grounds of public policy that it should be dealt with by the *present* Government. If therefore they bring in a proposal for settling the whole question of the future Government of Ireland, my desire will be, reserving of course necessary freedom, to treat it in the same spirit in which I have endeavoured to proceed with respect to Afghanistan & with respect to the Balkan peninsula (20.12.85).

In other words, a conditional promise of support, should Salisbury introduce a Home Rule bill. In so writing, Gladstone must have had in mind the previous great crisis of Victorian politics, over the Repeal of the Corn Laws in 1845–6. Sir Robert Peel, unable to persuade his Cabinet to accept Repeal, had resigned in November 1845. The Whig leader Lord John Russell had sought from Peel the same guarantee that Gladstone now offered Salisbury. On Peel's refusal to give it, Russell refused to form a government and Peel was back in the saddle (McLean 2001b, pp. 40–1).

Unlike Peel, Gladstone was too late. His son Herbert, to whom he had shown his hand on 14.11.85, revealed it all to the press. The 'Hawarden kite', flown on 17.12.85, announced that 'Mr Gladstone has definitely adopted the policy of Home Rule for Ireland' and went on to analyse what each other player should do: 'There is reasonable expectation that both Lord Hartington and Mr Goschen will come round to Mr Gladstone's view, and Mr Chamberlain and Sir Charles Dilke, in spite of their present attitude, could not consistently oppose it' (*Pall Mall Gazette*, 17.12.85, quoted by McLean 2001b, p. 85).

Telling them what they were expected to do guaranteed that they would not. Salisbury knew that he need not now come up with an Irish policy, and was spared the embarrassment of the Parnell-Carnarvon talks being revealed and the Tory Party splitting. Gladstone's appeal to him was a waste of ink. Salisbury was very happy to be defeated when the Commons met (on an unrelated issue deliberately chosen by Gladstone to be anything but Ireland) and watch Gladstone's party be split rather than his own. The year 1886 would not replicate 1829, 1845, 1846, or 1867.

Thus Gladstone resumed office in January 1886 full of ideas for Irish Home Rule, ideas which he dared not expose to his own Cabinet because the Liberals were so divided. Hartington and Goschen, after being told what to do in the Hawarden kite, refused to play. Chamberlain did so very reluctantly, to walk out as soon as the details of the plan were revealed to the cabinet in March 1886. The Queen vetoed Dilke because of his involvement in a divorce case. There was thus the barest Cabinet scrutiny of the Bill (*PP* 1886, II, 465–88), which was excellent on constitutional matters, weak on representation in the Commons, did not mention Ulster at all, and fudged finance.

In his resignation speech, Chamberlain gave as one of his grounds for resigning that the draft bill 'renounced all the exercise of the right of Imperial taxation in Ireland'. Although, he conceded, Gladstone had withdrawn this suggestion, Chamberlain stayed resigned (*Hansard* 09.04.86, cc. 1190–1; cf. Powell 1977, p. 8). In fact it was very hard to see how either giving or not giving fiscal freedom to Ireland could work. Ireland was truly not like Canada. By 1867 the Canadian colonies had been self-governing, and fiscally free, since the end of the American Revolution eighty years earlier. They raised what they spent; they spent what they raised. Ireland was not remotely in this position. In 1801, Gladstone stated, it had been assumed that Ireland would contribute 2/17 of UK tax receipts. It actually contributed only 1/12. He now proposed that the Irish contribution to the Exchequer should be 1/15 of UK tax receipts (*Hansard* 08.04.86, cc. 1073–80). However, as Colin Matthew (1999, p. 503) has pointed out, the Bill specified not proportions of receipts, but sums of money whose upper limit was fixed for 30 years, as due from Ireland to the UK for imperial services (GoI Bill 1886 cls. 13 (1) to 13 (3)). If the Bill had been enacted, the Irish would have had an extraordinarily cheap, virtually free, ride on UK services by 1916. The Irish share of the UK population was something like 31 per cent in 1801, and its share of tax receipts about 8 per cent. In 1886 its population share had dropped to 14 per cent (thanks to famine and emigration) and its proposed tax contribution was 7 per cent.[4]

These numbers show that giving, or refusing, control to Ireland over Customs and Excise rates was a red herring. Ireland could not have maintained the same standard of domestic public services and made an equal per capita contribution to the UK for Imperial services, whatever the rate of Customs and Excise duties. The gap was yawningly huge. About a third of UK public expenditure was on military services and a quarter on debt servicing (Table 1.4). If Ireland were to remain in the UK at all, it must take a free, or a cheap, ride on these public goods. If the channel forbade separation, then it also forbade fiscal autonomy. Furthermore, Gladstone copied the preceding Unionist government (and was copied by its successor) in proposing a huge public sector loan to Irish landlords, to buy them out of their estates if they so wished. This could have meant loan stock valued at as much as £50 million, secured on the very dubious security of Irish estates in an agricultural depression. However, these manoeuvres had no effect on the interest rate on Consols (the main form of government debt).

Gladstone's vision for the constitution was thus magnificent, but his vision for public finance was purblind. In that respect, nothing about Anglo-Irish financial relations would change until around 1999.

Not forgetting Goschen

Lord Randolph thought he was indispensable when Salisbury made him Chancellor in the Unionist government that succeeded the defeat of the 1886 Home Rule bill. His behaviour became more and more unpredictable, until Salisbury ruthlessly ditched him in favour of Goschen in December 1886. Churchill later confessed that, when he resigned expecting Salisbury to plead for him to return, he 'forgot Goschen'. He forgot that an unflamboyant Liberal Unionist could do the job as well as he could. Much better, in fact.

Goschen's 1888 Budget rivals Peel (1842), Gladstone (especially 1853 and 1860), and Lloyd George (1909) as a corner-stone of public finance in the UK, but Goschen remains the least-known of those four. He should not be. Unlike Lord Randolph, who, according to his son, said that he 'never could make out what those damned dots [decimal points] meant' (Churchill 1906, ii., p. 184), Goschen brought prior skills to the job of Chancellor. He became a director of the Bank of England in 1859, aged only 27; he was known to his City friends as the 'Fortunate Youth' (*source*: Old *DNB*). In 1870, while President of the Poor Law Board (a cabinet post) in Gladstone's first ministry, he had written a Report on Local Taxation for the Treasury; in 1905 he would publish a collection of economic policy speeches (Goschen 1872, 1905).

The full title of Goschen's report of 1870 (published as Goschen 1872) reveals its political impetus: it was a *Report ...on the Progressive INCREASE of LOCAL TAXATION, with especial reference to the Proportion of Local and Imperial Burdens borne by the different Classes of Real Property in the United Kingdom* relative to the same burden elsewhere. Goschen found that no good statistics on local government income and expenditure existed, but that the aggregate for England and Wales was an 'astounding total' (p. 5) of about £30 million income and expenditure annually (compare Table 1.3). These rates were levied and spent by a wide range of statutory authorities for special purposes (cf. Webb 1963), but the principal components (in the ratio of about 2:1 – p. 15) were the old one of Poor Rates and the new one of rates to provide sanitary facilities. The growth of expenditure was matched by a growth in the value of real property, and hence of rateable value. Therefore there was no true increase of the incidence of local taxation of real property; but there was still a relative transfer of the tax burden away from personal towards real property, because the value of other assets had gone up by more (p. 24). Geographically, the tax burden was shifting from south to north, as the new rates were dearest in the growing urban areas.

Though Goschen's Report was factual and made no recommendations, its lessons were very clear. It has a very modern ring, as the problem Goschen addressed in 1872 is exactly the same as that addressed by Deputy Prime Minister John Prescott and Chancellor Gordon Brown in 2003, when they commissioned the Balance of Funding Review to examine the imbalance between central and local government funding of local government services in England. The Balance of Funding Review (ODPM 2004: see http://www.local.dtlr.gov.uk/finance/balance.htm)

expired inconsequentially in 2004 with its questions raised (see later chapters of this book), but unanswered. By contrast, in his 1888 Budget Goschen answered some of the questions that he had raised in 1872. An 1870 Commons Select Committee of which he was a member had already called for more uniform local taxation, although it failed to adopt the detailed report that he drafted for it (Goschen 1872 pp. 151–76).

The County Councils Act 1888 set up 62 powerful, elected County Councils, to start operations in April 1889. The larger towns (some of which had had elected local governments since 1835) became islands in their surrounding counties, labelled 'county boroughs'. A county borough council was a unitary authority combining the powers of a county council with those of all the small-town and rural bodies that survived underneath county councils (and the powers of the Mayor of Casterbridge were in turn regularised, and rural district councils created, by the Liberals' Local Government Act 1894). The 1888 bill proposed only ten county boroughs, but lobbying in the committee stage increased their number to 61. Thus for the first time the whole of England and Wales (but not yet Ireland or Scotland) was covered by a uniform structure of elected local government. Wherever you were in England and Wales, you were governed by one top-tier local authority. The 1894 Act left County Boroughs unaffected as single-tier authorities and created two-tier government in the rest of England and Wales. Since then England and Wales have always had a patchwork of single-tier and two-tier local government, except between 1973 and 1986 when it was two-tier throughout.

In his 1888 Budget Goschen had to provide a funding regime for the new county and county borough councils. In doing so, he needed to address the imbalance of funding that his own report had identified back in 1870. Goschen was one of the first to see that not all local services can be financed from local rates. Some services (e.g. poor relief), are redistributive. They require rich people to be taxed so that poor people can benefit. In modern terminology, they are transfer payments. Other services (e.g. sewage and urban transport) provide local public goods, but with some spillover. They benefit those in the city, but not only those in the city. Insanitary conditions and urban congestion threatened the rich and out-of-towners as well as the poor and city-dwellers. Even the rich died of cholera and typhus.

Goschen understood that neither transfer payments nor local public goods could be financed out of the traditional sole source of local expenditure, namely property rates. Transfers could not come out of property rates because rich areas could raise the funds but had little demand for transfers, whereas poor areas could not raise the funds but had heavy demand. Local public goods should not be financed wholly out of the rates precisely because they were *public* goods – there needed to be a mechanism to get free-riders to pay. Accordingly, the 1888 Budget contains structures for transferring tax proceeds from central to local government; the first formula-based treatment of Scotland and Ireland; and a valiant but unsuccessful attempt to get the polluter to pay. Goschen's budget was the ancestor of both the Balance of Funding Review and the Barnett Formula discussed in subsequent chapters.

The sums that Goschen transferred were modest; the principles have lasted. He assigned two sources of revenue and proposed one new tax. 'Assigning revenue' means turning over the proceeds of a given tax to the localities, while retaining control of the tax rate and the mechanism of collection at the centre. As the tax burden for local services on land and real estate was excessive, Goschen stated that he was transferring 'a substantial sum … from personal property to the relief of local taxation' (*Hansard* 26.03.88, c. 288). The first assignment was of the proceeds of excise (a tax, mostly, on alcoholic drinks) to local authorities in Britain, but not Ireland. The second was to assign half the proceeds of probate duty (*Hansard*, 26.03.88; Redlich and Hirst i: 199–200). In an era where the obvious source (to us) of personal tax receipts, namely income tax, had narrow and controversial coverage, probate duty was not so outlandish a tax base as it may sound. After dismissing income tax as a base to assign, Goschen identified probate tax as the only source of 'realized personalty' – and a robust one (*Hansard* 26.03.88, c. 289).

Goschen tried to deal with the problem of urban local public goods by proposing a tax on 'wheels and vans', and on horses kept for pleasure rather than business. This made good economic sense. Carts and vans caused urban congestion. The streets of London and other cities were full of horse manure. Personal horses were the sports utility vehicles of 1888, imposing a negative externality on their neighbours which was not reflected in the costs their owners paid. But not for the first time, a tax which made economic sense proved politically impossible to implement. Nicknamed the 'veal and ham' tax, it was impossible to secure a parliamentary majority for it. Not until the London Congestion Charge of 2003 was Goschen's principle of taxing to alleviate local public bads implemented.

Just as today, the tax system was standard throughout the UK, but the arrangements for spending the proceeds differed sharply in

Scotland and Ireland from those in England. Both Scotland and Ireland had semi-independent administrations which would oversee public spending there. Goschen went on to give these administrations their first block grants, from the probate duty proceeds. He noted, however, that simply returning to them the share of probate duty raised there would not help to meet Ireland's greater demands for public spending. He found that 85 per cent of the proceeds came from England, 10 per cent from Scotland, and 5 per cent from Ireland, so if that amount was simply returned to the Irish administration, 'Ireland would come off very badly indeed'. Instead, he went on, he would

> give each country a share of it in proportion to the general contribution of that country to the Exchequer. On this principle, England will be entitled to 80 per cent, Scotland to 11 per cent, and Ireland to 9 per cent (*Hansard* 26.03.88, c. 301).

This is obscure. Goschen went on to say that Ireland's 'general contribution to the Exchequer' was less than 9 per cent. He said it was 8.7 per cent, but that is impossible to believe if the numbers in Gladstone's First Reading speech only two years before (see above) were anything like accurate. Given the poverty of Ireland, Gladstone's figures are more credible than Goschen's.

Nevertheless, formula funding for Ireland and Scotland made good sense for a politician who wished to retain the Union of the countries of the United Kingdom. The Union was at risk from peripheral grievances. But the peripheral countries contained the poorest regions in the Union. Therefore Goschen needed a device for quiet redistribution: enough to alleviate grievance in the periphery but not to provoke resentment at the centre. Redistribution by formula did the trick. The ratio 80:11:9 for England (with Wales), Scotland, and Ireland was the 'Goschen formula' or 'Goschen proportion' that was to dominate discussion between officials in Scotland, Ireland (later Northern Ireland), and the Treasury for nearly eighty years.

The Goschen formula was redistributive to Ireland, because the money assigned to the Irish administration far outweighed the relevant tax proceeds in Ireland. Further measures of 'killing Home Rule with kindness' followed, culminating in George Wyndham's Land Act of 1903, which completed the buy-out of Irish landowners by the (involuntary) British taxpayer. It was not enough to save Ireland for the Union. But assigned revenues continued (in theory) to finance expenditure in the remaining province of Northern Ireland from its creation in 1920.

As to Scotland, a myth grew up that the Goschen proportion was related to Scotland's population proportion. Reference to Goschen's speech (above) shows that this is false. In 1888, the transfer was more or less financially neutral, because Scotland's tax take was close to its population share. Thus the Goschen Proportion was not originally redistributive to Scotland, but it became so. It never governed the whole of Scottish spending, but it became a focal point (Schelling 1984, pp. 220–1) for all Scottish Office and Scotch Education Department lobbying of the Treasury. The most important step was that the Education (Scotland) Act 1918 wrote it into the funding formula for schools, at the same time as hugely increasing state funding for Scottish schools by a wholesale takeover of the Roman Catholic school system (Mitchell 2003, ch. 8; McLean 1999, pp. 189–92). This implied a step increase in expenditure in Catholic schooling; and also a higher per head expenditure in Scotland than in England. The Catholic population share is higher in Scotland than in England; and Catholics have more children than non-Catholics.

The Goschen Proportion gradually spread to other services, with Scottish politicians and civil servants always insisting that Scotland's entitlement should be at least 11/80 of that for England and Wales (equivalently, 11/91 of the total budget for Great Britain). When they could make a case for more than 11/80, as they came to do for education (Mitchell 2003, ch. 8), they did so. When they could not, they kept prudently silent and relied on Goschen. With a floor of 11/80, service by service, it followed that Scotland's spending on those services covered by the Goschen formula was higher than 11/80 of that for England and Wales, while Scotland's relative population declined.

Table 3.1 shows that the Goschen proportion gave Scotland a poor deal until 1901, but an increasingly good deal thereafter.

Enter Sidney and Beatrice

Sidney (1859–1947) and Beatrice (1858–1943) Webb were far from the only architects of the Edwardian Welfare State. But their exhaustive researches into the structure of British local government and their redistributive enthusiasms give them pride of place in this section. Other important players included:

- Chancellor, later Prime Minister, H.H. Asquith, architect of the first Old Age Pensions;
- his successor as Chancellor David Lloyd George, whose leading innovations on the revenue side came in his 1909 and 1914

Table 3.1   Relative populations of England & Wales and Scotland, censuses 1881–1971

Census	Population, 000s:		Scotland: England & Wales = 80	Value of Goschen Proportion per head in Scotland (England = 100)
	England and Wales	Scotland		
1881	25,974	3736	11.51	95.59
1891	29,003	4026	11.11	99.05
1901	32,528	4472	11.00	100.01
1911	36,070	4761	10.56	104.17
1921	37,887	4882	10.31	106.71
1931	39,952	4843	9.70	113.43
1939	41,460	5007	9.66	113.86
1951	43,758	5096	9.32	118.07
1961	46,105	5179	8.99	122.41
1971	48,750	5229	8.58	128.19

Source: British Historical Statistics, B.R. Mitchell (CUP 1988).
Note: 1939 mid-year estimate.

Budgets, and on the expenditure side for his National Insurance plan of 1911;

• and highly committed civil servants such as Sir Hubert Llewellyn Smith, W.J. Braithwaite, and the young William Beveridge, who created the new machinery (Braithwaite 1957; Harris 1997).

This disparate group had one thing in common. They all believed that the welfare state was a job for central government and its agencies, not for local government. In Beveridge's words of November 1909, 'local government areas are out of all relation to industrial needs and structure' (quoted in Harris 1997, p. 173). Although the Minister for local government, John Burns, came from a labour background, he had neither the drive nor the redistributive enthusiasm of his Liberal colleagues Lloyd George and Winston Churchill. Thus the Edwardian Welfare State was a redistributive engine of central government. So was the second Welfare State, created by Beveridge and others between 1942 and 1948.

On a walking holiday in Norway in July 1891, Beatrice gave Sidney the following ruthless evaluation of their prospects:

We are both of us second-rate minds – but we are curiously combined – I am the investigator, and he the executor; and we have a wide and varied experience of men and things between us. I have also an unearned salary. This forms our unique circumstances. A considerable work should be the result, if we use our combined talents with a deliberate and persistent purpose (Webb 1982, entry for 07.07.91).

Beatrice, the investigator, was tall, beautiful, upper-class, had an unearned salary, and had almost become the mistress of Joseph Chamberlain. Sidney, the executor, had none of these properties. But Beatrice's expectations of their combined talents turned out to be spot-on. They worked at first by 'permeation' of susceptible politicians of all parties and bureaucrats of none, before turning after 1910 to the Labour Party exclusively.

In social policy, their most famous contribution was the Minority Report of the Royal Commission on the Poor Law (1909). In 1905 the expiring Balfour government did what Harold Wilson was later to copy extensively. Faced with a difficult problem, it appointed a Royal Commission which would not report until long after the succeeding General Election. We examine below where Wilson's use of this tactic led, when he appointed a Royal Commission on the Constitution in 1969.

For the Balfour government, the difficult problem was poverty. Everybody could see that the New Poor Law of 1834 no longer worked efficiently (if it ever had). The 1834 law was supposed to provide incentives for the able-bodied poor to work by making workhouses worse than any possible alternative, while still keeping the inmates alive (but without second helpings of gruel). The problem was as old as the Elizabethan 'sturdy beggar' and as new as the welfare-to-work programme of the 1997 Labour government. Patently, the Oliver Twist solution of 1834 had failed. Secondly, as poor relief was a transfer payment, it was not a suitable function for purely local taxation. Thirdly, it could be overwhelmed by both cyclical and structural unemployment. Not only liberals and socialists worried about poverty. A moral panic about 'physical deterioration' had arisen during the Boer War of 1899–1902, when it emerged that a high proportion of Army recruits were too unhealthy and too stunted to fight. This gave Unionists as well as politicians of the left a stake in the poverty debate.

Beatrice was appointed a member of the Commission and permeated away busily for four years. She clearly intended from the outset to produce a personal manifesto rather than a consensus report. Her talent for publicity has ensured that the Minority Report, which she signed together with three other socialist members of the Royal Commission, became much better known than the Majority Report (although its public finance is utterly irresponsible).

The two reports actually contain quite similar recommendations, although the similarity was easily swamped under Beatrice's two-volume manifesto. Both Majority and Minority recommended the abolition of Poor Law Guardians, and subsuming both their functions and their powers of levying rates into the 1888 creations, County and County Borough Councils. The Majority wanted the function to come under a single, new, Public Assistance Committee of each authority; Beatrice and her colleagues wanted the function to be split among existing committees for health, education, and so on. However, as *The Times* commented, 'both the majority and the minority have gone beyond their brief' (*Times* 1909, p. 4) to make wide-ranging proposals on unemployment relief. Here in part is *The Times'* jaundiced summary of Beatrice's plan:

> Almost incidentally the [Minority] Report throws out the remark, as though it were indisputable, that the age for old-age pensions should be reduced to 65, if not to 60; ... the cost, taking 65 as the age limit, would be £27,000,000 a year; and we may assume that if 60 were the limit, that sum would be nearly doubled.[5] [L]abour must be not only regularised, but organised ... [by] a Minister responsible to Parliament, who might be designated the 'Minister for Labour'.... [T]his Ministry is to lay down a 'ten years' programme' of work for the unemployed in slack times.... In other words, the minority recommendations are the recommendations of State Socialism; and the State must be sick indeed before it has recourse to such desperate remedies (*Times* 1909, p. 6).

State Socialism or not, much of the minority programme was enacted before 1914, even though the socialist party (if that is what the Labour Party was) never held more than 42 seats, and unlike the Irish Party had no veto power. It was all in place by 1951, after two world wars and a majority Labour government. It had the profoundest effects on public finance – *The Times* was at least right about that.

The Labour Party had no power; the labour (i.e. working-class) voter had the power of the median voter. Therefore the Liberal governments of 1906–15 enacted substantial social legislation. Non-contributory Old Age Pensions came in 1908. They were only for people of over 70, and were relatively cheap for only as long as few people lived to that age.

As longevity improved throughout the 20th century, the state pension would absorb a larger and larger share of public spending. Labour Exchanges came in 1909, in a collaboration between Chancellor Lloyd George, Home Secretary Winston Churchill, and left-wing bureaucrats including Llewellyn Smith and Beveridge. National Insurance against sickness and unemployment came in 1911, due to Lloyd George and his 'ambulance wagon' (Braithwaite 1957) of committed civil servants. Since its first announcement in the 1909 Budget, Lloyd George had sold the scheme as something for nothing, or rather 'ninepence for fourpence' (contributors would get benefits worth 9d in exchange for contributions of 4d a week). His horrified officials demanded that any national insurance scheme must be actuarially sound. Lloyd George wanted a 'pay as you go' scheme, whereby current benefits were paid from current contributions. Although in the end he told his officials 'I am inclined after all to be virtuous' – i.e. to enact an actuarially sound funded scheme (Braithwaite 1957, p. 127) – his virtue was skin deep. Trade unions had contributory schemes, and were to be recognised as collecting agents under the 1911 Act. Lloyd George promoted a funded scheme in order to get trade union and Conservative support, and to differentiate himself from the Webbs' 'national minimum' scheme. His tactical alliance with the unions aimed to show that the Liberal government was closer to their interests than were the socialist Webbs. But he revealed his true preferences in a note to his private secretary in March 1911:

> Insurance necessarily a temporary expedient. At no distant date hope State will acknowledge a full responsibility in the matter of making provision for sickness, breakdown and unemployment It really does so now, through Poor Law; but conditions under which this system had hitherto worked have been so harsh and humiliating that working-class pride revolts against accepting so degrading and doubtful a boon. Gradually the obligation of the State to fund labour or sustenance will be realised and honourably interpreted (LG to Ralph Hawtrey, 07.03.1911 in Braithwaite 1957, p. 24).

Whether or not it was honourably interpreted, it was realised, by subsequent governments of all parties. The 1911 scheme covered only a narrow segment of the working class, those actuarially at the lowest risk of becoming sick or unemployed. Any extension would make the National Insurance Fund less of a fund and more of a pay-as-you-go pot. The first crucial extension was to widows and pensioners, by the Conservatives in 1925. The most general extension was under the Beveridge Report during the wartime coalition government in 1942, when one of the godfathers of the 1911 scheme got the opportunity to widen its scope to cover, essentially, the whole employed population and their families (Harris 1997 pp. 365–450). Since Beveridge, National Insurance contributions have been simply a disguised form of income tax. The National Insurance Fund has been a fiction, the scheme has been entirely pay-as-you-go, and transfers have been a function of beneficiaries' status and contribution record, the latter gradually diminishing in standing as a criterion.

What is now the Social Protection function of government, therefore – the largest single component of public expenditure – is a transfer from the relatively rich to (some of) the poor. It is geographical in so far as the rich tend to live in one place and the poor in another, but it is not formally a transfer from one region to another. Lloyd George was forced to concede territorial committees for Scotland, Wales, and Ireland (known in the ambulance wagon as 'the Celts' – Braithwaite 1957, p. 37); but rates did not vary by geography.

Some social services remained with local authorities, as both the Webbs and their majority colleagues had wanted. But the pressure has always been upwards and away from them. The 1920s debate on 'Poplarism' exemplified this. In 1921 the Labour-controlled London borough of Poplar, led by George Lansbury (later leader of the Labour Party), raised benefit rates beyond the proceeds of local taxation, deliberately driving the borough into bankruptcy and thirty Labour councillors to jail (Shepherd 2002). This was fine as gesture politics (later copied by the Militant leadership of Liverpool and Lambeth in the 1980s), but when Labour formed its first government in 1924, the minister responsible for local government, John Wheatley, would have none of it. Wheatley had extolled the Poplar councillors in opposition but gave no real ground to them in government. He rescinded the banning orders against them, but insisted that he would put machinery in place to stop a single London borough from repeating what they had done (McLean 1999, pp. 212–4). He failed to get round to doing that before the fall of the Government. Successive centralising governments had tried more and more to circumscribe the powers of local government to do things they disapproved of, a peak in centralism being reached in the face-off between Margaret Thatcher and left-wing Labour councils including Liverpool in the 1980s. Poplar shows that local authorities are not suitable bodies to deliver transfer payments, unless a robust equalisation system is in place, a matter to which we return in later chapters.

Lloyd George and public finance

Thus the Welfare State, created between 1908 and 1911 and vastly enlarged since then, created a uniform UK-wide set of entitlements funded by uniform UK-wide taxes. The main transfer programme – what is now called Social Protection – is not devolved to Scotland, Wales, or Northern Ireland, nor to local authorities in England. However, some domestic social services are so devolved, raising serious issues of geographical fairness.

Expenditure was one side of the story; taxation was the other. Here Lloyd George's genius was at its most fertile, aided by the incoherence of his unionist opponents. Before Lloyd George, there had been Liberal steps in the direction of progressive taxation, notably in the Budgets of 1894 (Harcourt) and 1907 (Asquith). In 1909 Lloyd George moved progressive taxation to the front line of the class war – and won.

He was lucky in his enemies, and (unlike with National Insurance) unlucky in his officials. The Treasury high command was so horrified at the unorthodoxy of their Chancellor and his ideas that the Permanent Secretary, Sir George Murray, openly complained about them to Lord Rosebery (Murray 1980, p. 123). This was as unconstitutional as Queen Victoria's attempts to block Gladstone from the Prime Ministership in 1886 and 1892. It was also as ineffective. Lloyd George had the good luck to inhabit a policy vacuum, because Unionist public finance was totally incoherent. It was partly that the Unionists had backed a noisy jingoistic campaign for warships ('We want eight [Dreadnoughts] and we won't wait') – which somebody had to pay for. More profoundly, Unionist public finance was entangled with Chamberlain's campaign for Tariff Reform, launched in 1903 (McLean 2001b, pp. 121–7). Chamberlain and his followers saw Tariff Reform as a panacea. Among other things, it would link Britain with the white Dominions; protect failing British industry; be nasty to horrid foreigners such as Germans; and fund social reform. Unfortunately, the last objective clashed with all the others. For if tariffs succeeded in keeping out imports, they would raise no revenue, and there would therefore be no alternative pot to fund social reform and transfers.

Therefore, however much Lloyd George's officials complained about him, he was not as bad as Chamberlain. In only two respects were the budgets of 1907, 1909, and 1914 unorthodox. The first, now thoroughly embedded in public finance, was the progressive principle: that is, a higher marginal rate of tax on high earners than on lower earners. Introduced as 'supertax' in 1907, it now underpins the variable rates of income tax used by all advanced countries. Progressive taxation has a geographical effect, symmetrical to that of transfers. Tax takes more money per head from rich parts of the country. Transfers move more money per head to the poor parts of the country. Probably, London has been the richest region of the UK continuously since 1907. In 1907, Ireland was the poorest; since the 1930s, the depressed industrial regions of northern England, Scotland, and Wales have been the poorest: although of course there is much poverty in rich regions and some wealth in poor regions.

Lloyd George's second principle was land taxation. Although he failed, we describe his Land Campaign here because the issues it raises will recur in later chapters. Like many politicians of the left at the time, Lloyd George was influenced by his namesake, the American journalist Henry George (1839–97). George lived in San Francisco during the Gold Rush, and therefore watched speculators and railway promoters become hugely rich as previously valueless land became valuable. Some of that value arose by chance: gold was found in previously worthless hills, and real-estate owners in San Francisco found themselves on top of another goldmine. Much of the value was conferred by the state, for instance in the 'eminent domain' (see Glossary) rights that Congress gave to the Central Pacific Rail Road, owned by sometime Governor of California Leland Stanford and four friends.[6] George concluded that as land value gains were either windfalls or were conferred by state action, it was appropriate for the state to tax them.

Henry George was the biggest influence on thinkers of the British left in his time – a far greater influence than Karl Marx. He visited Britain and Ireland during the agricultural depression of the 1880s to spread his message. His most effective ally was his namesake. In the 1909 Budget, Lloyd George announced the creation of a register of land values, as a preliminary to taxing them. The Duke of Buccleuch announced that the land tax would be so crippling that he could no longer afford the subscription to his village football club. A number of Liberal MPs held a whip-round to make it up (Jenkins 1968, pp. 88–9). Lloyd George hit back:

> [A] fully-equipped Duke costs as much to keep as two Dreadnoughts – and they are just as great a terror – and they last longer.

Anticipating (and helping to provoke) the House of Lords' rejection of the budget, Lloyd George went on

> The question will be asked 'Should 500 men, ordinary men chosen accidentally from among the unemployed, override the judgment – the deliberate judgment – of millions of people who are engaged in the industry which makes the wealth of the country?' That is one question. Another will be, who ordained that a few should have the land of Britain as a perquisite; who made 10,000 people owners of the soil, and the rest of us trespassers in the land of our birth[?]... These are the questions that will be asked. The answers are charged with peril for the order of things the Peers represent; but they are fraught with rare and refreshing fruit for the parched lips of the multitude... (At Newcastle upon Tyne, October 10, 1909, quoted by Jenkins 1968, p. 94).

The House of Lords rejected the Budget, as Lloyd George and Winston Churchill had hoped, because that action forced an election which the anti-Unionist coalition won, having previously been expected to lose. It also forced the issue of the Lords' own powers on to the agenda. The ensuing politics of the Parliament Act 1911, and the introduction of Irish Home Rule and Welsh disestablishment in 1912 in the knowledge that they would be enacted in 1914, took Lloyd George's eye off the fiscal ball. (He was also, of course, very busy with National Insurance). Not until the 1914 Budget did he reintroduce proposals to reform central grant to local authorities and to establish land value rating. They were a mess, and Lloyd George had to withdraw them in June. The former head of the Inland Revenue, who had been a strong ally of Lloyd George in 1909 ('I would like to festoon this room with their [the Lords'] entrails'), now vented his frustration at his former boss's ways of doing business: 'It all springs from the besetting sin of the creature that he will not work at his business beforehand & betimes, and it serves him perfectly right that he has got it 'in the neck'' (Sir Robert Chalmers, quoted [1909] by Murray 1980, p. 80; [1914] by Murray 1987, p. 1). Before the month was out, the Archduke Franz Ferdinand was assassinated in Sarajevo.

The Goschen proportion at work

In 1922, Winston Churchill said in the Commons that in the Great War, 'Every institution, almost, in the world was strained. Great

Empires have been overthrown... but as the deluge subsides and the waters fall we see the dreary steeples of Fermanagh and Tyrone emerging once again' (Churchill 1929 pp. 319–20). By then the dreary steeples of Fermanagh and Tyrone were in the province of Northern Ireland, created by the Government of Ireland Act 1920. That Act was enacted by Lloyd George's postwar coalition government – led in this case by its Unionist members Bonar Law and Walter Long. The Act also created a Government of southern Ireland, and a Council of Ireland that might bring the two together. However, neither of those institutions came into existence. Instead, the British government acknowledged the independence of the Irish Free State (now the Republic of Ireland) in 1921. Northern Ireland remains part of the UK, with its (highly unsatisfactory) boundaries exactly as they were set in 1920.

Its public finance is even more unsatisfactory, being more or less where Mr Gladstone left it in 1886. Sections 20–34 of the GOI Act 1920 (1920 c. 67) specified that the main revenue source for (Northern) Ireland was to be the transfer of assigned revenues. Northern Ireland was to have the power to tax, but by s. 20 all the important and buoyant taxes including income tax, corporation tax, Customs, and Excise were reserved to the Imperial Parliament. From the Northern Irish proceeds of assigned taxation, the UK government would first deduct an Imperial Contribution (Ireland's share of the cost of the services provided by the Imperial Parliament – mostly debt payments and defence). This contribution was initially set at £18 million for the whole of Ireland, 44 per cent of which (£7.92m) would be Northern Ireland's share (1920 c. 67, s. 23). It would then deduct the cost of providing reserved services in Northern Ireland. The rest would be for the Parliament of Northern Ireland to use as it wished. The Act gives a prominent place to a Joint Exchequer Board, to broker disputes.

It was all fantasy. The total revenue assigned to Northern Ireland was not enough to pay for devolved services. Northern Ireland never levied any taxes of its own, to speak of. And, as a poor area of the UK, it would have been fruitless for it to try. The Joint Exchequer Board was a nullity, whose chair was described in a Treasury note as 'an aged Scottish Judge ... who lives in Bournemouth' (PRO, T/233/1475, 07.04.52, quoted by Mitchell 2004a p. 8). The Royal Commission on the Constitution, reporting in 1973, summarised the situation as follows:

The intention of the [GOI] Act [1920] was that Northern Ireland should be provided with a comfortable income and left to its own devices. Its revenue would be sufficient both to finance the transferred services and to furnish a substantial contribution towards the cost of the services still operated by the United Kingdom Government. Very soon, however, the income provided by the Act became insufficient to finance even the transferred services.... This represented a complete reversal of what the Act intended. The method of financing provided in the Act was ... the revenue basis, in which a subordinate government is given certain predetermined sources of revenue and has to finance the devolved services out of the proceeds. The method actually operated was the expenditure basis, in which expenditure requirements are measured first and the subordinate government is furnished with the income necessary to meet them. (Royal Commission on the Constitution, 1973, paras 1273–4).

In fiction, Northern Ireland made an Imperial Contribution to the UK. In reality, the UK made an Imperial Contribution to Northern Ireland. Subsidising its standard of living was the price that successive UK governments were prepared to pay to keep Northern Ireland in the union and the Empire.

In Scotland, the shadow of Goschen was more substantial. Scotland, like Ireland, retained a separate administration. From 1707 until 1872, this was in the hands of the Lord Advocate. In 1872, the Gladstone administration created a Scotch Education Department, and in 1885 a(n initially separate) Scottish Office. Their officials went native – indeed, they were natives. Sir Henry Craik was Secretary to the Scotch Education Department from 1885 until 1904, and later the Unionist MP for Aberdeen and Glasgow Universities. Both as bureaucrat and as politician, he lobbied ceaselessly for his department, and for (at least) the Goschen share of education spending to be earmarked for Scotland. After one of these rows in 1926, the Permanent Secretary to the Treasury minuted the Prime Minister as follows:

Sir H. Craik was himself a Civil Servant from 1870 to 1904, during the last nineteen years of the period being Secretary to the Scottish Education Department. He conceived that position as one of great importance and the contemporary Treasury (unfortunately) never seems to have disguised its view that neither Sir Henry nor his post was of any particular importance. Hence an abiding resentment on his part.... (Sir W. Fisher to S. Baldwin, 16.02.26, quoted by Mitchell 2003, pp. 150–1).

But Sir Henry had the last laugh. He and his successors relentlessly lobbied the Treasury to ensure that Scotland never got less than its Goschen proportion of 11/91 of any new spending programme. The Secretary (of State) for Scotland did the same – it was his job. Whenever they could, they argued for more than Goschen, although even 11/91 was after 1901 more than Scotland's population share (Table 3.1; Mitchell 2003 ch. 8 *passim*). The only department in a position to resist these claims was the Treasury itself. But with Scotland directly represented at the Cabinet table, by a Secretary of State who could always play the Home Rule card, the Treasury would not even start to get its revenge until the 'Needs Assessment' of 1979, described in later chapters. As noted, Scotland's greatest Goschen triumph was to get the entire Catholic school system taken over by the state in 1918, perhaps (unspokenly) for the same reasons of public order as the Maynooth Grant of 1845. Mitchell (2003) gives numerous examples of Secretaries of State for Scotland playing the Goschen card, which I have previously labelled as the 'Johnston gambit' after its most successful player.

Tom Johnston (1881–1965: Johnston 1952; Walker 1988; McLean 1999) was a Labour MP and journalist, whose *Forward* newspaper had defined Red Clydeside between 1914 and 1922. He became Secretary of State for Scotland in the wartime coalition government in 1941 and stayed in that post until 1945. He formed a bipartisan Council of State uniting all his living predecessors. Most of these were Conservatives; all had done the same as Johnston when in Cabinet, demanding more for Scotland in order to head off any Home Rule agitation. Johnston's Cabinet colleague Herbert Morrison described Johnston as:

> [o]ne of the most able men in the technique of getting his own way at cabinet committees…. He would impress on the committee that there was a strong nationalist movement in Scotland and it could be a potential danger if it grew through lack of attention to Scottish interests. (Morrison 1960, p. 199).

Considering that the allegedly 'strong' nationalist movement came nowhere near winning a by-election until April 1945, at the very end of Johnston's term, and then only because of the wartime truce between the major parties, this was a fine trick with smoke and mirrors.

Johnston also played a role in embedding the parliamentary over-representation of Scotland in 1944 (McLean 1995). The Speaker's

Conference on redistribution of seats had fallen for the Johnston gambit:

> It was strongly urged that ... it would be very desirable, on political grounds, to state from the outset quite clearly that the number of Scottish and Welsh seats should not be diminished. The absence of any such assurance might give rise to a good deal of political feeling and would lend support to the separatist movements in both countries.

In the debate, Johnston said:

> At the time of the Union of the Parliaments – it is sometimes forgotten that we are here by Treaty rights – we had reserved to us a proportion of the Members of the House. In 1707 we had 45 Members. That was when we had a population of just over a million. It is now well over 4,500,000 and we have 74 Members. (Both sources cited from McLean 1995).

He omitted to add that England's population had gone up by more and her proportion of seats by less. He either created, or reinforced, a pervasive myth that Scotland was guaranteed over-representation in 1707. It was not. It was guaranteed over-representation in 1944, a guarantee that lasted until 2004.

In summary, Scotland and Northern Ireland did at least as well as their Goschen proportion, and usually better, from 1888 until the rise of nationalism created a new set of tensions in the 1960s. Even though overt nationalism was quiescent, their politicians possessed a *credible threat* of trouble from nationalists. In Northern Ireland the threat never reached the UK Cabinet, because it was wielded by Stormont ministers in their discussions with the Treasury. In Scotland it did reach the Cabinet, and the Cabinet listened. Fundamentally, public spending depended on threat potential, not on Goschen nor on any other formula. In the 1960s the threat sharpened. In the next chapter we shall see how that led from Goschen to Barnett.

4

The Origins of the Barnett Formula

Nationalism awakes and reawakens 1966–74

Labour won the General Election of 1966 with a comfortable overall majority of seats. All the events described in previous chapters seemed to belong to the remote past. Public finance in Northern Ireland was a private game between the Stormont government and the Treasury. The Goschen Proportion no longer formally applied in Scotland, but it had created the baseline for higher expenditure per head in Scotland than in England on all or most domestic services. This was a little secret, which Scottish Secretaries and St Andrews House knew and loved; the Treasury knew and hated it, but was powerless to do anything about it. Wales, meanwhile, had been given administrative devolution in 1964, as the result of a low-key manifesto commitment of the incoming Labour government. The commitment had caused little stir even in Wales and none elsewhere. The story was that it was incoming Prime Minister Harold Wilson's way of getting rid of an elderly, popular, but ineffective lieutenant, Jim Griffiths. A former deputy leader of the Labour Party, Griffiths became the first Secretary of State for Wales in October 1964. Almost all Whitehall departments had operated on an 'England & Wales' basis. Therefore the powers of the Welsh Office, to begin with, were practically restricted to housing and land-use planning, as these were the already-geographical matters most easily hived off from the Ministry of Housing and Local Government to the new department.

The Wilson government hit economic difficulties in July 1966. Its first by-election was caused in that month by the death of Megan Lloyd George, daughter of the Prime Minister and Labour MP for the Welsh-speaking constituency of Carmarthen. In the by-election, the Welsh nationalist party Plaid Cymru ('Party of Wales') won its first seat on a swing of 18 per cent. Plaid Cymru has always drawn its strength from cultural issues (the Welsh language; the survival of chapels and family farms) and in the thinly populated Welsh-speaking west and north of Wales. It was lucky in its first by-election. The credibility conferred by winning Carmarthen enabled it to do well in by-elections in the non-Welsh speaking and traditionally safe Labour seats of Rhondda West (1967: 29 per cent swing) and Caerphilly (1968: 29 per cent swing). An even bigger upset for Labour occurred in Scotland. In November 1967, as the Labour government handled its second bout of bad economy news culminating in the devaluation of the £, it lost its safest Scottish seat of Hamilton to the Scottish Nationalists on a swing of 38 per cent – to this day still the third-worst by-election defeat in the Labour Party's history.[1] In Northern Ireland, a series of civil rights marches, drawing attention to discrimination against Catholics, degenerated during 1969 into sectarian rioting, which sucked the British Army into the province, initially to protect Catholics under attack in the ghettos of Belfast and Derry.

The unionist parties both reacted to these events. Labour had a strongly unionist Secretary of State for Scotland, Willie Ross. Ross bitterly opposed devolution and had played (and would continue to play) the Johnston gambit with distinction. Its Welsh Secretary by the end of the parliament, George Thomas, was strongly opposed to concessions on language or culture; but more of his time was spent on the aftermath to the Aberfan disaster of October 1966, in which 144 people, mostly schoolchildren, had been killed when a colliery waste tip crushed a school. In the aftermath of Aberfan, it became clear that the new and very junior Welsh Office was at the bottom of the Whitehall playground hierarchy, bossed around by the Ministry of Power, whose mission was to protect the National Coal Board from the consequences of its negligence (McLean and Johnes 2000). However, the Rhondda and Caerphilly by-elections showed Harold Wilson that some concession to nationalism in Wales as well as Scotland might be desirable, and as Richard Crossman's diary reveals, spread alarm and despondency in the Cabinet.

To avoid confronting these conflicting pressures and forcing a solution on a deeply divided Cabinet (Crossman 1977, e.g. entries for 29.04.68, 06.05.68, 09.05.68, 27.05.68), Wilson appointed a Royal Commission on the Constitution in 1969

> to consider, having regard to developments in local government organisation and in the administrative and other relationships

between the various parts of the United Kingdom ... whether any changes are desirable in those functions or otherwise in the present constitutional and economic relationships; to consider, also, whether any changes are desirable in the constitutional and economic relationships between the United Kingdom and the Channel Islands and the Isle of Man (Royal Commission on the Constitution 1973, pp. iii–iv).

Crossman objected to the appointment of this Commission but recorded that 'Callaghan had submitted a paper, signed by Willie Ross and George Thomas recommending a commission. Those two have been bought over very easily, because they are anti-nationalist and this is a way of doing nothing' (Crossman 1977, 23.10.68). Adding the Channel Islands and Isle of Man to the remit ensured that the Commission would not report before the ensuing General Election, which occurred in June 1970.

The Conservatives were more sympathetic to devolution. Under the influence of the Scot Sir Alec Douglas-Home, the leader previous to the incumbent Edward Heath, they drew up a 'Declaration of Perth' in 1968, announcing the party's support for an elected Scottish Assembly. A committee chaired by Home proceeded to draw up a plan for a 125-member assembly, which they published in 1970. That the most unionist party should have proposed this 'is still the subject of some mystery in the annals of Scottish political history' (Kellas 2003). But I do not find it mysterious. In the 1968 Scottish local elections, the SNP had won more votes than either of the unionist parties (McLean 1970). The Conservative & Unionist Party, which cared more about the Union than any other, was the first to show flexibility in order to save the Union. Labour was six years behind it.

The 1970 General Election seemed to show that the nationalist threat had been contained. The nationalists lost Carmarthen and Hamilton, although they gained the quirky and tiny seat of Western Isles, the only constituency in the UK in which the Gaelic language remained viable. Northern Ireland seemed a more immediate threat to the union. The Catholic communities that had welcomed the Army as their saviours turned against them. Paramilitary violence by Protestants against Catholics, Catholics against Protestants, both against the British Army, and the British Army against both, escalated. The new Conservative government under Edward Heath requested the Stormont government to cede control over their security forces to the UK government. When the Stormont government refused to do so, in 1972 (the worst year for sectarian violence), Heath prorogued Stormont, and Northern Ireland came under direct rule. The financial arrangements for running Northern Ireland did not change, except that military and policing costs were now borne directly by the UK government.

The Royal Commission under Lord Kilbrandon reported in 1973, recommending devolved assemblies for Scotland and Wales. By then the SNP was rising fast again, because it had discovered its most effective slogan ever. North Sea Oil had been first brought ashore in 1971, So, to the SNP, 'It's Scotland's Oil...'. As one version of the poster, featuring a haggard-looking old lady, went on: 'so why do 50,000 people in Scotland a year die from hypothermia?' International lawyers gravely disputed whether it was in fact Scotland's oil. Should Scotland declare independence, the international boundary would run north-east, not due east, from Berwick-on-Tweed, thus putting a third of the North Sea oilfields into the English sector (Grant 1976, pp. 86–123). Another third was off Shetland, which was then making the same demands for separation from Scotland that the SNP was making for separation from England. These subtleties did not spoil a great slogan. The SNP won another by-election in 'safe Labour' Govan (swing: 27%) within a week of Kilbrandon reporting.

Labour politicians started to panic. At this point, there were few principled devolutionists in the national party, although one influential one was the Oxford academic Norman Hunt (Lord Crowther-Hunt), a member of the Kilbrandon Commission who was to be Wilson's key adviser in the events that followed. The rest of the national Labour leadership were like Tory peers in 1911, divided into hedgers and ditchers. The hedgers, led by Harold Wilson, believed that making some gestures to devolution would head off the Scottish Nationalist threat. For them, devolution was a purely pragmatic move, to be taken with no deep thought as to its constitutional implications. The ditchers, led by Willie Ross and (in a quite different way) by the MP for West Lothian Tam Dalyell, believed that any concession to the SNP was dangerous. For them, devolution was a dangerous precedent, a slippery slope, the start of the break-up of Britain.

In the February 1974 General Election, the SNP held Western Isles and gained six more seats, four from the Conservatives and two from Labour, while just failing to hold its by-election gain in Govan. It won 22 per cent of the Scottish vote. Astute politicians knew that, while the electoral system had protected Labour by giving the SNP only 10 per cent of the Scottish seats for its 22 per cent of the vote, it would swing round viciously if the SNP vote share were to rise by another 10 percentage points or so. On a vote share of somewhere between 30 and 35 per cent, the SNP would flip from victim of the electoral system to its beneficiary. With an evenly distributed 35 per cent of the vote, it could win more than half of the seats in Scotland (Labour had just won 40 out of 71 seats (i.e. 56%) in Scotland on 37 per cent of the vote). Were it to do so, it would start to negotiate for Scottish independence. Bang would go the United Kingdom and (more importantly for national Labour politicians) Labour's chance of forming a governing majority, which utterly depended on its 40 Scottish seats.

The battle of Dalintober Street

Through the year 1974, Labour's national elite focused on these governing realities, while its Scottish elite focused more on the pros and cons of devolution *per se*. This led to the confused events of June to August. On June 22, 1974, Scotland were playing Yugoslavia in the World Cup. A thinly attended meeting of the Labour Party's Scottish Executive was evenly divided between hedgers and ditchers when, in Tam Dalyell's account:

> all eyes turned to ... the petite and comely Mrs Sadie Hutton of Glasgow, who had drifted in after doing her morning's shopping. Loyal to her [ditcher] Chairman, and resentful of the pressure that was being put on him from Transport House, she raised her hand.... So, by six votes to five, the Scottish Executive of the Labour Party reaffirmed their policy that an Assembly was 'irrelevant to the real needs of Scotland' (Dalyell 1977, p. 101).

Pandemonium ensued. To reverse this embarrassing decision, the national leadership of the Labour Party called on their trade union shock troops. In July, the national executive of the party resolved that it 'recognise[d] the desire of the Scottish people for the establishment of an elected legislative Assembly within the context of the political and economic unity of the United Kingdom'. The shock troops were sent with their card votes to a special Scottish conference on 17 August in the Dalintober Street Co-operative Halls in Glasgow. (All these events happened during the summer holidays). This duly reversed the Scottish Executive's position. By command of the National Executive, the un-devolved Scottish Executive announced that it was now in favour of devolution.

Tam Dalyell's bitter but entertaining diary account of this meeting records John Smith as having said that devolutionists 'could not have their cake and eat it, by insisting that they keep the office of Secretary of State for Scotland, and all seventy-one MPs'. But that was precisely the position the party adopted. In Keating and Bleiman's words (1979, p. 167), 'the difficulties over which devolutionists had agonised for years were solved at a stroke by incorporating in the successful propositions the principal demands of both devolutionist and unionist factions'. Smith, the most successful and only committedly devolutionist Labour Minister in the ensuing struggle to legislate, helped to enact the Scotland and Wales Acts 1978, which provided precisely for devolved assemblies in each country while retaining its Secretary of State and its full slate of Westminster MPs.

Harold Wilson's and his officials' determination to enact the Dalintober Street coup, and reverse the party's position on Scottish devolution, arose after they had commissioned private polls in the summer which appeared to show that there was a groundswell of demand for devolution in Scotland. Analysed more carefully, they do not show that, but rather that there was a groundswell of demand for more public spending. (The polls did not ask whether the Scots would like to pay more tax). In the October 1974 General Election, the SNP advanced further, to 11 seats and 30 per cent of the Scottish vote (Table 4.1). Then the most extreme pro-devolutionists in Scottish Labour split off to form the Scottish Labour Party. It seemed that the ditchers had been right, and that the Union was not to be saved by the Battle of Dalintober Street. The initial Scotland and Wales Bill 1976 was therefore designed to grant devolution while preserving Labour's capacity to govern the UK. So it retained 71 seats for Scotland and 36 for Wales in the House of Commons, whereas the number proportionate to population would have been about 57 and 31. If Scotland and Wales had been given devolution on the lines of the Government of Ireland Act 1920, their seats would have been cut further, to about 2/3 of their population share (say 40 and 25) in recognition that they

Table 4.1   UK General Election of October 1974: seats and votes in Scotland

Party	Vote share, %	Seat share, %
Labour	36.3	56.9
SNP	30.7	15.3
Conservative	24.7	22.2
Liberal	8.3	4.2

would have a devolved assembly. In finance the Bill did not propose any alteration to the block grant arrangements that still echoed Goschen, notably in higher public spending per head.

The Scotland and Wales Bill, though described as the flagship legislation of the Government (by now led by James Callaghan), fell in February 1977 on a guillotine vote, victim of an English backlash (Guthrie and McLean 1978). The backlash was strongest in the North-East of England, which had a long border with Scotland; similar social and economic problems; and according to a government-sponsored survey, the North Region Strategy Team (NRST 1976), less public spending per head than Scotland. As it seemed to local leaders, a Labour government was punishing the Geordies for voting Labour and rewarding the Scots for voting SNP. Furthermore, they believed that devolution would entrench Scotland's advantage, with its continuing 71 MPs, its Secretary of State, and its devolved assembly.

The Government reintroduced two separate bills (which were enacted as the Scotland and Wales Acts 1978 but, in effect, fell at the change of government in 1979) and looked for ways to damp the English backlash. The most important of the latter were the Needs Assessment and the Barnett Formula.

The immediate pre-Barnett situation is best summarised in the terms of the Scotland Act 1978. Its financial clauses are astonishingly meagre – less informative even than the sheet of Lord Rosebery's notepaper on which Gladstone had first sketched Irish Home Rule in 1885. Section 48 of the Scotland Act merely says:

48.–(1) The Secretary of State shall from time to time make out of moneys provided by Parliament payments into the Scottish Consolidated Fund of such sums as he may determine by order made with the consent of the Treasury.

(2) No order under this section shall be made unless a draft of it has been laid before the House of Commons and approved by a resolution of that House; and there shall be laid before that House, together with the draft, a statement of the considerations leading to the determinations to be made by the order.

One of the White Papers leading up to the Act (Cmnd 6890/1977, 'Financing the Devolved Services') had rejected devolving taxation powers. It announced the Government's intention to set up a nonstatutory needs formula. The Bill was little discussed in the Commons and much of such clause-by-clause discussion as took place was in the

Lords. There, a Scottish Office Minister of State said: 'The method of determining the block fund will have to be discussed and agreed with the Administration, but it may be possible to devise a formula approach to this also' (Lord Kirkhill, *Hansard*, Lords, vol. 391 c. 281, 03.05.78). The authoritative commentary on the Act by Bradley and Christie (1979) notes that the financial section of the Act

> contains merely the legal framework necessary to make block grants for expenditure on the devolved services to be paid from the UK Exchequer to the new Scottish Executive.... [I]t contains no provision enabling the UK Government directly to control the choice of expenditure proprieties within the devolved services. (Bradley and Christie 1979, 'General Comment on Part III').

However, as they go on to note, s. 48(2) requires the appropriations to the Scottish Executive to be laid before the Commons. In the event of a conflict between the UK and Scottish governments, this would have given the former a veto over the actions of the latter.

Even in the dry text of their notes on the clauses, the eminent constitutional lawyers Bradley and Christie make no attempt to disguise their opinion, which I share, that the Act would have been utterly unworkable. Luckily for all, it was not put to the test. Labour rebels had inserted, first, an amendment requiring the proposed Scottish and Welsh Assemblies to be put to a referendum in each country; and, later, the 'Cunningham Amendment', moved by an expatriate Scottish MP, requiring 40 per cent of the electorate to vote 'Yes' before the Acts could be implemented. In the Welsh referendum, the proposed Assembly was thrown out by a majority of 4 to 1. In Scotland, the 'Yes' side just barely won, by 51.6 per cent to 48.4 per cent, but was supported by only 32.9 per cent of the electorate. The Conservatives proposed a motion of no confidence in the Government, which the SNP perforce supported. In March 1979, it succeeded by one vote. This forced a General Election, won by Mrs Thatcher's Conservatives. The Nationalists did badly. Mrs Thatcher immediately repealed the Scotland and Wales Acts, and devolution went into cold storage.

But the funding of the Scottish, Welsh, and Northern Ireland Offices was an issue that would not go away. The Labour Government had signalled its intention to fund these territories by formula. This gave the Treasury the incentive it needed to put that funding on a more defensible footing. And it would give Ministers a weapon to deal with any future English backlash.

The needs assessment and the Barnett Formula

The engine-room of the 1977 rebellion was Tyneside. It turned on the alleged privilege of Scotland *vis-à-vis* the Northern region. Scotland and the Northern Region had roughly equivalent deprivation. Each of them had a regional GDP per head of about 84 per cent of the UK average. But mean spending in Scotland on the services which were to be devolved was 117.0 per cent of the GB average per head, whereas that on the Northern region was only 112.4 per cent of the GB average. It seemed that the (Labour) government was rewarding the Scots for voting SNP, while failing to reward the Geordies for voting Labour. (NRST 1976, Table 4.3; Guthrie and McLean 1978).

The Treasury responded with the Needs Assessment and the Barnett formula. In so doing, they were pursuing their own bureaucratic agenda, but they were also helping the Unionist politicians of both the outgoing Labour and the incoming Conservative government to save the Union by heading off future English backlashes. The main finding of the Needs Assessment is in Table 4.2.

Thus, if (a big if) the figures were reliable, Scotland was spending above her 'needs' at the time of the Geordie revolt, and Wales below.

The origins of the Barnett Formula are mysterious and controversial. Joel Barnett, Chief Secretary to the Treasury, applied it from 1978. Its existence was first publicly revealed in 1980 (Heald 1980). Though Barnett has said that he did not initially think his formula would last 'a year or even twenty minutes' (House of Commons Treasury Committee 1998, evidence Q1), and also that it was intended to be a transitional device until a needs-based formula could be put in place, it has not only survived but has been embedded in the post-1997 devolution settlement. Both the Scottish and Welsh White Papers (although not the respective Acts) setting up their devolved administrations promised that the Barnett formula would continue to cover the assignment of blocks of spending to the devolved territories. Northern Irish spending is also governed by the formula. Ministers frequently repeat that,

Table 4.2   HM Treasury 'Needs Assessment', 1979 (data for 1976–7)

	England	Scotland	Wales	Northern Ireland
Relative needs assessment	100	116	109	131
Actual spending levels 1976–7	100	122	106	135

Source: HM Treasury (1979), esp. para 6.5. Crown copyright.

although the Barnett Formula is not 'set in stone', yet 'there are no plans to change it'.

The Barnett formula is much misunderstood, often wilfully, but see Edmonds 2001; Bell 2001; Bell and Christie 2001; Heald 2001. The Treasury has also published on the Web its operational manual for applying the Barnett formula to the devolved administrations (HM Treasury, current (4th) edition 2004). The formula originally had two purposes. It was an *anti-rounding-up device*; and a *convergence formula*. Early justifications of it, including Joel Barnett's, concentrated on the first. Now, only the second is noticed. It has completely succeeded in the first aim and largely failed in the second.

The Treasury wanted an anti-rounding up device after many years of battle with Scottish departments over the Goschen proportion (Mitchell 2003, chapter 8), and with Northern Ireland financial civil servants, whom they saw as mendicants. They were terrified that the mendicant mentality might spread to Wales. When spending was negotiated with the territorial departments one programme at a time, the territorial department could use the Goschen proportion as a floor. If it could make a special claim for the particular service being negotiated (say, that Scotland had more teachers to pay or a sparser population), it did; if not, it could refuse to be budged below Goschen, and could often call on Cabinet support. Barnett therefore forced the territorial Secretaries of State to argue for a block, not for programme-by-programme increments. According to the Scottish Office civil servant who was in charge of devolution policy at the time, the formula

> reflected the conviction of all Departments other than the Scottish Office and all MPs other than Scottish ones that the Scots had been getting away with murder.... The purpose of Barnett was both to simplify the Treasury's bargaining processes and to ensure that, when increases in Votes were negotiated, the total Scottish increase over all Votes should be no more than a reasonable one. (J. Ross, 1985, quoted in Mitchell 2002, p. 5)

As Barnett himself has said, this made the Chief Secretary's life easier; it also placated English spending departments. But eighty years of Goschen and credible threats had left Scottish and Northern Irish (although not Welsh) spending per head above 'needs', if the Needs Assessment was correct. Therefore Barnett was designed to operate also as a *convergence formula*. As such, it worked, and continues to work, not on absolute public spending, but on increments to public spending. Each time there was an increment in public spending in England on a domestic service that would have been devolved,[2] Scotland, Wales and Northern Ireland were each to get an unearmarked increment in their block grant proportionate to the ratio between their population and that of England.

As all three territories were receiving higher public spending per head (on 'devolved' services) than England when the formula began, the operation of the formula should, in the sufficiently long term, have led to convergence on equal public spending per head in each of the three territories.[3] In Scotland, there has been little convergence, as Table 1.1 and Figure 4.1 confirm. In Wales, any convergence will have worsened disparities between Wales and England, if the initial numbers in the 1979 Needs Assessment were correct. In Northern Ireland, there seems to have been divergence in the early 1990s, followed by some convergence. All of these trends may be seen graphically in Figure 4.1.

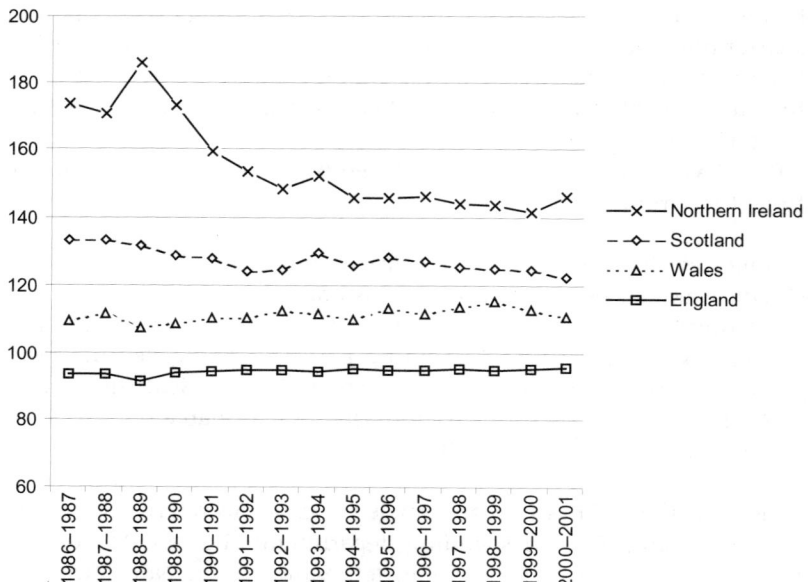

Figure 4.1   Spending on devolved services in England, Scotland, Wales and Northern Ireland 1986–2000 (UK spending = 100)
Source: PESA various years.

A mechanical reason why there was no convergence in Scotland was that the initial population relativities (set, arbitrarily in Goschen fashion, at 85:10:5 for England:Scotland:Wales) were wrong. Scotland has less than 10/85ths of England's population. Chief Secretary Michael Portillo made a one-off correction in 1992 to align the Barnett ratios with population shares (and therefore slightly reduce the flow of goodies to Scotland); it has been rebased biennially since 1997, after each Comprehensive Spending Review (HM Treasury 2004, para. 3.7). Another mechanical reason was that until the mid-1980s public expenditure was planned from year to year on a volume, not a cash, basis. On a volume basis, only *real* increases on spending in England (which were few) would trigger convergence in the territories; real decreases would trigger divergence. On the cash basis that has operated since the mid-1980s, *nominal* increases on spending in England lead to the formula being applied, thus producing a smaller real increase (and perhaps a real cut) in the territories. This effect has continued through the Treasury's recent further move from cash to resource accounting.

However, the reasons for non-convergence are political as well as mechanical. Scotland continued to pose a credible threat to the Union, which any SNP resurgence would bring back to life. Conservative governments were particularly sensitive to this threat. Their Secretaries of State continued to protect Scotland from the full rigour of the Barnett Formula until 1997. Secretaries of State Lang and (especially) Forsyth boasted about the spending differential in order to warn Scots that devolution would threaten it. Prime Minister Major seems to have been uneasy at this strategy (Major 2000, esp. p. 419). In effect, politicians could rely on the quiet convergence of Barnett when it was safe to do so, but any perceived threat to the Union would arm the territorial Secretaries of State to bypass Barnett and counter its convergence effect. One result of this, discussed in the next chapter, is that in the poorer regions of England the 'iniquitous Barnett formula', as it is always labelled by the Newcastle *Journal* and the *Northern Echo*, is seen as the cause, not as the mitigation, of Scotland's spending advantage.

Nobody lobbied for faster convergence in Northern Ireland. Any such suggestion could have imperilled the peace process there. However, Wales was the weakest of the three territories. Wales' administrative devolution dated only to 1964. It also presented no credible threat to the Union. Plaid Cymru could not foreseeably win a majority of Welsh seats, and it was not certain that, even it if did, it would open negotiations for independence – Plaid Cymru being primarily a party of cultural protest, whereas the SNP has always been primarily an economic movement. Perversely, therefore, Wales, which remained poor, may have seen spending converge under the Barnett formula, whereas Scotland, whose GDP per head is now almost at the UK average, did not. Evidence on this is in Chapter 5 below.

Up to 1997, therefore, the Barnett Formula operated as a more dynamic version of the Goschen Proportion, with the same fundamental advantage for unionist politicians. It was an engine of quiet redistribution. Optimally, it would keep down anti-Union feeling in the three non-English territories without arousing anti-Celtic feelings in England. Until 1997, it succeeded wholly in the second aim (because nobody in England outside the Devolved Countries & Regions team in the Treasury understood it), but only partly in the 'Territories', as the Treasury calls them. In the next chapter we examine Barnett after the resurgence of devolution that began in 1989.

5
Barnett and Devolution Today

The third awakening of the Territories, 1989–97

The Conservative victory in 1979 sent devolution to sleep for ten years. In Wales, the crushing defeat of devolution in the 1979 referendum had apparently revealed it to be the pet project of only the Welsh-speaking 20 per cent of Welsh people, with little or nor support among the remaining 80 per cent. In Scotland, the expected howls of outrage that devolution had been approved, but not implemented because of the 40 per cent rule, did not occur. This was superficially puzzling. The entire Scottish political class had been preoccupied with devolution for five years; and the 40 per cent rule was plainly a wrecking amendment – it has never been applied to General Elections, where the only party since 1945 to get more than 40 per cent of the electorate to vote for it was Labour when it *lost* the 1951 General Election.

However, the collapse of devolution not with a bang but with a whimper maybe showed the wisdom of Harold Wilson's strategy of looking busy, without committing himself to anything. Support for devolution had been broad – but not deep. Politicians had mistaken a Scottish wish for more spending with a Scottish wish for more self-government. Analysed more carefully than had Labour leaders in the panicky summer of 1974, the polls carried out for the Royal Commission and Labour's own private polls actually showed no more discontent with the constitution in Scotland than in any other part of Great Britain.

From 1979 to 1989, therefore, devolution was not an issue. Formula funding for the Territories continued to go by the Barnett block, except when territorial Secretaries of State found ways of by-passing Barnett in order to quench any revival of peripheral nationalism.

It is, nevertheless, rather surprising that it remained quiescent for as long as it did. For, although public finance suited politicians in the Territories, their representation in government did not. As throughout our period since 1800, the governing Conservatives were a predominantly English party, and southern English at that. Table 5.1 shows the party balance of seats in the four territories of the UK in the four parliaments of Conservative rule from 1979 to 1997.

Table 5.1 shows an imbalance of representation that Gladstone, Parnell, and Salisbury would have recognised with perfect clarity. In each parliament, the Conservatives won more than half of the seats in the UK, and therefore formed a single-party government. But their majority depended entirely on England. In none of the other three territories, and in none of the four parliaments, did they win as much as a plurality of either seats or votes. If Scotland, Wales, and Northern

Table 5.1   Seats and votes in the four territories of the UK, 1979–97

After General Election of		Conservative		Labour		Other	
		% vote	% seats	% vote	% seats	% vote	% seats
1979							
	Eng	47.2	59.3	36.7	39.3	16.1	1.4
	Scot	31.4	31.0	41.5	62.0	27.1	7.0
	Wales	32.2	30.6	48.6	61.1	19.2	8.3
	NI	0.0	0.0	0.0	0.0	100.0	100.0
	UK	**43.9**	**53.4**	**37.0**	**42.4**	**19.1**	**4.3**
1983							
	Eng	46.0	69.2	27.0	28.3	27.0	2.5
	Scot	28.4	29.2	35.1	56.9	36.5	13.9
	Wales	31.0	36.8	37.5	52.6	31.5	10.5
	NI	0.0	0.0	0.0	0.0	100.0	100.0
	UK	**42.4**	**61.1**	**27.6**	**32.2**	**30.0**	**6.8**
1987							
	Eng	46.2	68.3	29.5	29.6	24.3	2.1
	Scot	24.0	13.9	42.4	69.4	33.6	16.7
	Wales	29.5	21.1	45.1	63.2	25.4	15.8
	NI	0.0	0.0	0.0	0.0	100.0	100.0
	UK	**42.2**	**57.7**	**30.8**	**35.2**	**27.0**	**7.1**
1992							
	Eng	45.5	60.9	33.9	37.2	20.6	1.9
	Scot	25.7	15.3	39.0	68.1	35.3	16.7
	Wales	28.6	15.8	49.5	71.1	21.9	13.2
	NI	5.7	0.0	0.0	0.0	94.3	100.0
	UK	**41.9**	**51.6**	**34.4**	**41.6**	**23.7**	**6.8**

Sources: Butler *et al.*; 1979; 1983; 1987; 1992; *The Times* 1979; 1983; 1987; 1992.

Ireland had had devolution during this period, not one of their devolved governments, over the eighteen years of Conservative rule in the UK, would have been Conservative. As they did not have devolution, they were all three governed by Ministers of a party that had won few seats (no seats, in Northern Ireland) in the territory. Furthermore, some controversial policies were tried first in the Territories. The most prominent example is that the Poll Tax (Community Charge) was piloted in Scotland in 1986, a year before England. Although all the Scottish Ministers who had piloted it lost their seats in the 1987 General Election, Mrs Thatcher persisted with it until her deposition in 1990. Can Unionism withstand such strains? In 1885, Gladstone thought not.

Nevertheless, the territorials were surprisingly quiescent for a surprisingly long time. Even the Poll Tax affair did not stir the Scots from their torpor immediately. Nobody attributed the Conservative losses in Scotland in 1987 to the poll tax (Butler and Kavanagh 1988, pp. 89–113). Throughout Britain in that election, Labour was extremely quiet about the Poll Tax. Its leader, Neil Kinnock, had just publicly and noisily expelled the hard left of the Militant Tendency from the party, and the party desperately wished to avoid being seen as the patron of 'loony left councils'. But as the extent of the poll tax disaster for the Conservatives unrolled during 1988, so did their legitimacy in Scotland. The poll tax had been enacted by a party holding 21 of Scotland's 72 seats, but after the General Election it had been reduced to 10 (Table 5.1); as noted, every Scottish Minister involved in enacting the poll tax had lost his seat. At long last, this revived the constitutional issue of devolution. The Scottish Nationalists derided the 50 Scottish Labour MPs elected in 1987 as the 'Feeble Fifty'. To contain the nationalists, the Labour Party and its allies had to show that they could protect Scotland from another poll tax.

In 1988, the Labour Party in Scotland therefore helped promote a Claim of Right for Scotland, followed by a Constitutional Convention. The Claim of Right intoned:

We, gathered as the Scottish Constitutional Convention, do hereby acknowledge the sovereign right of the Scottish people to determine the form of Government best suited to their needs, and do hereby declare and pledge that in all our actions and deliberations their interests shall be paramount.   (Quoted in Scottish Constitutional Convention (1995), preamble)

Labour worked together with the Liberal Democrats, the churches, trade unions, and other civil society bodies on the Constitutional Convention. The Scottish Nationalists hesitated but stayed outside. The Conservatives stayed out without hesitation. The Constitutional Convention's final report in 1995 recommended a 129-seat parliament elected by an additional member system of proportional representation (AMS). It would have a power to vary the UK rate of income tax up or down by 3p in the pound. Public finance should continue to be governed by the Barnett formula. All of these provisions went into the Labour manifesto and, almost unaltered, into the Scotland Act 1998, so that they now govern the Scottish Parliament. Because the Scottish Constitutional Convention was a Scottish body, not a UK body, it did not have to consider whether its recommendations on public finance made sense from an all-UK point of view.

In Wales, the heirs of Nye Bevan, including for a while Labour leader Neil Kinnock, repeated Bevan's argument (shared with Beveridge and all the other founders of the Welfare State) that devolution imperilled redistribution. It was an argument endorsed by future-Chancellor Gordon Brown in his doctoral thesis (Brown 1981). There was no Welsh Constitutional Convention. Welsh Labour was deeply divided, so that the blueprint brought by its leader, Ron Davies, for the 1997 Labour manifesto was a painful compromise, offering powers over secondary but not primary legislation, and no power to tax nor assignation of UK taxes, to the proposed Welsh Assembly. No pressure group of any consequence, not even Plaid Cymru, was calling very hard for independence or devolution of tax powers. As ever, Plaid Cymru's gaze was fixed on culture rather than on public finance. On the cultural front, things moved faster in Wales than in Scotland. In the 1979 referendum, the *No* campaign had made effective use of the complaint that devolution would privilege a Welsh-speaking elite, who they alleged would monopolise public-sector jobs and force children in Newport to waste time learning Welsh at school. Though the *Yes* campaign used an old Lloyd George trick, viz., saying in their Welsh-language literature that devolution would protect the language while denying in their English-language literature that it would (Ellis 1979), the 'Welsh mafia' objection was probably decisive.

But things changed between 1979 and 1997. After the obstinate George Thomas ceased to be Secretary of State for Wales, UK politicians realised that language concessions in Wales were what economists call cheap talk. They did not cost much to implement, and most of the costs could be spread thinly around the rest of the UK. The most costly innovation was Welsh-language television. S4C (Sianel Pedwar Cymru) has been a great political, as well as broadcasting, success. It increased the visibility of the language, gave non-Welsh speakers an attractive incentive to learn it – and most of the costs were absorbed by the 95 per cent of UK licence payers and consumers of advertising who are not in Wales. Likewise, the Welsh Language Act 1993 proved to be successful cheap talk. And the inclusion of Welsh in the national curriculum, although it causes problems in recruiting primary school teachers, was an enormous step in safeguarding the future of the language. The language, so explosive (sometimes literally) in the years up to 1979, had ceased to be an issue by 1997. As in 1974, therefore, the government that came to power in 1997 decided to offer devolution to Wales as well as to Scotland.

In Northern Ireland, as always, the political dynamics were very different although the financial dynamics were remarkably similar. John Major, Prime Minister from 1990 to 1997, launched the peace process there with substantial help from US President Bill Clinton, in the light of evidence that republican paramilitaries were prepared to give up violence. The process was long and tortuous, and incomplete at the change of government in 1997. However, on Good Friday 1998, the Belfast (or Good Friday) Agreement recreated an elected assembly in Northern Ireland on condition that all parties represented there renounced violence. As in Wales, public finance was at the front of none of the negotiators' minds.

Barnett in operation since 1997: principalities and powers

Labour fought the 1997 General Election with a manifesto commitment to introduce devolution to Scotland and Wales. As explained above, in Wales the commitment was heavily qualified. In Scotland, it had the backing of the Constitutional Convention but apparently only lukewarm support from Labour leader Tony Blair, who said in Edinburgh during the campaign that 'Sovereignty rests with me as an English MP and that's the ways it will stay'. He went on to pooh-pooh the proposed tax-varying power of the Scottish Parliament, which, in the words of the *Scotsman* newspaper, he 'likened to those of an English parish council' (*Scotsman* 04.04.97, quoted by McLean 2001c, p. 437). He had earlier insisted that the tax-varying power must not be conferred on the Scottish parliament unless supported in a referendum; and (apparently in defiance of the whole idea of devolution) he pledged that a Labour administration in Scotland would not use the power.

After its landslide victory in the 1997 General Election – a landslide in which the Conservatives lost every single seat in Scotland and Wales, so that they were now represented only in England – Labour moved quite fast on devolution. It issued White Papers outlining its plans in July 1997. It held referenda in Scotland and, a week later, in Wales in September 1997 on its devolution and (in Scotland only) tax-varying proposals. The purpose of staggering the dates was quite plainly to create a bandwagon from Scotland, which was expected to endorse the plans by a large majority, to Wales, which was not. In the event, the Scottish Parliament was endorsed by 74 to 26 per cent of the vote (and the tax power by 63 to 37 per cent). Wales was a cliffhanger, with the *Noes* ahead all evening, but after the last declaration the National Assembly was endorsed by 50.3 to 49.7 per cent of those voting.

So Scotland and Wales were destined to get their devolved governments: but under what financial arrangements? Simply by default, the Barnett formula would continue. The minds of English and Welsh politicians, who probably stood to lose from this decision, were elsewhere. The Scots, for whom Barnett guaranteed largesse for at least a couple of decades to come, were keen that it should continue.

The report of the Scottish Constitutional Convention had stated:

> The principle of equalisation will continue. This means resources will be pooled on a UK basis and distributed on the basis of relative need. The establishing Act will embody the principle of equalisation – which has provided a stable, long-term foundation for government expenditure in Scotland for many years, receives the support of all the UK parties, and has served Scotland and the UK well. Thus, Scotland will continue to be guaranteed her fair share of UK resources, as of right.
>
> The current formula for the calculation of government expenditure in Scotland – the Barnett/Goschen formula – will continue to be used as the basis for the allocation of Scotland's fair share of UK resources.   (Scottish Constitutional Convention 1995, p. 27)

These two paragraphs are problematic. 'Relative need' was the principle behind the 1979 Needs Assessment. It was not the principle behind Barnett. And Barnett was not the same as Goschen. Because Barnett accepted the higher baseline for Scottish spending it was initially generous to Scotland. Because increments in English spending would be matched on a population – not a needs – basis in Scotland, the formula was convergent and unrelated to relative needs.

Nevertheless the two White Papers of July 1997, that introduced the proposals on which the Scots and Welsh were to vote that September, both announced the continuation of Barnett.

> [T]hese arrangements, based on the Block and Formula, have pro-
> duced fair settlements for Scotland in annual public expenditure
> rounds and have ... largely removed the need for annual nego-
> tiation between the Scottish Office and the Treasury. The Govern-
> ment have therefore concluded that the financial framework for
> the Scottish Parliament should be based on these existing arrange-
> ments with, in future, the Scottish Parliament determining spending
> priorities.
>
> Changes to the Welsh block will be calculated by the population-
> based formula used at the moment. These arrangements based
> on the Block and Formula have worked in practice, producing
> fair settlements for Wales in annual public expenditure rounds.
> (Cm 3658/1997 (Scotland); Cm 3718/1997 (Wales); both as quoted
> in HM Treasury 2004a, para. 3.2)

As Professor Joad might have said, it depends what you mean by a fair settlement. At any rate, these were the Government statements available to any Scots or Welsh voters who cared to consult them as they voted in the referenda. A case can be made for saying that Barnett is entrenched in the devolution arrangements on the grounds that it was the known rule on which people voted in September 1997. Malcolm Bruce MP, a Scottish Member, argued this case very force-fully in an attempt to quash the Commons Treasury Committee's unhealthy interest in Barnett in November 1997 (House of Commons Treasury Committee 1997, *passim*).The detailed arrangements were set out, for the first time in public, in a Commons written answer in December 1997, three months after the referenda, and now more elaborately in a publicly available Treasury manual, now in its 4th edition (HM Treasury 2004a). Although there was no White Paper for Northern Ireland and the Written Answer of December 1997 antedates the Good Friday Agreement, the Government used, and intended to continue using, the same Block and Formula procedure there.

However, it was not enshrined in statute. The financial clauses of the Scotland and Wales Acts 1998 are as bare and formal as those of 1978 – or indeed 1886. The Scotland Act 1998 (1998 c. 46), for instance, states at s. 64:

> 64.–(1) There shall be a Scottish Consolidated Fund.
>
> (2) The Secretary of State shall from time to time make payments into the Fund out of money provided by Parliament of such amounts as he may determine.
>
> (3) Sums received by an office-holder in the Scottish Administration shall be paid into the Fund.
>
> (4) Subsection (3) is subject to any provision made by or under an Act of the Scottish Parliament for the disposal of or accounting for such sums.
>
> (5) The Treasury may, after consulting with the Scottish Ministers, by order designate receipts of any description specified in the order which are payable into the Fund (or would be but for any provision made by or under an Act of the Scottish Parliament).
>
> (6) The Scottish Ministers shall make payments to the Secretary of State, at such times and by such methods as the Treasury may from time to time determine, of sums equal to the total amount outstanding in respect of designated receipts.
>
> (7) Amounts required for the payment of sums under subsection (6) shall be charged on the Fund.
>
> (8) The Fund shall be held with the Paymaster General.

The parallel between s. 64(2) of the successful 1998 Act and s. 48(1) of the abortive 1978 Act (Chapter 4) is striking. In both cases, the Parliamentary drafting allows the UK government maximum latitude to fund the devolved assemblies by any mechanism it unilaterally chooses. The sinister implication for the Territories is that what the Treasury gives, the Treasury may take away.

But not straight away. Since 1998, the attitude of Ministers in all departments other than the Treasury, and the English local government department, now known as ODPM (Office of the Deputy Prime Minister), has been that devolution is a done deal (apart from the periodic suspensions of the Northern Ireland Assembly, one of which is in force as I write). It is not to be reopened.

The Treasury has continued to operate Barnett in bilateral discussions with the finance ministries of the three Territories. It undoubtedly has some private frustrations. For instance, the Barnett arrangements do not allow the Treasury to control the Territories' capital spending. Devolution implies that they may switch their block grant at will between capital and current spending. Capital spending brings benefits over a long time – mostly after the next election. Current spending brings benefits over a short time – mostly before the next election. Therefore a rational politician, with her gaze fixed on winning the next election, is always tempted to starve public sector capital formation to the benefit of current public expenditure. It was precisely to avoid such temptations that the incoming Chancellor, Gordon Brown, bound himself to the mast in 1997 with two spending rules:

The **Golden Rule** states that, on average over the economic cycle, the government will borrow only to invest and not to fund current expenditure. This means that, over the cycle, the surplus on current budget must not be negative.

The **Sustainable Investment Rule** states that public sector net debt as a proportion of GDP will be held at a stable and prudent level.   (HM Treasury 2004b, 'Glossary of Terms')

The Golden Rule and the Sustainable Investment Rule are self-imposed rules for macroeconomic fiscal management. Under the devolution settlement it is plain that the UK government is alone responsible for macroeconomic management – as is inevitably the case in all federations, including the USA, Australia, and Canada. The Territories are not responsible for fiscal policy. Therefore, they have no Golden Rules of their own. But, if they yield to the temptation of sacrificing capital formation in favour of current spending, the UK government can do nothing to stop them – even though such behaviour could put the UK's adherence to its self-imposed rules at risk. A possibly significant addition to the 4th edition of the Treasury's manual (HM Treasury 2004a, new text in para. 6.4) announces that 'prudential borrowing regimes for local authorities ... have been introduced in 2004–05', but does not touch this virement issue directly.

Another possible friction point between the Treasury and the Territories is local taxation. The centre has taken powers to cut the Barnett block if local authorities in the Territories (raise and) spend too much (Written Answer, 09.12.97 para. 8e, in HM Treasury 2004a p. 39). But there is an opposite danger – of the Territories making *too little* tax effort. Unsurprisingly in view of its history, this seems to have arisen in Northern Ireland. Northern Ireland was not affected by the Poll Tax affair, and has continued to levy property rates. House prices are relatively low there, and wages (at least in the public sector, which accounts for 60 per cent of the NI economy) are the same as in the rest of the UK. Therefore the cost of living is cheap and the material standard of living high. It seems that the Treasury has been putting sustained pressure on Northern Ireland to make more tax effort with the rates. But the structure of Barnett fails to give politicians there an incentive to raise rates, which would make them unpopular. This is what seems to underlie a statement in the most recent Comprehensive Spending Review: '**A major programme of reform to modernise water, rating and public administration will be introduced in Northern Ireland**' (HM Treasury 2004c, para. 23.18; stress in original). This could be code for the following: 'While the NI Assembly is suspended, the unelected direct rule ministers will introduce the rating reform that elected politicians in the Province have never dared to do'.

The other department with a stake in Barnett is the ODPM, on this subject strongly led by its Secretary of State, Deputy Prime Minister John Prescott. Prescott could be described as 'Secretary of State for the English backlash'. Himself a Northern English MP, he shares and reflects the resentment of politicians in northern England that the Territories – or at least Scotland – are getting an unfairly high share of public expenditure, given their respective levels of deprivation. In April 2001, Prescott announced that there would be 'blood on the carpet' on this issue, before being summarily slapped down by the Prime Minister's press spokesman Alastair Campbell (Hetherington 2001; Mitchell and Nelson 2002). It was in order to level this particular playing field that Prescott sponsored elected English regional assemblies. Early in the term of the Labour government, the already-existing regional development agencies (RDAs) and Government Offices for each of the nine standard English regions were strengthened. The nine standard regions are shown in Figure 5.1.

In each region, the GO contains the regional officials of several Whitehall departments with territorial functions. In each region outside London, the RDA is a central government body with the remit of promoting the economic development of its region. Because London, uniquely among the nine regions, has had elected government since 2000, the London Development Agency is under the control of the Mayor of London and the Greater London Authority, not of central government; however, the Government Office for London remains a multi-departmental agency of central government. A White Paper (DTLR 2002) and then a Bill were published in 2002–3 to empower those regions that so wished to have a directly elected regional assembly. Here, Prescott's agenda clashed with Tony Blair's

Figure 5.1   The nine standard regions of England
Source: DTLR 2002, accessed at http://www.odpm.gov.uk/stellent/groups/odpm_
regions/documents/source/odpm_regions_source_607900.doc on 05.08.2004.

and others' *Realpolitik* and came off badly. Blair, with little interest in English regionalism even though he sits for a seat in the most deprived region of England, perceived that elected assemblies would be attacked as 'talking shops', and 'another layer of politicians paid for out of taxes'. Therefore he is said to have insisted on the following provision in the White Paper.

> 17. Elected assemblies are not another form of local government. They will have a different role and different priorities; almost all of their functions will be taken from central government, not from local level. Nonetheless, a regional assembly would add a third tier of elected government region, county, district below national level in some areas. This would be one tier too many. Thus, in any region where the Government decides that a referendum on an elected assembly should be held, there will first be a review of local government structures which will deliver proposals for a wholly unitary local government structure for the region as there is in Scotland, Wales, and London to be implemented if an elected assembly is established. Voters in the referendum will be aware of the implications for local government when choosing whether to have an elected regional assembly.   (DTLR 2002, summary)

Unitary local government has a lot to recommend it. But introducing it in this way was not good for the prospects of either local or regional government. For it set the Labour councillors of Barsetshire County Council to fighting like ferrets in a sack with the Labour councillors of Barsetshire East, North, Central, South, and West District Councils over which tier would survive if Barsetshire were to become part of a region with an elected assembly. The only thing that might unite top- and lower-tier councils would be a fight against the elected assembly coming into existence at all, as it threatened the material interests of both groups of councillors. In the autumn of 2003 the Government announced that referenda on whether to introduce elected assemblies would be held in the three northern English regions (North-east, North-west, and Yorkshire & the Humber). Despite the accession of a powerful ally to Prescott, namely Chancellor Brown's right-hand man Ed Balls, who was adopted in summer 2004 as prospective Labour candidate for Normanton (Yorkshire) and who was clearly keen on regional government in the North of England for the same reasons as Prescott, the policy hit the rocks in July 2004. The proposed referenda in two of the three regions (North-west and Yorks & Humberside) were withdrawn, ostensibly because of problems with possible fraud in the proposed all-postal ballots, but actually because Prescott could not longer be confident that they would vote Yes. This left only the North-east, where feelings about the 'iniquitous Barnett formula', as the region's newspapers call it,[1] run strongest. The North-east referendum is due to be held after this book goes to press and its result will be known before publication.

Thus, at most two of the nine English regions will have elected regional government in at least the near future. However, the regions remain essential building blocks for any policy which looks to inter-regional equity (if policy ought to do that). I return to this in later chapters.

Barnett in operation since 1997: financial implications

Figure 5.2 shows the frequency of mentions of the string 'Barnett formula' in UK newspapers since the Lexis-Nexis database began in 1989. It shows a minor peak in 1992, perhaps because of Michael Portillo's recalibration (Chapter 4), but a tenfold increase in 1997 – when the Formula came out of the shadows – and further increases since then, peaking in 2000 and 2001.

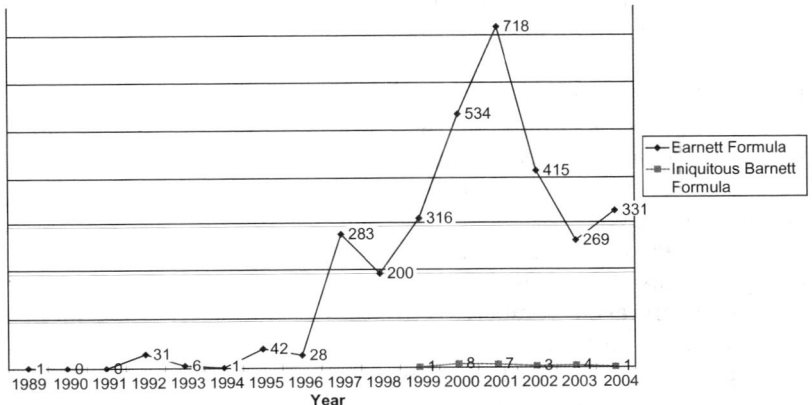

Figure 5.2 Mentions of 'Barnett Formula' in UK press, 1989–2004
Source: Lexis-Nexis database.

The Commons Treasury Committee held an inquiry into the Barnett Formula in the 1997–8 session. Although it led nowhere – its arbitrarily curtailed report bears the marks of Whips' interference in a topic deemed too hot to air in public – it uncovered a good deal of interesting evidence about how Barnett operated as devolution was coming into effect. Most importantly, a 'Supplementary Memorandum submitted by HM Treasury' confirmed that the Formula had been tightened in two important respects in 1992 – presumably by Chief Secretary Michael Portillo at the same time as he corrected the population relativities. Before 1992, if there was a UK-wide pay increase for some category of public sector workers (nurses, for example), extra-Barnett funding would go to the Territories to deal with the consequences; and inflation allowances were given in the third year of three-year expenditure plans. In 1992, it turns out, Portillo and/or his officials withdrew both of those concessions (Treasury Committee 1997, p. 39).

These changes should have made the 'Barnett squeeze' more painful. But for the first three years of the new government it did not bite. Incoming Chancellor Brown decided to hold public spending down to the previous government's announced totals for the first two fiscal years of the new government. Recall that Barnett only operates on *increments* of spending. If there is extra expenditure in England on a domestic programme, then the Territories each get a 'consequential' to enable them to spend more (not necessarily on the programme where spending has increased in England). Because these consequentials are proportionate to the population of each Territory, and they come on top of a baseline of higher spending per head, they tend to lead spending to convergence on equal spending per capita between England and the Territories. Hence, *if there is no increase, there is no convergence.* Because public expenditure was by now measured in cash, not volume, terms, there was a small increase in each year for inflation. But inflation was low during those years, and therefore there was little Barnett convergence.

Public expenditure planning in the new administration was made in Comprehensive Spending Reviews (SR200x). One of these would take place in every even-numbered year, and it would set department's expenditure limits for thee fiscal years. The last year of (SR200x) would overlap as the first year of (SR200x+ 2). Beginning with SR2000, the Blair-Brown government decided to pour substantially increased real resources into public services. There were substantial real increases in SR2000 and SR2002, and smaller real increases in SR2004, which were made subject to the Barnett Formula. This has produced a 'Barnett squeeze' on the Territories, although in Scotland Figure 4.1 suggests that in practice it has been little more than a gentle hug. The mechanical operation of Barnett will lead to convergence in Scotland and England, but not for several years. In any case, simple convergence is neither equitable nor efficient.

The unacknowledged purpose of Barnett was always to bring down relative public spending in Scotland (and to a lesser extent Northern Ireland), where as we saw in Chapter 4 the Treasury thought it was unjustifiably high. As in other devolution matters, Wales was swept in almost by accident. And yet, if the Needs Assessment numbers were right, showing that in 1976–7 Wales had 'needs' calibrated at 109 against England = 100, but expenditure per head only at a ratio of 106 to 100 (Table 4.2), then *the Barnett Formula ought never to have been applied to Wales, and any application of it would tend to exacerbate Welsh disadvantage.* When the Labour government opened the public spending tap, there was always likely to be trouble in Wales. Trouble also loomed in Northern Ireland.

In 2000, the Labour minority First Minister of Wales, Alun Michael, was dismissed by the National Assembly after failing to promise extra-Barnett matching spending that was required in order for the Valleys and West Wales to claim EU 'Objective One' funding.[2] In July 2000, his successor Rhodri Morgan and the Secretary of State for Wales jointly announced that 'the Government has accepted our special case for funding outside the Barnett Formula' on the grounds that the Welsh Objective One areas contained 65 per cent of Wales' population. As no such claim could be made in Scotland, this was the first occasion on which spending in Wales and in Scotland trended in different directions. As Morgan had the support of a majority of the National Assembly, the UK government had no choice in the matter.

In Northern Ireland, Sean Farren (SDLP), Finance Minister in the first Assembly (1999–2003) until its suspension, was the most outspoken and perhaps the most perspicacious of the territorial finance ministers. He argued, as did his officials, that although Northern Ireland had traditionally done well out of public spending, nevertheless rapid Barnett convergence would cause a lot of trouble, because spending on devolved services had to be high. In particular, Northern Ireland has a high school-age population (30 per cent higher than in England, according to the senior NI official in charge of Barnett – Constitution Committee 2002, p. 332, evidence of Dr Andrew McCormick) and two separate publicly-funded school systems. After the suspension of the Assembly, the Northern Ireland Civil Service continued to make the point with vigour in various places, including seminars at Stormont; bilateral meetings with the Treasury; and an appearance before the House of Lords Committee on the Constitution in June 2002 (House of Lords Constitution Committee 2002, pp. 331–41). Northern Ireland has one extra-Barnett programme, the Peace Programme from European Structural Funds. But that is much smaller than Objective One in Wales, and gives Northern Ireland little relief from its Barnett squeeze.

Northern Ireland officials have therefore led the call for the 1976–79 Needs Assessment to be repeated. There is some evidence that the Treasury has kept data enabling it to repeat the exercise (e.g. Treasury Committee 1997, Minutes of Evidence, p. 22 n.1). But there has not been a full – let alone a public – discussion with the Territories or with outside specialists. One is overdue, as the strains within Barnett cannot be contained for long.

Ministers have become less coy about the purposes of Barnett:

> However, for those who have concerns about the Barnett formula, I point out, first, that it is not the formula that is responsible for the inequalities in funding about which people are worried. Those are historic matters which, of course, the Barnett formula addresses. It is a convergence formula – something on which we receive representations from other parts of the United Kingdom (Andrew Smith MP, then Chief Secretary to the Treasury, *Hansard*, Commons, 19.07.01, col. 425).

But the more Ministers say this to the English, the more the Scots notice, as shown by the peaks of press comment logged in Figure 5.2. Most of that comment is in the main papers circulating in the Territories, but a significant proportion in English regional papers.[3] The Barnett formula has failed to allay resentment in Scotland, because it cannot. It has failed to protect Wales, because it was structurally unsuited to do so. And it has failed to quell resentment in poor regions of England, because the numbers which gave rise to the 1977 government defeat have stubbornly failed to change. In 2000, the Newcastle-upon-Tyne *Journal* claimed that the secondary school in Duns (Borders region) had a pupil: teacher ratio of 13:1 and one computer per 5 students. The secondary school in socially identical Alnwick (Northumberland) had a pupil: teacher ratio of 18:1 and one computer per 13 students. Health spending per head, in fiscal year 1998/9, was £692 in Northumberland and £945 in the Borders (McLean 2001a). It is this disparity that Joel Barnett has repeatedly called an 'example of terrible unfairness' (e.g. in the House of Lords debate on his formula, 7 November 2001, *Official Report*, col. 228). Whereas in 1997 he seemed rather proud of 'his' formula (Treasury Committee 1997, Minutes of Evidence, p. 1), by 2001 he had disowned it.

The latest data on the effects of Barnett available at the time of writing are as shown in Table 5.2, which is derived from SR2004, published in July (HM Treasury 2004c).

The percentage increases calculated in Table 5.2 demonstrate the Barnett squeeze at work. Wales gets the highest increases (as it should); but in all three countries, the increases fall off sharply in the last fiscal year of the planning period, 2007–08. This confirms that, in Wales and Northern Ireland, Barnett is becoming unsustainable. Scotland is then left as its one beneficiary. One territory out of the 12 standard regions

Table 5.2 Departmental expenditure limits for the Territories, July 2004

	£ million			
	2004–05	2005–06	2006–07	2007–08
Scotland				
Resource Budget	19,676	21,198	22,535	23,700
Capital Budget	1,893	1,783	1,980	2,172
Total Departmental Expenditure Limit	21,338	22,757	24,202	25,549
% increase from previous year		6.65	6.35	5.57
Wales				
Resource Budget	10,275	11,044	11,927	12,625
Capital Budget	918	998	1,083	1,195
Total Departmental Expenditure Limit	10,985	11,826	12,753	13,557
% increase from previous year		7.66	7.84	6.30
Northern Ireland				
Resource Budget	6,699	7,077	7,554	7,862
Capital Budget	373	412	476	534
Total Departmental Expenditure Limit	7,004	7,420	7,913	8,296
% increase from previous year		5.94	6.64	4.84

Note: The Wales and Northern Ireland baselines shown above for 2004–05 and 2005–06 exclude the above-Barnett formula additions of £106 million a year for Objective 1 in Wales and £62 and £80 million for the PEACE programmes in Northern Ireland. These figures are however in spending plans for these years.
Source: HM Treasury 2004c, Table 23.3. Crown copyright. Author's calculations.

of the UK is very vulnerable in inter-territorial bargaining. Barnett must go: but what should replace it?

Before we can address that question, we must devote two chapters to the spatial distribution of public expenditure in England. Chapter 6 deals with health, where most experts agree that regional distribution works reasonably well. The following chapter deals with local government services, where most experts agree that regional distribution works badly.

6
Health – Getting it Right

Introduction

In this chapter and the next, we turn our attention to formula funding in England. Most 'British' books about social policy turn out to be 'English' books, because the authors have data for England only, or because England is by far the largest part of the UK, or – at worst – because the authors are barely aware that the Territories exist, or that they may do things differently there. In this book, the reason for separate treatment of England is different. Both the Territories and England have formula funding for domestic services. However, in the Territories the formula is Barnett. In England it is very different. There are formulae for health, and a set of formulae for services delivered by local authorities, which includes most of the other big-ticket domestic services (school education; personal social services; police; fire; most highways; social housing). The formulae are, or purport to be, needs-based. Because needy people tend to live in different places to non-needy people, they therefore have strong geographical implications.

We face a preliminary but extremely important data problem. Whereas governments have known how much is spent per head in the Territories for many years, they have not known how much is spent per head in the regions of England. The Treasury and the territorial departments have always needed the data so that they can argue over whether the Territories are getting too much, too little, or just the right amount of public spending. They have ministers to police the argument – the Chief Secretary to the Treasury, and the territorial Secretaries of State. None of this applies in the English regions. Previous chapters have shown how this became sharply political in the 1970s, culminating, first, in official data on regional public spending in the

North of England (NRST 1976), and, then in the guillotine defeat of the Scotland and Wales Bill in 1977. However, as devolution vanished from the policy agenda in 1979, so did interest in the regional footprint of public expenditure in England. It has only recently revived.

In 2002, I was commissioned by the then DTLR, now ODPM, to study the flow of domestic and European public expenditure into the nine standard English regions (see Fig. 5.1). The study (McLean *et al.* 2003) was co-sponsored by the Department of Environment, Food, and Rural Affairs (DEFRA) and HM Treasury. A team of about twenty researchers examined data supplied by departments to the Treasury, and undertook two waves of interviews in departments in order to find out how departments derived the data. We had (what we believe was) unprecedented access for an outside academic team to the process of compiling data on regional public expenditure and we are extremely grateful to our sponsoring departments and to our respondents in all departments.

Our full report is freely available (McLean *et al.* 2003), as is an academic paper summarising the main findings (Cameron, McLean, and Wlezien 2004). Readers who need more detail than is given in the next few paragraphs are referred to those.

Two government departments collect and publish data on regional economic statistics for the UK, including public expenditure: the Office for National Statistics (ONS) and HM Treasury. However, for various reasons, the Treasury series, known by the acronym *PESA* (for Public Expenditure – Statistical Analyses) is in principle a more reliable guide to public expenditure. It is collected by the Treasury directly (or, in the case of money spent by English local authorities, indirectly) from the departments and local authorities that actually spend the money, and is reported by the financial year, the basis on which expenditure is both planned and accounted for.

PESA had published breakdowns of regionally relevant public expenditure in each of the English regions, as well as the Territories, beginning with fiscal year 1998–99. However, we found that the quality of the data base varied dramatically by department. The worst (indeed practically non-existent) data were for European public expenditure. Although the distributive politics of public expenditure from the European Union budget is intense, there seemed to be astonishingly little interest either in EU or UK government offices in tracking the outturns. As over half of EU expenditure is on the Common Agricultural Policy, however, our educated guess is that European public expenditure flows most to the most agriculturally-intense regions of the UK, by which we mean the regions with the highest agricultural output per head, not the regions with the highest prevalence of farmers. The East of England region is therefore probably the highest recipient per head of EU public expenditure in the UK.

With regard to domestic departments, we found that those departments which saw their mission in regional terms tended to keep better records than those that did not. The Department of Work and Pensions (DWP) administers benefits to individual recipients. It is the largest-spending department, but its spending almost wholly comprises transfers, plus administration costs. The *Social Protection* function of government, which maps largely on to the expenditure of DWP, accounted in 2002–03 for 13.6 per cent of GDP and 36 per cent of total expenditure on services, TES (*PESA* 2004, Table 3.4). As the main transfer programme to individuals, social security is not devolved. Payments are made by the UK government to qualifying individuals irrespective of location. The Department knows where its payees are, can group them into any spatial aggregate including standard region, and has a defensible methodology for allocating its administrative costs to regions also. It could be regarded as a model for other departments to follow.

The next largest programmes are *Health* (in 2002–03 accounting for 6.3 per cent of GDP; 17 per cent of TES) and *Education and training* (in 2002–03, 5.2 per cent of GDP; 14 per cent of TES). Since 1911, and notably since 1945, these three functions of government have grown hugely and the 19th-century staples of defence and debt interest have shrunk. For the latest available year of 2002–03, *Defence* accounts for only 2.5 per cent of GDP (7 per cent of TES), and *Public sector debt interest* for only 2.0 per cent of GDP (5 per cent of TES: *PESA* 2004, Table 3.4). One consequence is that, whereas defence and debt interest are public-goods expenditure which is presumed to benefit each citizen of the UK to an equal extent and cannot be apportioned by region, the large programmes of 21st-century government spending can be and are apportioned to the UK's regions. If the regional distribution of public expenditure on health and education were robustly known, we could start to draw inferences about the regional effects of formula funding to the Territories and the English regions, as these are by far the largest programmes that are devolved in the Territories and supplied by local public bodies (Primary Care Trusts and local authorities) in England.

Unfortunately, at the time of our investigation, neither the health nor the education data for the English regions in PESA were trustworthy. The Department of Health supplied only the barest details to the Treasury, although our field research showed that it kept reliable and comprehensive departmental records of its own. The Department for Education and Skills (DfES) was one of a number of departments that reported the English regional breakdown of its direct expenditure[1] on an equal per capita (EPC) basis. In other words, whatever the truth on the ground may have been, DfES reported that it was spending the same amount per head on its big programmes, especially higher and further education, in each region of England. Data readily available in the public domain, on the location of universities, colleges, and their students, showed that this was not the case. We estimated more accurate figures for education among other services.

In 2004, the Treasury announced that Ministers had accepted our recommendations for data improvements, which were implemented by departments in time for the *PESA* 2004 report (*PESA* 2004, para. 8.2). Accordingly, Table 6.1 shows the latest available (2002–03) data on expenditure per head on services by country and region of the UK. The data have been recalculated on the new basis back to 1997–98.

Albeit with more accurate data, Table 6.1 confirms the picture that we and other researchers have previously drawn (Table 1.1; Fig. 1.1; McLean and McMillan 2003). Public expenditure per head in the 12 regions of the UK, and indeed in the nine standard regions of England, correlates poorly with GDP per head, although one would expect a strong inverse relationship between the two. Table 6.1, like Table 1.1, shows that the upward outliers are Scotland, Northern Ireland, and London; the downward outliers are Wales, and the eight English regions outside London. This pattern obtains for all services together, and for the particular services of *Health* and *Education and training*, which are the main focus of this chapter and the next.

Health spending and the inverse care law from Lloyd George to RAWP

As related above, all the founders of National Insurance in 1911 envisaged a national scheme in which entitlement to health care would depend on sickness and national insurance status, not on wealth. The 1911 scheme was therefore the first state attempt to upset what Julian Tudor Hart (1971) has influentially labelled the 'Inverse Care Law':

> The availability of good medical care tends to vary inversely with the need for it in the population served. This inverse care law operates more completely where medical care is most exposed to

accruals per head, £

Table 6.1 UK Identifiable expenditure on services, by function, country and region, per head, 2002–03

2002–03	General public services	International services	Defence	Public order and safety	Enterprise and economic development	Science and technology	Employment policies	Agriculture, fisheries and forestry	Transport	Environment protection	Housing and community amenities	Health	Recreation culture, and religion	Education and training	Social protection	Total
North East	83	–	–	387	166	14	107	87	197	101	81	1203	105	1012	2920	6463
North West	56	–	–	371	97	17	77	71	204	103	103	1181	85	953	2725	6043
Yorkshire and Humberside	60	–	–	285	122	13	57	87	185	96	81	1081	93	955	2423	5538
East Midlands	67	–	–	300	86	13	37	102	147	90	49	946	79	882	2213	5011
West Midlands	63	–	–	300	91	13	47	84	169	84	61	1045	77	923	2417	5374
South West	74	–	–	263	62	15	38	148	140	98	56	999	68	797	2219	4976
Eastern	65	–	–	247	40	41	28	82	156	95	23	990	66	799	2065	4697
London	95	–	–	470	51	23	43	17	563	102	230	1282	146	1085	2416	6522
South East	62	–	–	269	48	41	26	54	174	105	61	1005	71	813	1970	4699

accruals per head, £

Table 6.1 UK Identifiable expenditure on services, by function, country and region, per head, 2002–03

	General public services	International services	Defence	Public order and safety	Enterprise and economic development	Science and technology	Employment policies	Agriculture, fisheries and forestry	Transport	Environment protection	Housing and community amenities	Health	Recreation culture, and religion	Education and training	Social protection	Total
England	69	–	–	323	77	23	47	75	230	98	89	1085	88	911	2337	5453
Scotland	154	–	1	362	105	24	136	131	231	200	143	1262	164	1038	2629	6579
Wales	129	–	–	320	208	12	48	100	183	168	88	1186	185	970	2881	6479
Northern Ireland	146	–	1	720	328	12	26	236	191	184	166	1214	54	1215	2774	7267
UK identifiable expenditure	81	–	–	338	93	22	54	86	226	112	96	1109	99	934	2401	5652

Source: HM Treasury 2004b, from Table 8.10. Crown copyright. Source has heading 'accruals per head, £ million', but HMT has confirmed that this is an error.

market forces, and less so where such exposure is reduced. (Tudor Hart 1971, Abstract).

If health care is entirely left to the market, then those who can most afford to pay will get the most care. Those who can most afford to pay are the wealthy, who are least likely to be ill. Similarly, an insurance-based approach will see the best risks pay the lowest premium for the highest benefit – again, an instance of the inverse care law. The Welsh radical Lloyd George tried to abolish it in 1911. A second Welsh radical, Aneurin Bevan, tried again in 1946. A third Welsh radical, Tudor Hart, argued that it persisted in 1971. He continued:

> The market distribution of medical care is a primitive and historically outdated social form, and any return to it would further exaggerate the maldistribution of medical resources.

He underestimated the generality of his law. Not only market-based health provision but most non-market forms suffered from it.

Both Lloyd George and Bevan had to negotiate with the relevant producer groups in order to implement their schemes. In 1911, the most relevant groups were the friendly societies and the British Medical Association (BMA). The friendly societies, which included trade unions, wanted to administer the scheme, because it gave citizens an incentive to join the societies. Like any other insurance company, therefore, the societies had an incentive to insure the best risks and hope that someone else would take on the worst risks. The doctors were more obdurate. A few weeks before the sickness insurance scheme under the 1911 Act was due to come into force, the BMA announced that it held pledges from 27,000 of its 32,000 members to refuse to take part in the scheme. Lloyd George called their bluff, but the price was a 'panel system', where each National Insurance patient was registered with just one doctor, to whom the state paid a capitation fee of a fixed amount per patient per year. The perverse incentive effects of this outcome dismayed the boldest member of the ambulance crew, W.J. Braithwaite (Braithwaite 1957, pp. 293–6). The incentives for doctors were to cherry-pick the best risks (healthy National Insurance and private patients) and leave the worst risks uninsured and un-doctored.

The Beveridge reforms of 1942 assumed a national health service with universal cover of the population, free to the patient at the point of use. Civil servants during the war worked extensively on the possibilities for what was already called a 'national health service', and the spirit of wartime cooperation made this an uncontroversial national consensus. But the form it should take remained undefined at the accession of the Labour government in 1945. The Labour manifesto had called for a 'national ... salaried, pensionable service'. But, as in 1911, the BMA had rallied in opposition to that idea. Bevan may have wished for a salaried GP service. But in getting his way and making the concessions he had to, he was in the Lloyd George class. Both Welshmen faced the threat of a doctors' strike from the BMA. Both faced it down. But both made concessions to the doctors' producer-group demands that made it less likely that their schemes would invalidate the inverse care law.

Bevan's masterstroke was to get the hospital consultants on his side, and then use them to call the bluff of the BMA, which mostly represented GPs. His first move was to nationalise the hospitals. In 1945, UK hospitals were either voluntary (charitable) or municipal. The voluntary hospitals varied in size and competence but at their apex were the great teaching hospitals, concentrated in London: medically eminent but financially exhausted. They would have been bankrupt but for wartime emergency funding. Municipal hospitals, run by local authorities, tended to be the reverse – financially sound but clinically undistinguished. Bevan faced hostility in Cabinet from protectors of (Labour) local authorities – especially from the Deputy Prime Minister, Herbert Morrison.

The argument between Bevan and Morrison was in part an argument about the appropriate level at which medical services should be provided. Bevan argued in a Cabinet memorandum for 'the complete takeover – into one national service – of both voluntary and municipal hospitals', which would entail 'the centralising of the whole finance of the country's hospital system, taking it right out of local rating and local government'. In the terminology of this book, hospital treatment should be regarded as a national, not a local, public good. Morrison countered that

> It is possible to argue that almost every local government function, taken by itself, could be administered more efficiently in the technical sense, but if we wish local government to thrive ... we must consider the general effect on local government of each particular proposal. It would be disastrous if we allowed local government to languish by whittling away its most constructive and interesting functions. (Bevan, CAB 129/3, 05.10.45; Morrison, CAB 129/3, 12.10.45; both quoted by Klein 1989 p. 30).

Bevan got his way, and his was the better argument, but Morrison had a point. The small local authorities of 1945 would have been inappropriate health authorities because they would have magnified the effects of the inverse care law. Rich areas would support good hospitals and poor areas would support bad ones. Rates were a weak tax base. An extremely heavy national rate support and equalisation system would have been needed to supplement them, which would itself have deprived the authorities of most of the autonomy that Morrison wanted – because central government would have demanded accountability for the great slugs of rate support and equalisation finance that it would have to put in. But Morrison was right that the centralising instincts of government stunt local government, as they have continued to do to this day.

Bevan struck up an alliance with Lord Moran, the president of the Royal College of Physicians, who became the spokesman of the hospital consultants', as opposed to the GPs', interests. The consultants were not opposed to nationalisation, so long as they ran the show and had enough money to do so. This Bevan offered: 'I stuffed their mouths with gold', he famously said – and he left the running of the medical profession to the medical profession, which in practice largely meant to the consultants. The 'Appointed Day' on which the NHS was to come into operation was fixed for 5 July 1948. As in 1912, up to a few weeks before the Appointed Day the BMA stated that it held pledges from the majority of its members to refuse to take part in the scheme. As in 1912, they almost all did, having been outbluffed by their second wily Welshman in 36 years. If the Royal Colleges, controlling the hospitals, were in, then individual GPs, who needed to be on good terms with consultants for referrals, could scarcely stay out. But they, too, got concessions which helped to protect the inverse care law. They remained self-employed contractors to the Health Service, paid mostly by capitation fees. Neither a salaried service – maybe Bevan's true aim – nor a local government service was politically feasible in 1948.

For its first three decades, therefore, the NHS was a doctor-run service in which, each year, money went essentially to the same places as it went the year before. The dominance of Lord Moran and his colleagues also meant the dominance of London teaching hospitals, despite the hollowing-out of London's population from the 1940s to the 1970s. On the GP side, Bevan took powers to prevent GPs from setting up in 'over-doctored' areas (powers that the BMA railed against but may have privately welcomed, as they tended to protect the fees of existing doctors in rich areas, which were of course the over-doctored areas).

But there was no effective mechanism to direct them to 'under-doctored' areas. Bevan's skills in finance did not match his skills in negotiation. He naively expected that as the NHS would tackle the killer diseases of poverty such as diphtheria and TB, its cost would then decline. It did tackle diphtheria and TB with rapid success: so that those patients survived to live longer and die, later, and more expensively, of something else. And the new service unleashed pent-up demand: in December 1948 Bevan was already conceding that 'the rush for spectacles, as for dental treatment, has exceeded all expectations' (CAB 129/131, 13.12.48, quoted in Klein 1989, p. 33). Supplementary estimate followed supplementary estimate; Bevan was forced to concede the introduction of charges for dental and optical treatment, but when Chancellor Hugh Gaitskell capped these expenditure items in 1951, Bevan resigned from the government. The problem of the so-called infinite demand for medical services was out in the open.[2]

During the 1950s the problem was smothered by cutting capital expenditure to almost zero and restraining salaries, which rose by less than the average for all pay in the UK (Klein 1989, ch. 2). But this was not an equilibrium solution, and it only made cost pressures worse when they broke out again. A pattern of expenditure frozen into the spatial contours of 1948 meant that even a universally popular national health service with care free at the point of delivery and markets operating only on the fringe, in the supply of GP services, fell foul of the inverse care law.

Change in the 1970s required policy entrepreneurs. The principal ones seem to have been Brian Abel-Smith, one of the influential products of the 'Titmuss school' of social administration scholars at the London School of Economics, and a political adviser to the Labour governments of 1964–70 and 1974–9; Barbara Castle, a forceful Secretary of State for Social Services (which then included the NHS); and David Owen, a forceful and medically-qualified junior minister under Castle:

> Expenditure did not seem to be well correlated with the regional distribution of death rates, waiting lists, and so on.... This began to be discussed more and more between first academics and then politicians.... The story goes that Owen summoned officials into his office and told them that he was not happy with the Crossman formula and that they were to go away and come back with something better. Officials went away for a week or two and returned

stating that there did not seem to be a problem. Owen told them to go away and try again. Their second suggestion was to establish RAWP (a senior DoH civil servant interviewed by Glennerster *et al.* 2000, quoted at p. 135).

RAWP stood for Resources Allocation Working Party. Its report (DHSS 1976) marked the first attempt to tackle the inverse care law head-on, and has shaped all subsequent attempts. The basic idea behind RAWP and all subsequent attempts at formula funding of the NHS has been that objective spatial data about indicators of sickness are available from the Census (e.g. mortality; prevalence of vulnerable groups in the population, and of bad housing) and from NHS administrative data (waiting times, waiting lists). Therefore money can be accurately targeted at need.

RAWP reallocated funds at a gross level, from relatively overfunded regions of England to relatively under-funded regions. As Glennerster *et al.* (2000, p. 56) shrewdly note, the main losers from RAWP were the London and other southern teaching hospitals, whose relative over-funding dated back at least to the deal between Bevan and Moran. But they could not directly attack the principle of allocation by need. However, they employed the best academically-qualified members of NHS staff, and therefore the best statisticians and computer experts: 'So the attacks took the form of technical criticisms of the formula itself. Those who made the criticisms were often well-equipped to do so and had valid points'. The fortunate side-effect was continuous refinement of the formulae, to which we now turn.

Health spending and the inverse care law since RAWP

Two powerful and influential reports (Black 1982; Acheson 1998) showed that the inverse care law remained alive and well. The Black Report was commissioned from the Chief Scientist of the Department of Health and three other eminent health policy specialists by the outgoing Labour government in 1977. When it reported under the new Conservative government in 1980, its message was felt politically embarrassing. The half-hearted government attempts to suppress it by issuing it only as a restricted-circulation typescript on August Bank Holiday provoked such a storm that it became better known than if it had been published in the regular way, and a Penguin edition was reprinted three times.

Black and his colleagues found that mortality varied significantly by class, housing tenure, and region (Table 6.2a and b). It is hard to argue that some regions are inherently healthier to inhabit than others in a country as small as the UK – too small for a Shire and a Mordor. Therefore the regional differences, which persisted even after controlling for the class and age composition of their populations, must have been due to, for example, differential lifestyles, and/or differential access to health care, of their populations.

Table 6.2a   Standardised mortality ratio, controlling for age and class composition, regions of the UK, 1970–72

Region	SMR
North + Yorks & Humber	113
North–west	105
East Midlands	116
West Midlands	94
East Anglia	104
South–east	90
South-west	93
South Wales	117
North and West Wales	113
England & Wales	**100**

Source: Black 1982, Table 2.
The standard regions in 1972 differed from the present ones as follows:
Cumbria: in 1972 in North[-east]; now in North-west.
Essex, Bedfordshire, Hertfordshire: in 1972 in South-east, now in East.
Greater London: in 1972 in South-east, now a region in itself.

Table 6.2b   Mortality by housing tenure and class, males 15–64, England & Wales, 1970–75.

Class	Mean = 100 Tenure		
	Owner-occupied	Private tenant	Local authority tenant
I	79	95	99
II	74	104	99
III non-manual	79	112	121
III manual	83	99	104
IV	83	100	106
V	98	126	123

Source: Black 1982, Table 4.

In 1997 the incoming Labour government commissioned another chief scientist, the retired Chief Medical Officer Sir Donald Acheson, to produce another review of health inequality in England & Wales. Its report (Acheson 1998) shows both continuity and novelty. It mentions the inverse care law and adds an 'inverse prevention law' (p. 112), although without directly citing Tudor Hart. It also warmly praises the Black Report. It continues Black's series on standardised mortality rates by class (Table 6.3) but not by region. By inference, Acheson and his colleagues found the problem of inequality of access to health care within region more pressing than that between regions. They mention particularly the poor quality of inner-city health services.

Table 6.3 shows that class inequality of premature death had actually increased since Black. Although classes IV and V were certainly much smaller in 1991–93 than in 1970–72 (Acheson gives no data about class sizes), and although absolute premature male mortality had declined by a third, from 0.624 per cent to 0.419 per cent, in twenty years, its ratio between the highest and the lowest social class had spread from 1.79:1 to 2.88:1. Even more than Black's, Acheson's recommendations concentrate on environmental factors (attack child poverty; reform the Common Agricultural Policy in order to cut food prices; concentrate both health and poverty interventions on the most vulnerable groups). His recommendations are so much in tune with the policy of the new government, especially that wing of it dominated by Chancellor Gordon Brown, that one suspects something more than coincidence. Acheson does not consider regional inequality, and his recommendations for formula reform are comparatively minor (improve the estimation of

Table 6.3 Standardised mortality rates, England & Wales, men aged 20–64, per 100,000 by social class

Class	Rate per 100,000		
	1970–72	1979–83	1991–93
I	500	373	280
II	526	425	300
III non-manual	637	522	426
III manual	683	580	493
IV	721	639	492
V	897	910	806
All	624	549	419

Source: Acheson 1998, Table 2.

under-enumerated groups in the Census including the homeless; recognise ethnic and cultural needs – p. 116).

The Labour government hails the Acheson report as another landmark (see, e.g. speech by then-Minister Lord Hunt at the Royal College of Physicians, 13.11.01, at http://www.dh.gov.uk/NewsHome/Speeches/ SpeechesList/SpeechesArticle/fs/en?CONTENT_ID=4000629&chk=HHD 2KE). Its favoured target-setting method for government is the Public Service Agreement (PSA). Several of these bear on reducing inequality, including health inequality. The 2004 restatement of PSAs includes:

- *Department of Health Objective 1.2:* Reduce health inequalities by 10% by 2010 as measured by infant mortality and life expectancy at birth.
- *ODPM Objective II, joint with DTI and HM Treasury:* Make sustainable improvements in the economic performance of all English regions by 2008, and over the long term reduce the persistent gap in growth rates between the regions, demonstrating progress by 2006.

The Treasury has also solipsistically imposed on itself a PSA (with itself) to *improve public services by working with departments to help them meet their PSA targets* (HM Treasury 2004d). It has not been revealed how the Treasury will punish itself if it fails to meet its PSAs with itself.

How have governments sought to beat the inverse care law since RAWP? And have Conservative governments (1979–97) acted differently from Labour governments (1976–9 and 1997–2005)? One might *a priori* expect their attitudes to health policy to be very different. It is a stylised fact that right-wing politicians care more about efficiency than equity, whereas left-wing politicians care more about equity than efficiency. The Conservative administrations encouraged private medicine, for instance by tax breaks for private health insurance. Labour in 1976–9 (but not since 1997) tried to restrict it, vainly trying to unpick the deals Bevan had struck with Moran, which allowed NHS doctors and resources to be used to treat private patients. Since 1997, Labour's main use of private medicine has been to buy in operations and procedures, in order to cut NHS waiting lists.

The central focus of Conservative health policy after 1989 was the split between purchasers and providers. Health authorities and fund-holding GPs were to become purchasers of health care, and other parts of the NHS were to provide it. The idea was to introduce market competition into the NHS while leaving it free at the point of use. This conception fitted well with the Thatcher administration's conception of public choice. Influenced by a report from the American health economist Alain Enthoven, Mrs Thatcher and her ministers saw the purchaser-provider split as a way of breaking producer-group dominance in the NHS. Providers would compete for purchasers' funds, and only the most efficient would survive.

However, the similarities between Conservative and Labour health policy are far more important than the differences. On coming to office in 1997, Labour promised to dismantle the purchaser-provider split, but has in fact re-erected it to form a larger part of the NHS architecture than under the Conservatives. A purchaser-provider regime forces the ultimate funder (the UK government) to consider closely on what basis purchasers themselves are funded. Should it be a flat sum per patient, or something more sophisticated?

Above all, policy converges because of the median voter theorem. Since opinion polling started, and almost certainly since 1948, the NHS has been overwhelmingly popular. No politicians aspiring to run the UK may say anything against it. Mrs Thatcher, no less, insisted that 'The NHS is safe with us' – and went on 'indeed it is only safe with us'. That precludes a government of any party from moving substantially away from a universal, tax-funded, service, free at the point of use.

Furthermore, efficiency and equity are not always enemies. A right-wing government wants to ensure that tax revenue is spent efficiently, and that neither health workers nor patients face perverse incentives that would lead them to behave more expensively than they need. A left-wing government wants to ensure that health care goes first to those who need it most. Both operate within the constraint that no UK politicians may alter the basic structure of the NHS as the patient sees it. In UK healthcare, as Chancellor Brown (or his speechwriters: Brown 2003) eloquently point out, efficiency and equity considerations point in the same direction. Both efficiency and equity – both right-wing and left-wing politics – point towards formula funding of health services, with a formula designed to ensure that scarce resources go to those who need them most, and that there are no, or minimal, incentives for anyone to behave perversely. Therefore, a modern government of any party can be expected to mount a sustained attack on the inverse care law. If the rich are getting health care that they need less than the poor, that is a waste of public expenditure.

There is just one possible risk. Sophisticated governments may take the median voter theorem *too* seriously. An unsophisticated government might want to divert funds into its heartlands – Labour to

Northern cities, Scotland and Wales; Conservative to southern suburbs. A more sophisticated government would divert funds into marginal constituencies. There are 659 seats in the House of Commons. If arranged in order from the safest to the most hopeless, each party must control at least from seat 1 to seat 330 in its ranking if it is to win a Commons majority. The 330th safest seat for Labour is likely to be very similar to – may even be the same seat as – the 330th safest seat for the Conservatives. Alternatively, if funds go through, or impact on, local authorities, then an unsophisticated government may try to reward 'its' authorities; a more sophisticated one, swing authorities that might go either way. Formula funding is therefore vulnerable to political manipulation. For this to occur, the would-be manipulator must know the effect of a change in formula, and must be able to present the change plausibly as a reflection of 'need', not politically motivated. In the remainder of this chapter and in Chapter 7, we examine funding formulae by the harsh light of the median voter theorem and its implications for rational politicians. In Chapter 7, we also must look at some more technical criticisms of regression-based formulae.

Regression-based needs analysis is itself a recent art, and it required computing and statistical tools that did not become available until the late 1960s. It is unfortunate that Karl Pearson applied the word 'regression' in this sense in 1897, because it has no connection with other meanings of the word. While very familiar to anyone trained in research methods, the concept of (especially multiple) regression will not be familiar to all readers of this book. The basic idea is as follows. If the value of one quantitative variable depends on the value of another, then the first is called the 'dependent' (sometimes 'response') variable, and the second is called the 'independent' (sometimes 'predictor') variable. For example, the more elderly people there are in a given area, the more costly will be health care per head in that area. The cost of health care per head is the dependent variable; the prevalence of elderly people is the independent variable. Multiple regression simply allows for more than one predictor variable to have an effect on the dependent variable. Thus the cost of healthcare per head may be expected to be a function of multiple predictors, such as the prevalence of elderly people; the prevalence of young children; the proportion of smokers; the class composition of the area, and so on.

One of the first attempts to show that a needs formula could be derived by regression analysis of appropriate predictor values was by another member of the Titmuss school, Bleddyn Davies (1968; cf. Glennerster *et al.* 2000, p. 12). Davies wrote (1968, p. 31):

> We define ... the statistical condition for territorial justice as a situation in which there is a perfect positive correlation between indices of standards of provision and the index measuring the relative needs of each area for the service, the relative inequality of the standards indices being the same as that of the index of relative needs.

Working on personal social services, which are delivered by local authorities, Davies (writing at a time when the structure of English local government was essentially as Lord Salisbury and G.J. Goschen had left it in 1888) calculated a 'needs index' for each county borough for both old people's services and children's services. The predictors were such things as overcrowding, infant mortality, mortality rate from bronchitis, and class composition (Davies 1968, Table 25).

Allocation on historical grounds had led to a huge concentration of resources in areas with political power rather than in areas with poor health. The initial years of RAWP redistribution were therefore painful. RAWP itself assigned funds only at the level of the fourteen Area Health Authorities in England. The Department and NHS did not then use the standard regional boundaries – indeed, although by 2002, when we investigated the flow of public expenditure into the English regions, their boundaries were very close to those of the standard regions, they were still not identical (McLean *et al.* 2003 section 4.2).[3] In particular, in the era of RAWP the NHS divided the London area into four compass-point segments meeting at the Thames. The advantage of this arrangement for the NHS was presumably that patients from Kent tended to use facilities in south-east London, from Essex, those in north-east London, and so on. However, it makes regional comparisons between health and other services for the 1970s impossible. The summary RAWP numbers are in Table 6.4.

As expected, the effect of RAWP was to withdraw resources (or, more accurately, to restrict the growth of resources) in rich areas and to reassign them to poor areas. The crude population was weighted for its class composition and mortality rates. Morbidity rates would have been better than mortality rates, but data were not available on morbidity, so the RAWP team argued that standardised mortality ratios were a good surrogate for morbidity except for illnesses that did not normally kill the patient (skin conditions, pregnancy-related conditions, mental illness), for which different weightings were used.

Table 6.4   Population and weighted population for NHS resource allocation purposes, Regional Health Authority areas in England, 1975

Region	Crude population, 000s	Fully weighted population, 000s	Ratio
Northern	3126.1	3233.7	1.03
Yorkshire	3576.9	3740.2	1.05
Trent	4545.4	4514.4	0.99
East Anglia	1780.4	1700.9	0.96
NW Thames	3475.3	3279.7	0.94
NE Thames	3717.7	3614.0	0.97
SE Thames	3603.2	3668.8	1.02
SW Thames	2880.3	2896.1	1.01
Wessex	2644.9	2558.8	0.97
Oxford	2199.3	1944.3	0.88
South West	3148.7	3243.2	1.03
West Midlands	5178.1	5005.5	0.97
Mersey	2499.3	2610.1	1.04
North West	4078.1	4444.0	1.09

Source: DHSS (1976), Table C21. Crown copyright. Final column: author's calculations.

The battles that must have lain behind the report leave their mark in odd places in the text. The formulae allowed for higher costs in London, as reflected in London weightings, but 'the problem that the London Weighting adjustment does not fully compensate for market variations should be taken into account subjectively in determining actual allocations ... [to] the Thames RHAs' (DHSS 1976, 2.34). On the other hand, when the committee came to add a weight for the extra cost of teaching medical students, they noted that a medical qualification from any English university was equally valuable to the NHS, and they refused to assign more than a standard weighting based on the median cost per student. Almost all below-median medical schools were outside London (Newcastle was the cheapest); almost all the expensive ones were in London. These two parts of the report comprise a 1–1 score draw between London and the rest of England.

As an attack on the inverse care law, the RAWP had some other limitations. It assigned grant only to the 14 top-tier authorities (regions), rather vaguely saying that they could use the same methodology to assign grant to their smaller units (areas and districts). The top-tier assignment was not based on a regression equation, but on relatively simple weighting (Table 6.4): the same method as used by the Australian Commonwealth Grants Commission (Chapter 9). For grant assignment, each person in the most under-resourced region (North

West) was to be treated as 1.09 persons, and each person in the most over-resourced region (Oxford) as 0.88 persons. The North West was thus Tasmania to the Oxford region's Victoria. But this method could not simply be applied downwards through the tiers of the NHS. The data on population characteristics required for a weighting would become too unreliable, and the problem of cross-boundary patient flows would become insuperable. Lower-level grant assignment would have to use a regression methodology, whose problems were already becoming apparent as they were applied to local government services. These problems are discussed in Chapter 7. Finally, RAWP only concerned hospital services, about 3/4 of NHS spending (Glennerster *et al.* 2000, p. 55). Money for GP and community dental services continued to flow to where the doctors and dentists were – the battles of 1912 and 1948 therefore still cast their long shadows.

The next round of revision of RAWP, under the Conservatives, concentrated on the problem of high costs. Making more allowance for those of course shifted resources from the (Labour) north to the (Conservative) south. However, a senior administrator involved told the LSE research team investigating the history of needs-based funding that 'RAWP is incredibly arcane and I would seriously doubt that a busy minister could foresee what would come out of the review' (quoted by Glennerster *et al.* 2000, p. 59). It might be argued that, although ministers are busy, the spatial impact of spending is exactly the sort of thing they make themselves busy about. Some evidence on this is presented below and in Chapter 7.

The Conservatives' moves towards a purchaser-provider split in the late 1980s meant that the methodology of RAWP had to be refined. Allocation to 14 units might reasonably be made on weighted capitation ratios; allocation to over a hundred needed a more sophisticated technique, if it was not simply to reward historic (over-) spending. As a result of the sophisticated criticism of RAWP, the process has become smoother. The formula currently used derives from work by the Centre for Health Economics at the University of York. It is a regression formula whose main technical properties are:

- the data on 'need' are derived from small area statistics, mostly from the Census. They are *not* derived from the administrative units (health authorities) that receive grants. To derive the data from the same units as receive the grant creates serious problems of perverse incentives, circularity, and ecological fallacy, which we discuss in Chapter 7 (Smith, Rice and Carr-Hill 2001, esp. pp. 224–7).

• it is a multi-stage model to cope with the problem of 'simultaneity in the determination of supply'. To derive need from supply is to commit the error mentioned in the previous point. Yet supply may itself reflect need (as well as other stuff). The two-stage method enabled the York group to 'capture... not only the direct effect of the selected needs variables on utilization but also the indirect effect, to the extent that supply reflects legitimate needs' (Smith, Rice and Carr-Hill 2001, quoted at pp. 234 and 235).

The York group note that

> the Government at the time of implementation [of the hospital services formula] was a Conservative administration, with voting strongholds in the areas that were most likely to lose from the new formula.... [The formula was therefore diluted, with 24 per cent of revenue] distributed on the basis of the age-weighted population alone. The researchers and others questioned this effective dilution of the needs indices.... The then Minister agreed to explore the unweighted 24 per cent, and since then the methods used in this study have been extended to virtually all health care expenditure needs' (Smith, Rice and Carr-Hill 2001, p. 237).

That is a frank (and unusual) statement of a triumph of statisticians over politicians. It also suggests that the busy ministers at the time of the earlier RAWP revision may have been busy with a spatial purpose.

Readers who have got thus far may wonder at the title of this chapter. I do not claim that the spatial allocation of funds for the NHS around England wholly reflects relative need. But it certainly comes closer to doing so that does either the Barnett Formula or the formula for distributing finance for local government services around England. It is to the latter that we now turn.

7
Local Government – Getting it Wrong

Local government finance from Goschen to the Poll Tax: the expenditure side

Local government finance in the UK is one of the dustier corners of social science. Local government has never had very high status in British politics, but in the nineteenth century it had more than now. Between around 1850 and 1914, self-confident cities with buoyant rate income erected the great town halls, such as Leeds (Cuthbert Brodrick, 1858); Manchester (Alfred Waterhouse, 1887); Oxford (T.G. Jackson, 1897); South Shields (Ernest E. Fetch, 1910): cathedrals of municipal self-confidence. The most self-confident English city of all was Birmingham. Joseph Chamberlain was Mayor of Birmingham from 1873 to 1876, in his radical Nonconformist phase. He was an active executive mayor. Under him and his followers, Birmingham became a showpiece of municipal socialism. The city took over and invested in its gas and water supplies, developed the commercial centre of the city using the Disraeli government's Artisans' Dwellings Act 1875 (but provided few artisans with dwellings), patronised the arts, and controlled the licensed trade. Chamberlain's Birmingham is still visible in its late-19th-century commercial district centred on Corporation Street – wonderful name. Perhaps, if Beatrice Potter had after all married Chamberlain instead of Sidney Webb, the British left would have been more localist.

The county councils created in 1888 did not build so grandly for themselves, although later Durham and Devon built stately County Halls. But they tended to share the self-confidence of the cities. Mostly, they were run by the landed aristocrats, used to giving orders and not to taking them, who had governed their predecessor authorities. The

Macclesfields ran Oxfordshire and the Ridleys Northumberland until the 1960s. Why then has the self-confidence of English local authorities declined even as their service responsibilities have grown, for the century since Chamberlain?

Because their finance was always unstable. In this section and the next we look at local spending and local taxation from Goschen to Margaret Thatcher. Governments have long tried to distribute funding for local government equitably across England. However, the task is difficult, and from time to time a great explosion – most spectacularly over the Poll Tax in 1990 – scatters past work to the winds.

Goschen's assignation of tax revenue recognised that in aggregate local authorities spent more than they raised. He could have changed this either by increasing their powers to tax or by reducing their duties to spend. If the balance of taxation matched the balance of spending, citizens could choose the quantity of government that they wanted. The median voter would determine the volume of national services supplied, because both a proposal to spend more than the median voter's optimum and one to spend less would lose to one which spent exactly the optimum. In local government, the Tiebout (1956) effect would come into play. Citizens would move around until each was in the jurisdiction that offered her the optimum package of taxes and services.

But this median-voter-plus-Tiebout model is crassly over-simple. It assumes a world of perfectly informed voters with zero transaction costs. The Tiebout model is at best in unstable equilibrium, because rich people would always try to move to low-tax, low-spending jurisdictions. Poor people would rationally try to follow them there in order to vote for higher expenditures from their generous tax base. If unable to move because of high property prices in rich areas, poor people would be stuck in high-tax jurisdictions which would like to fund generous services, but could not afford to. In which case, poor people would have a rational interest in voting to redistribute resources from rich areas to poor ones, and then the model is destroyed because equalisation grants have to return. Perhaps both the attractiveness and the internal contradictions of the model explain why reformers from Lord Goschen to Sir Michael Lyons (of whom more later) have been striving to get there.

In 1888 there was already a plethora of central grants to local authorities:

> a fixed grant based on average attendance, a special-merit grant in three categories of merit (fair, good, and excellent), a grant for

singing by ear, and one for singing by note (the latter worth twice as much per head as the former). There was a special grant for needlework (only for girls), and one for cookery (worth four times that for needlework). (Foster, Jackman and Perlman 1980, p. 173).

Although Goschen did end non-educational specific grants, Lord Salisbury's first government sounds remarkably like Tony Blair's first government. Central government set detailed performance targets and rewarded local government in proportion as it achieved them. But grants tied to detailed performance targets have many drawbacks. They become so complex that nobody, not even Sidney Webb, can classify or rationalise them (ibid.); they encourage actors to game and to pursue targets; and they clash with equity objectives. A teacher in a slum school in 1888 would have an incentive to teach her children singing by note rather than personal hygiene. And she would get less grant per pupil than a teacher in a prosperous area where the children attended without having to be rounded up, and where they sang by note anyhow because their governesses taught them to.

Equalisation grants were first proposed by Lord Balfour of Burleigh, Secretary for Scotland and local government finance specialist in the Salisbury cabinet, in the Minority Report of the Royal Commission on Local Taxation (Cd. 638) in 1901.[1] He proposed to define a minimum 'need' in terms of the smallest amount per head spent by any actual authority, and maximum 'resources' by the largest amount per head raised by any authority. Grant could then be calculated by these two reference points in order to enable each authority to deliver a standard level of service. Ten years later, the Webbs (see ch. 3) talked airily about a national minimum, but displayed Leninist insouciance[2] as to who would determine what the national minimum standard of service provision should be, and how they would decide. Equalisation grants, with a needs and a resources component, were enacted and refined in 1929, 1948, 1958, and 1988 (Foster, Jackman, and Perlman 1980, pp. 182–204; CIPFA 1996, ch. 6). The needs component recognises that authorities in (mostly poor) areas have higher needs per head than others. The resources component recognises that authorities in poor areas have a weaker tax base per head than those in rich areas. Recently, a third element has entered grant calculations, to allow for the varying costs of delivering public services. As in health (Chapter 6), it is recognised that it is more expensive to deliver a given standard of service in some parts of England than in others. How much more expensive remains an open question. We examine this Area Cost Adjustment in the next chapter.

Throughout these decades of battles, the centre wanted to allocate block grants whose level it could easily control, and the local authorities preferred grants based on their own expenditure. Each system would maximise the information advantage of the side that promoted it. No system from 1901 to 2004 has yet given an equitable and efficient distribution to all authorities. The reasons for the failure of systems up to 1980 to do so are given fully by Foster, Jackman, and Perlman 1980. Their book was itself a catalyst for later changes, many of which were neutral or beneficial, but one of which proved disastrous. To understand why, we have to move from expenditure to tax.

The tax side

As already noted, the sole tax base of any consequence for UK local government services has always been the rating of real property. Already in the 19th century, it was clear that rates were not buoyant; raised questions of equity; and confused three conceptions of what local taxation was for.

The buoyancy and equity issues are linked. Property values may rise either faster or more slowly than incomes. If they rise more slowly than incomes, then the tax base is insufficiently buoyant. As and when they rise faster than incomes, this may be because of windfalls, the improvement of areas through infrastructure improvements, or (since 1947) by the increment in the value of land conferred when planning permission for development on it is given. Governments have often sought to tax these windfalls but never succeeded. The windfalls have, however, ensured that every time there is a property revaluation for rating purposes, those whose property has risen relatively in value have a strong and direct motive for protesting, to the detriment of the incumbent government.

Most commentators assume that tax liability should be related to ability to pay, whether out of income or wealth. But in the case of local taxation, two other concepts are tangled up with 'ability to pay'. The first is what Foster *et al.* call 'beneficial rating'. The second is the concept of the taxation of economic rent.

The idea behind beneficial rating is that local taxes are a charge for local services. Everybody in a city or county gets the local public goods secured by the council (public health, street lighting) to the same extent. Some, too, of the private goods delivered by councils, such as libraries and rubbish disposal, are arguably similar in that respect. They are equally available to all. True, the rich produce more rubbish, and read more books, than the poor, but there is a case for saying that these services should be funded by a flat-rate charge. Foster *et al.* (1980, pp. 44–7, 153–7) class local government services as 'beneficial' (essentially the provision of public goods) and 'redistributive' (everything else they do). This could imply that beneficial goods should be financed by beneficial (flat-rate) taxation, and redistributive goods by central government equalisation grant.

The third concept is the taxation of economic rent. Economic rent is the payment that the owner of a factor of production can command from its scarcity value, over and above the amount payable for its next most profitable use. David Ricardo (1817) argues that as land is inherently scarce, the economic rent it commands rises inversely as that from other factors of production tends to zero:

> The rise of rent is always the effect of the increasing wealth of the country, and of the difficulty of providing food for its augmented population. It is a symptom, but it is never a cause of wealth; for wealth often increases most rapidly while rent is either stationary, or even falling. Rent increases most rapidly, as the disposable land decreases in its productive powers. Wealth increases most rapidly in those countries where the disposable land is most fertile, where importation is least restricted, and where through agricultural improvements, productions can be multiplied without any increase in the proportional quantity of labour, and where consequently the progress of rent is slow. (Ricardo 1817, 2.18, cited from http://www.econlib.org/library/Ricardo/ricP.html)

Therefore, for Ricardo, as later for the American journalist Henry George (George 1879/[1911]), land rents were inherently monopolistic. Landowners as landowners contributed nothing, unlike suppliers of capital and of labour, to the productive economy, and their rents rose with prosperity. An abundant factor of production commands a zero rent. An abundance of capital will tend to reduce profits or interest to a minimum, similarly an abundance of workers will tend to reduce wages to a minimum. However, because land is inherently scarce (and prime locations even scarcer) Ricardian (economic) rents will tend to increase to the maximum that production and the economy can bear. Economic growth and increasing population increase rent because the demand for housing and other building increases.

Rates were a tax on real property: that is, land with or without buildings. After 1880, landowners argued that they paid excessive rates. They could use the beneficial principle to argue that land, as such, received few local government services, and therefore they were overtaxed. They founded the Country Landowners Association, which to this day holds an annual game fair at Blenheim Palace, to be their lobby. Those who did not own land needed a counterblast. Henry George, the most important intellectual influence on the British Edwardian left, supplied the ammunition. Lloyd George and Winston Churchill fired it.

In his 1909 budget, Lloyd George introduced taxation of land values, to be implemented when a land valuation register was ready. This inflamed the dukes and provoked Lloyd George's finest oratory:

[A] fully-equipped Duke costs as much to keep as two Dreadnoughts – and they are just as great a terror – and they last longer.

Anticipating (and helping to provoke) the House of Lords' rejection of the budget, Lloyd George went on

The question will be asked 'Should 500 men, ordinary men chosen accidentally from among the unemployed, override the judgment – the deliberate judgment – of millions of people who are engaged in the industry which makes the wealth of the country?' That is one question. Another will be, who ordained that a few should have the land of Britain as a perquisite; who made 10,000 people owners of the soil, and the rest of us trespassers in the land of our birth[?]... These are the questions that will be asked. The answers are charged with peril for the order of things the Peers represent; but they are fraught with rare and refreshing fruit for the parched lips of the multitude... (At Newcastle upon Tyne, October 10, 1909, quoted by Jenkins 1968, p. 94).

Winston Churchill, then the Home Secretary, went beyond Ricardo:

Roads are made, streets are made, services are improved, electric light turns night into day, water is brought from reservoirs a hundred miles off in the mountains – and all the while the landlord sits still. Every one of those improvements is effected by the labour and cost of other people and the taxpayers. To not one of those improvements does the land monopolist, as a land monopolist, contribute, and yet by every one of them the value of his land is enhanced. He renders no service to the community, he contributes nothing to the general welfare, he contributes nothing to the process from which his own enrichment is derived. (Winston Churchill, 1909, quoted by Barker 2003, p. 116).

The neo-Ricardian argument for land tax was thus that landowners gained windfalls not only from the scarcity described by Ricardo, but also from the deliberate action of (local) governments. The argument acquired yet more force in 1947, when the Attlee Labour government introduced the UK's current system of land-use planning (zoning). Planning permissions, even more than street lighting and water supply, add value to land. The Attlee government tried to devise a tax that would capture some of the resulting gains in land values for the Treasury. It failed, as has every government since (Barker 2003).

The argument over local taxation might thus be characterised as a mainstream assumption that tax should be related to ability to pay, flanked by two unorthodox alternatives. To its left,[3] the view that local government should tax economic rents in land. To its right, the view that local government should charge citizens a flat rate per head for its services. The left-wing view is currently experiencing a modest intellectual revival, signalled by Kate Barker, a monetary economist commissioned by Chancellor Gordon Brown in 2003 to investigate the stickiness of the UK housing market. Her report dabbles in Georgism (Henry and David Lloyd) but then pulls back. The right-wing view exploded into British politics in 1986. The UK still lives with the consequences of the poll tax. The Conservative government first elected in 1979 was not the first to encounter a ratepayers' revolt. But it was the first since 1381 to reach for the 'beneficial' principle of financing local services, and (against the advice of all specialists including Foster and his colleagues) attempt to finance *all* services (not just beneficial ones) from a flat-rate charge.

The burden of rates had also exercised its predecessor, the 1974–79 Labour government. Local government finance was squeezed from multiple directions. The structure but not the finance of local government had been reformed by the Conservatives in 1972. There was a rating revaluation in England in 1973. As always, those whose properties had risen in relative value screamed blue murder; the gainers either did not know who they were or stayed silent. It was a time of rapid inflation, and government did not have an effective mechanism for preventing local authorities from increasing their spending even faster than central government increased its own. Secretary of State for the Environment Anthony Crosland told councils that 'the party's over' but did not know how to end it. He set up the Layfield Committee of Inquiry into Local Government Finance, which reported in 1976 (Layfield 1976; Cmnd 6453). Layfield posed a choice between centralism and localism, which governments of both parties since 1976 have ducked:

> [A] decision now needs to be taken to place responsibility firmly either with the government or with local authorities. This means either adopting a financial system which frankly recognises a need for strong central direction or taking positive steps to increase the ability of local authorities to manage local affairs (Layfield 1976, p. 74).

In 2003, the local government minister in the ODPM, Nick Raynsford, set up and chaired a Balance of Funding Review to consider the balance of central and local taxation. That review expired inconsequentially in July 2004, when the Chancellor of the Exchequer and the Deputy Prime Minister announced a review to review the review, to be undertaken by a safe pair of hands, belonging to Sir Michael Lyons. Sir Michael is a former local authority chief executive who undertook two other jobs for Chancellor Brown in 2003–4, one on locating civil servants outside London and the other on discovering and selling off unneeded parts of the public sector real estate portfolio.

One member of the Layfield Committee, Professor Alan Day, pointed out in a note of dissent that the principle of accountability applies at the margin. For accountability, citizens need to know not which level of government spends the average pound on each service, but which level spends (or saves) the *marginal* pound. Some services provided by local government are better regarded as national than as local public goods. Day argued that central government should mandate (and pay for) floor standards, leaving local government free to choose (and pay, and tax for) higher standards. It is an interesting and subtle contribution, reaching back to Balfour of Burleigh and forward to attempts by the government elected in 2001 to define floor standards. An eye-witness has said that Day's arguments reflected views long held in the local government department (then called the Department of the Environment – DoE), but were resisted in the Treasury, because the logic of Day's and the DoE's view was that a substantial proportion of tax must be transferred from central to local control.

However the Conservative government elected in 1979 ignored Layfield's main report (as had its predecessor) and understood the Day dissent, if at all, only in a half-baked way. They attempted to increase accountability for local spending and succeeded in reducing it. Initially, although the Conservatives were committed to abolishing rates, they concentrated more on successive attempts to force local authorities to cut their spending. As the Conservatives had been deeply unpopular between 1980 and 1982, when unemployment soared, most local authorities were controlled by Labour, which at the time was under the dominance of the far left. Labour councillors therefore regarded it as an honour to spend as much as they could, and the Conservative government regarded it as a duty to stop them. In the end, in a unitary state, central government was bound to win, but at the cost of imposing more and more restrictions on authorities' power to spend. However, a Scottish rating revolt in 1985, in which those whose property had gained in value objected to a perfectly appropriate readjustment of tax liability, provoked the government to look for more radical solutions. The government had made the Scottish revolt worse by reducing rates on industry in Scotland, which meant that householders in aggregate would have to pay more.

Unfortunately, nobody had found a convincing alternative base for local taxation. Layfield had considered local income tax (LIT), but there were two serious problems with that. One is that it would impose an administrative burden on the Inland Revenue and employers: a burden which in the 1970s was prohibitive and even now would be serious. Most income tax is collected by employers and pension providers. But one employer may have the citizens of many different local authorities on the payroll. Income from sources other than employment (or pensions) could not feasibly be subjected to LIT at all. Secondly, the spatial pattern of receipts from LIT would be the same as that from national income tax. Therefore the equalisation problem would remain, and might well become more acute. Sales tax is the other hardy perennial. But the UK is too small, and within the UK local authorities are too small, for sales tax to work. Shoppers would always nip over to the council which operated a lower sales tax, leaving a commercial wasteland on the other side of the boundary. Local sales taxes would also bring a member state into conflict with the European Union.

As Butler *et al.* (1994) make clear, therefore, the Poll Tax largely arose by default, because it was not rates, LIT, or sales tax. In so far as it had an intellectual godfather, it was Sir Christopher Foster (as he became in

1986), although his support for it was heavily qualified. Foster *et al.* 1980 (p. 233) take their argument about paying for beneficial services to the logical conclusion that 'the most efficient tax is a poll tax since such a lump sum does not affect the quantity of the tax base demanded'. Yet even that falls far short of an endorsement of poll tax as the base for all local services – only, at most, for 'beneficial services', which excludes education and personal social services. They also warned presciently that 'the equity objections to a poll or per house-hold tax to finance even beneficial services are likely to be over-whelming' (pp. 240–1).

However, another idea implemented at the same time continues to affect the balance of funding between central and local government. This was the nationalisation of business rates, now known as NNDR (National Non-Domestic Rate). Enacted in 1988, and in force since 1990, this change removed local authorities' power to vary the rate they could charge on non-domestic properties. There were two ra-tionales for nationalisation. The first was that local authorities had pre-viously had an incentive to load local taxes on to businesses, which had no votes, in order to subsidise domestic ratepayers, who had votes. The second was that prosperous city authorities, especially London boroughs, could generate huge revenues from business rates and strug-gling ones could generate relatively little. Heathrow airport (in the London borough of Hillingdon) alone has a higher business rate base than the whole of Liverpool.

No such clear rationale accompanied the poll tax. Every economist teaches in Economics 101 that a lump-sum tax is the least distorting of taxes. But no one expected a government to make a lump-sum tax the sole base for local government finance. Foster *et al.* argue explicitly that the argument for a charge applies only to beneficial services. And the equity objection seems, as they say (p. 241), quite overwhelming.[4] The duke and the dustman were to pay the same tax if they lived in the same council area, which seemed totally unfair (even though brave Conservatives pointed out that they paid the same for their TV licences). And, had anybody in local government been consulted, they would have pointed out that the tax, requiring an entirely new register, would be vastly more expensive to collect, and easier to evade, than rates. So it proved. The tax led (as had its predecessor in 1377 – McLean and Smith 1997) to riots in the West End of London, to the corruption of the electoral register and the Census, and to the downfall of the monarch's principal adviser. Margaret Thatcher resigned on Thanks-giving Day 1990. The poll tax was replaced by Council Tax. Under council tax, every house is classed into one of eight bands – A to H – according to its capital value in 1991. The ratio of tax rates between these bands is fixed by law, but councils set their own tax level for the reference band D. Council tax is less regressive than the poll tax, but more regressive than domestic rates. It has strong regional effects, being a considerably higher burden on households in poor areas than in rich areas of England (Muellbauer 2004). A council tax revaluation is due in 2007. This means that whatever party is in government then can expect a furious reaction from all those whose houses have risen in value since 1991, relative to others in their council area. All parties should therefore be preparing their local taxation reforms now, so as to have them ready for 2007. The remainder of this book attempts to help.

Expenditure: formula funding after the Poll Tax

We return to the inequitable distribution of public expenditure around England first highlighted in Chapter 1. Figure 7.1 shows the trends in identifiable spending, in the English regions, on the services that are devolved outside England. It therefore includes health, education, and other local government services, but excludes social security, a non-devolved transfer programme. The data antedate our report on data inadequacies, and the re-estimation of PESA numbers (Chapter 6). However, those re-estimations would not change the relative picture shown in Figure 7.1. It shows that London has received much more public spending per head than any other English region, although its relative advantage is diminishing.

London is by far the richest region of England; the North-East is by some way the poorest. On the face of it, therefore, Figure 7.1 suggests that something is wrong in the way the formulae work. In Chapter 6 we argued that the health formulae worked tolerably well. So the problem seems to lie with local government services.

The ODPM operates the system, but other spending departments provide the resources in their fields – e.g. the Home Office for police, and the Department for Education and Skills for schools and colleges. These departments are responsible for most[5] grant to pay for what Figure 7.1 labels as 'devolved' services: that is, services that outside England are the responsibility of the devolved administrations. Neither the tax system (apart from the Scottish Variable Rate of Income Tax, not so far used) nor the social security system are devolved. The vertical distribution for the Health Service began controversially and has

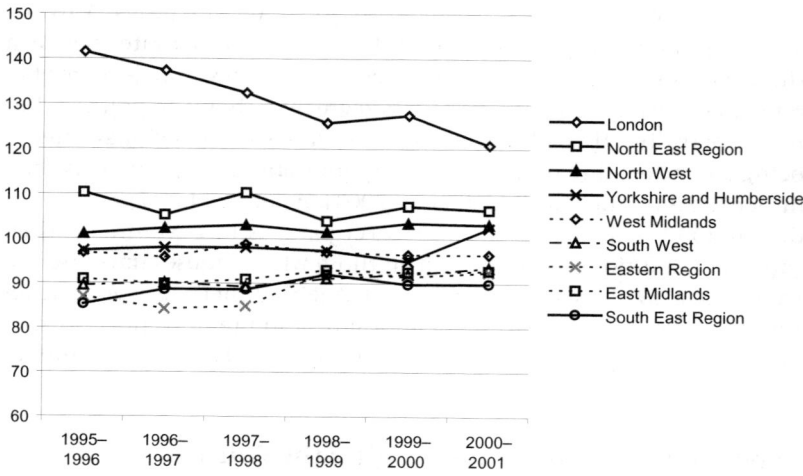

Figure 7.1   Spending per head on devolved services in the English regions 1995–2000 (identifiable English spending = 100)
Source: PESA, various years.

become less controversial (Chapter 6). The vertical distribution for local government spending began controversially and has become more so, with the Government conceding the weaknesses that academic critics had been pointing out since the early 1990s.

The formula for local government services is now called the Local Government Finance Formula Grant Distribution (LGFFGD). As that is such a mouthful, we follow the Department's Web addresses and retain the acronym of its predecessor, Standard Spending Assessment. SSA and LGFFGD are the latest of a set of regression formulae that have controlled the distribution of grant to English local authorities since the 1970s. SSAs were introduced in 1990, which was a particularly fraught time in UK central-local government relations. The poll tax was collapsing (Butler, Adonis & Travers 1994; Besley, Preston, and Ridge 1997). Local government's penultimate tax base, non-domestic rates, was transferred to the centre. It is left, essentially, with only domestic real estate (Council Tax). Only London has so far pioneered an alternative tax base, with the Congestion Charge introduced in 2002. Like any other tax on an economic bad, the more successful it is at cutting congestion, the less money it raises directly.

SSA had to meet some very specific political needs. From the wreckage of the poll tax, the governing Conservatives salvaged what they could. They pointed to a small number of Conservative-controlled 'flagship authorities', where (they said) the poll tax had worked as intended. Those councils[6] set low poll tax rates and ran services cost-effectively. The Opposition claimed that the low poll tax rate in the flagship authorities resulted from Government manipulation of the new SSA formula. Not only anecdote,[7] but also subsequent academic analysis, supports the Opposition claim. Ward and John (1999; cf. John and Ward, 2001) found that, as well as population and needs, the following factors increased grant to a local authority in 1994/5:

- being a large unitary authority;
- being a shire (i.e. not predominantly urban) county;
- containing marginal Parliamentary seats;
- having been a Conservative flagship authority in 1990;
- being Essex.

Although these conclusions themselves derive from a multiple regression analysis, their predictors are not ones that a government would have dared to enter directly into the formula. All five of these predictors favoured the incumbent Conservatives. The continued significance of the 'flagship' factor suggests that there are lagged effects. As with any time series, grant at t_1 is usually one of the best predictors of grant at t_2. This could explain the continued significance of the 'flagship' variable four years after the death of the poll tax.

In their later paper, John and Ward find two sets of political variables significant. One points to a political business cycle, in which the incumbent government spends more on local authorities when a General Election is pending. The other points to the same political effects as the earlier cross-sectional model, although marginality of parliamentary seats works only for the period after 1988 (John and Ward 2001, Table 2, Model 3).

The York health economics group (see Chapter 6) designed the SSA for personal social services. They report that

> the needs element of the new formula resulted in major shifts of assessments, most notably an average 20 per cent reduction in needs assessments in inner London, an 11 per cent reduction in outer London and a 7 per cent gain in other areas... To some extent these shifts were moderated by the introduction of the new area costs adjustment. It is of course a matter for speculation whether the Government would have searched for a revised area cost adjustment

with such vigour if the results of the needs analysis had not implied such a marked shift of resources (Smith, Rice and Carr-Hill 2001, p. 233 (source of quotation); Carr-Hill, Rice, and Smith 1999).

Gibson (1998, pp. 645–6) found 'pure (that is, unadulterated) political manipulation of the Education SSAs by the Conservative government in 1990.... [T]he large redistribution of Education SSAs in 1990 ... must have a cumulative value of well over £1 billion'.[8] In a later paper he added that the SSA system 'generated at least two issues – the increased role of ethnicity in additional educational needs (and the reduced role of indicators of economic deprivation) and the sudden large increase in the allowance for additional labour costs in London and the South-East' (Gibson 1999, p. 29).

Most of these examples predate the change of UK government in 1997. But the incentives facing any government are identical. It wishes to be re-elected; it must attract the median voter in the median constituency. SSAs for local government have proven to be more manipulable than the formula for health spending.

Needs are an essentially contested concept. Since there is no objective definition of a need, it is always open to politicians to argue that whatever the median voter in the target constituency lacks is a 'need'. In health, it is reasonably easy to define outcomes (death, morbidity). In local government services, it is much harder, and it is correspondingly easier to confuse outputs (miles of road, home visits), with outcomes. In local government, the only evidence as to the cost of providing a service is often the vector of costs which local authorities have actually incurred in providing it. Also, the cost of providing capital goods is reflected in the vector of local authorities' interest charges. To incorporate these into an index of need is to reward inefficiency (Audit Commission 1993; Smith, Rice, and Carr-Hill 2001, p. 224; Gibson 1998, pp. 631–5; ODPM 2002 *passim*, e.g. para. 52). This is the fundamental problem that the Department calls 'regression against past spending'. Day complained about it in his note of dissent to Layfield (Layfield 1976; Foster *et al.* 1980, p. 427).

The risk of moral hazard is particularly acute when the predictors in the regression equation come from the same unit as the recipient of grant. The health formula could avoid this by deriving its predictors from the Census. For local government services, the most convenient, and sometimes the only possible, reporting unit is the local authority. Furthermore, once a historic pattern is frozen into the system of regression equations, it is difficult to break its hold – witness the shadow that the Conservative flagship authorities continued to cast over SSA for years after 1990.

In 2001, the government conceded all the points made by the academic critics of SSA (DTLR 2001, part II paras 3.21–3.24). In the consultation paper that preceded LGFFGD (ODPM 2002) it tries to move away from regression against past spending, but some of the replacement formulae are still regression-based. The most recent example of the problems to which this continues to give rise is another ODPM discussion paper (ODPM 2004b). Here the Department admits that as late as 2004, the Department was not yet proposing to use population figures from the 2001 Census as its baseline for grant, but to 'to continue to use the regressions based on the 1991 Census-based mid-year population estimates' for most services (ODPM 2004b, para. 26). This is pretty remarkable. The 2001 Census was highly controversial, as it seemed to undercount the urban population in several places. But so was the 1991 Census, which was seriously corrupted by the Poll Tax fiasco. People believed (reasonably, although wrongly as it happens) that if they hid from Census enumerators, as well as from the electoral register, their chances of evading Poll Tax liability were increased (McLean and Smith 1992). If such a fundamental datum point as population of each authority is uncertain, what hope is there for valid inferences from regression formulae?

A former Conservative minister once whispered confidentially to me, 'Look at the exemplifications!' Whenever the Department proposes a formula change, it publishes a set of tables of maybe five columns and 400-odd rows, one table for each block of services (education; police; fire; and so on). These tables show the effect of each proposed formula change (the columns) on each local authority in England (the rows). In the case of health authorities, it has been argued even if Ministers wished to fiddle RAWP and its successors the task would be just technically beyond them (Chapter 6). But for local government services it is only too easy. The Minister need only decide which local authority, or class of authorities, she wishes to reward, run a finger across the table, find under which formula the favoured authorities do best, and choose that formula – without, of course, mentioning anything about its impact on her favourite councils.

This is a truly intractable problem. The Department insists, reasonably, that it must have exemplifications as a reality check. If a formula change had a very abrupt effect on the grant payable to a particular authority, there would be trouble for the minister, who would then reasonably complain to her officials that they had failed to warn her of the consequences. Therefore exemplifications must stay. It would be hard in the light of the Freedom of Information Act for the Department to keep them secret. But as long as they are there, rational political agents will use them politically. I believe that this may be the fundamental reason why the formula funding of local government services is less successful than the formula funding of the NHS. Ironically it arises in part because local authorities are elected, whereas health authorities are not.

Providing a framework in which spending is allocated at a regional level based on a robust and general indicator of needs would ensure that local biases have a limited effect, and that the general pattern of spending is transparent and equitable. Therefore this book proposes that formula funding for local government services should go to each standard region. It would be for regions to allocate downwards to the authorities in their patch. This is the procedure adopted for health in the 1976 RAWP. It is also the procedure used in Australia (Chapter 9). The mechanics must wait until Chapter 11, after we have described the Australian system.

A possible solution to the problem of regression on past spending is emerging. Ideally, your determinants of grant should measure outcomes – say, how much happier people have become since social workers called on them. If you can't do that, should at least measure outputs – say, the number of people seen by social services departments per annum. When you cannot even do that, you have to measure inputs – say, the amount that each council has spent on social services. If you can only measure inputs, you are regressing against past spending. If a council has spent unusually highly in the past, it will get an unusually high grant in the future. But its high past spending may be due to high need, or low efficiency, or high costs, or a political decision to give priority to that service. Multiple regression cannot tell those apart. It is at severe risk of rewarding councils for past inefficiency. Central government, and particularly the Treasury, has laid great stress on performance indicators. The emphasis increased at the 1997 change of government. The new government set great store by Public Service Agreements (PSAs) for government departments and both PSAs and performance targets for local authorities. The first were policed by the Treasury and the second by the Audit Commission.

Few people outside central government are true believers in the PSA/Audit Commission regime. The traps are well known. Like teachers in 1888, public servants in 1997 have an obvious incentive to respond to targets rather than to act in a socially optimal way. As we argued in a recent pamphlet:

> Inspectees will improve their performance on the target that is measured, at the cost of neglecting things that are not measured. When it was announced that hospital throughput would be monitored in a certain week in March, hospital managers moved heaven and earth to shift patients – *in that week*. That is the rational strategy for any public service manager.... [G]overnment by inspection will always and everywhere generate perverse incentives of that sort. Therefore, government by target will never even achieve a correct measure of what is targeted, let alone of what is not. (McLean and McMillan 2003b, p. 15).

However, the regime has improved. The number of targets has dropped, and government is attempting more and more to focus on outcomes rather than outputs or inputs. In a foreword to the latest government list of PSAs, the Chancellor of the Exchequer writes:

> Now we can measure how effectively resources are being used and whether services are delivering the outcomes that will really make a difference to people's lives.... By setting minimum standards across a range of public services, including health, education, and crime, 'floor' targets ensure that everyone benefits from improvements. In this way we are continuing to ensure both equity and excellence in the provision of public services (HM Treasury 2004d p. [iii].

Up to a point, Chancellor. Even Chancellor Brown and his officials have not yet found how to measure whether personal social services have improved people's happiness. But by 2004 the PSA targets have become considerably more defensible than they were in 1997 (or 1888). Here are three that apply from 2004 to 2006:

- Raise standards in English and maths so that:
  - By 2006, 85 per cent of 11 year olds achieve level 4 or above, with this level of performance sustained to 2008; and
  - By 2008, the proportion of schools in which fewer than 65 per cent of pupils achieve level 4 or above is reduced by 40 per cent....
- Reduce crime by 15 per cent, and further in high crime areas, by 2007–08.... (HM Treasury 2004d pp. 11, 19).

These targets are in the domain of local authorities. Yet the PSAs bind Departments, not local authorities. What is the transmission belt? The document continues:

> Floor targets for key government departments are aimed at levering up the performance of public services towards the national average in areas where delivery is unacceptably weak, particularly in deprived areas (HM Treasury 2004d, Box 2).

There is a hint here of the Day minority report in Layfield, or of the implicit prescription of Foster *et al.* (1980). But schools, police, fire, and local transport are delivered by local authorities, not directly by government departments. If, therefore, government is to adopt a 'floor standards' approach, it will need to alter both central-local government relations and local government finance. In the Day-Foster model, central government would fund local government to a level which would enable an averagely competent authority to deliver at least the floor standard for each of its main services. What it did beyond that would be up to itself, and its citizens. But central government would have to provide the finance for floor standards. The local share of tax revenue could, and would, shrink yet further. The dynamics of floor standards, for better and worse, are that once they have been achieved, government raises the floor. This would make local services better and better, but less and less local. As local tax effort should probably be improved, not relaxed, this is itself one of the problems with the implicit Day-Foster model. Thus we return to the options for local taxation.

Taxing: some answers to Layfield's questions

As noted elsewhere in this book, the UK has one of the highest vertical fiscal imbalances (VFI) of any country in the democratic world. As Layfield and many others have observed, this divides responsibility for taxing from responsibility for spending. Obviously it gives local authorities, who spend more than they tax, an incentive to spend irresponsibly. Less obviously but equally truly, it gives central government, which taxes more than it spends, an incentive to tax irresponsibly.

Layfield liked local income tax (LIT) but it was administratively unfeasible at the time. Inland Revenue computer systems for assessing and collecting personal income tax are now quite robust. And in 2004, the Liberal Democrats committed themselves to 'axe the [Council] tax' and bring in LIT in its place. Does that make LIT an idea whose time has come? I think not. The 2003–04 ODPM Balance of Funding Review considered this question and came to no clear conclusion. It commissioned two reports from the specialist organisation of local authority treasurers, CIPFA. LIT has two advantages. It is probably more progressive than council tax, and more buoyant. Against that, it has crippling disadvantages. If anything, the Balance of Funding report underplays them, and it omits altogether a serious cross – boundary problem.

The first disadvantage is that either answer to the question *Would LIT supplement or replace property tax?* is problematic. If it replaced it entirely, as proposed by the Liberal Democrats, government would be giving up domestic real estate as a tax base – unless they nationalised it, which the Liberal Democrats do not propose. This would be highly imprudent for three reasons.

- house prices are extremely, perhaps unsustainably high, in the UK, and to abandon tax on them is irresponsible;
- council tax is cheap to collect because houses do not move and cannot hide;
- it is much easier to abandon a tax base (and cease collecting the relevant information) than to reinstate it.

But if LIT *supplements* council tax, then local tax collection costs must rise (and so must the costs of equalisation over more than one tax base, as in Canada (Chapter 10)). Computerisation of the Inland Revenue does not magic away the problem of collection. LIT could only feasibly be levied on the component of income that is at present taxed on the PAYE (Pay as you Earn) system. This includes income from employment and employers' pensions, but not from savings, dividends, and self-employment. LIT enthusiasts might pass over savings and dividend income but self-employment is an intractable problem. The state imposes many of the collection costs for income tax on employers, who have to operate the PAYE system, and send the tax thus deducted from their employees' pay to the Inland Revenue. A national or multinational company would of course have employees all over the UK. A medium-sized English employer with all its offices on one site might still have employees living in 30 local authorities, not all of them in England.[9] A small employer, who typically operates the PAYE system manually, would be hit, proportionately, even harder by the extra administrative costs. The CIPFA report to the Review estimates the additional annual costs to business of running LIT at £110 million, on a baseline of £800 million – an increase of 14 per cent (ODPM 2004a, 5.22).

Next, the Review ignores Scotland and Wales. Even if Northern Ireland is regarded as self-contained, Scotland and Wales cannot be. Thousands of people live in England and work in Scotland or Wales, or vice versa. The Scottish Executive has the power to levy an LIT – the Scottish Variable Rate of Income Tax, which may be levied at any level from –3p to 3p in the pound, but on the standard rate of income tax only.[10] The National Assembly for Wales does not. Scotland and Wales could not be forced to introduce LIT just because the UK government decided to introduce it in England. Now revert to the fact that Wigan Council employs people domiciled in Wales and Scotland, and work out a procedure for collecting LIT on the assumptions (a) that the Scottish Variable Rate is levied; (b) that it is not. Report your answer to the Director of Finance.

Finally, LIT would put greater pressure on the equalisation component of central grant to local authorities. This is the flip side of its greater progressivity. Poor areas would need even more support from the centre than at present, and rich areas even less. This is, of course, a feature of any progressive tax, and must not be held against LIT in particular. But the other drawbacks listed should be enough to kill it as a practical proposition for the UK.

The argument against sales tax is as good as it was when Layfield reported, and it need not be considered further. This leaves two serious options. One is relocalisation of business rates, considered by the Balance of Funding review; the other is land tax, not seriously considered.

In response to business lobbies' complaints about taxation without representation, central government promised that NNDR would increase annually by at most the rate of price inflation. Therefore it is, by fiat, non-buoyant. But it pays for local government services which are delivered by people. Wage costs go up each year more than prices. Therefore, NNDR is doomed to pay for a lower and lower proportion of the costs of local government. When a new storm broke out in 2003–04 about steep increases in council tax, Ministers were quick to blame local government. But they had themselves contributed to it. NNDR is nobody's tax. Central government does not own the proceeds and has no interest in keeping it buoyant. Local government cannot control the rate at which it is set.

A well-designed tax gives the government that owns it an incentive to behave so as to maximise the proceeds of the tax without distorting other economic activity. NNDR fails that test. It would be good if local authorities encouraged industrial and commercial development where there is no overriding planning objection to it. To do this, it should reject 'NIMBY' (Not In My Back Yard) objections. But if it gets no gain from the new development, because it sees none of the increase in rates that the development generates, it lacks the incentive to face down Nimbies. In recognition of this, ODPM has designed a fearsomely complicated Local Authority Business Rate Growth Incentive scheme (See http://www.local.odpm.gov.uk/finance/labgi.htm). However, the scheme is tiny, complicated, and self-contradictory. A more radical government would re-localise NNDR, while meeting the business objection to taxation without representation by forbidding an authority to raise its business rate by any proportion larger than the rise in its domestic property tax.

Neither Layfield nor the Balance of Funding Review spent long on land taxes, although the Review at least mentioned them, as did a summer 2004 report from the Select Committee on the ODPM (House of Commons Select Committee 2004). Foster *et al.* (1980, pp. 458–82) have a long discussion of site value rating, which unlike their comments on poll tax was totally ignored. It was the Barker Review of housing supply, reporting to the Chancellor of the Exchequer (Barker 2003), that disinterred Winston Churchill's 1909 enthusiasm for taxing monopolistic landowners. The Liberal Democrats, the party of Churchill and Lloyd George, have however moved in the opposite direction. Although they retain a shadowy commitment to site value rating, their headline policy at the time of writing is to 'Axe the Tax', namely council tax. This may be good politics, but it is bad policy for reasons listed above. So let us explore land value tax.

By 1914 the register of land holdings was still not ready. Lloyd George therefore returned to land taxation in his 1914 Budget, relying on his capacity for brilliant improvisation to work out the details. That had worked when he introduced National Insurance in 1911 (McLean 2001b, ch. 6). This time, on a very complicated subject with powerful vested interests in opposition and no support from his own Treasury officials, he failed. The outbreak of World War I put paid to land value tax in the UK until 2003.

Three recent reports (the Review, the ODPM Select Committee, and Barker) engaged with the arguments for land value tax – something that no UK government had done since 1947. The Town & Country Planning Act of that year created a system of rationing land use by planning law, and a system of taxing those who benefited from this created scarcity – i.e. holders of planning permission. The first limb of the Act lives on. The second withered and was amputated when the Conservatives returned to power in 1951. Therefore owners of land with planning permission, or land on which the market believes that planning permission for change of use will be obtained, derive far more economic rent from it than even Ricardo can have imagined possible.

The standard text on the UK tax system, one of whose authors is now the Governor of the Bank of England, insists that 'the underlying intellectual argument for seeking to tax economic rent retains its force' (Kay and King 1990, p. 179). Since 1947, land value in the UK has depended on its planning status. If a field is zoned for agriculture, it is worth a few thousand pounds per hectare. If it is zoned for business or housing, it may be worth millions of pounds per hectare. Land value taxation is efficient (because it does not distort the incentives to develop land) and equitable (because it returns some of the economic rent to the people who created it, namely the local authority and its electors). Henry George (1879/[1911], p. 290) recognised both of these properties. As Kay and King go on (p. 181):

> Suppose the award of planning permission increases the value of a plot of land from £5000 to £1 million. Then even if the resulting gain were taxed at 90 per cent, the developer would still be better off by almost £100,000 using the land for housing than retaining it for agricultural purposes. Substantial incentives to bring projects forward would remain.

Property interests have always seen off past attempts at land taxation. This happened not only in 1909 and 1914, but also, as Barker (2003, Box 7.3) notes, in 1947, 1967, and 1974. On each occasion property owners had an incentive to delay transactions in the hope that the tax would be repealed. On each occasion, it was. The lesson is not Barker's inference that land taxation is unfeasible. It is that any tax should be a tax on capital (or rental) value, not a tax on transactions.

The second objection to land value taxation is the cost of assessment. However, the same difficulty faces NNDR and council tax, the two taxes that land value tax would replace. Both of these taxes are linked to valuations that rapidly go out of date. Council tax bands are determined by houses' value in 1991. The next Council Tax revaluation is not due until 2007. The base for NNDR is revalued only every five years, next in 2005. The more time that elapses between valuations, the more those whose assets have risen in relative value have an incentive to block revaluation. It was just such a revolt against rating revaluation in the 1980s in Scotland that led to the poll tax disaster. Losers from revaluation are more likely to be members of political parties than gainers, because both losers and party members are more likely to be rich than poor.

Enough houses change hands every year that the capital value of the land underneath every house could be calculated annually. Estate agents do it all the time, in their ordinary business. Therefore the existing Valuation Service or a successor could do the same. Commercial and industrial property changes hands less often, so that annual valuation of every parcel of land may not be feasible. But this is not an insuperable objection. At worst a government could stick with the existing five-yearly revaluation, which could be updated whenever a sale took place. A National Land and Property Gazetteer is already being constructed, by uniting databases from the Ordnance Survey, the Royal Mail, and local and central government. In principle it can identify every taxable hereditament in the UK. And it is not a snooper's charter, because it contains information only about places, not about people. Land value taxation is not an option for tomorrow. But it could be an attractive option to announce in 2007 and introduce in 2009, to celebrate the centenary of the People's Budget.

A third objection, currently politically salient, is that any property tax including land tax penalises the 'asset-rich but cash-poor' – who in current debate are characterised as 'Devon pensioners'.[11] The first, robust, answer, is that Devon pensioners should face the real opportunity cost of continuing to live in large houses, and they have the options of taking in lodgers or trading down to smaller houses. A softer answer is that the tax liability on a freehold house could be deferred if the householder cannot pay, and become a charge on the estate when the house is sold. Local authorities would be able to borrow against this debt owed to them, and would therefore not be deprived of a cash flow.

Land tax would be a tax on land value (LVT), or more strictly on the economic rent deriving from land value. Therefore it should be levied at a zero rate at land that has no capital value above baseline agricultural use. A zero rate band up to £20,000/hectare has been proposed (Muellbauer 2004, p. 15). Above that, it should not depend on whether land had a planning permission, but on whether the market believed that it would get planning permission – thus it would catch speculative appreciation in land values on urban fringes. A fourth objection is therefore that if it is partly a local tax (which on balance I think it should be), land tax gives cash-strapped councillors an incentive to permit sprawling developments from which the 1947 system protects the UK. The answer to that objection is that councils, like Devon pensioners, should face the true opportunity cost of their decisions. And so should the people they represent. Refusing development comes at a cost which at present local citizens do not bear. They should face the open choice: Permit development and face lower local tax rates, or refuse it and face higher local tax rates. The ballot box should decide.

This argument works both ways. If an authority proposes a development that reduces land values – say an incinerator or a tannery next to a housing estate – it is right that those who take the decision should face the true costs in a reduced land tax income flow.

Finally, as a land tax would tax Ricardian rents, it must be a tax on land, not on the structures that sit on the land. This means that a future valuation regime would have to separate those two. In the case of houses, that is both fair and uncomplicated. Every house is priced for insurance purposes at its rebuilding cost. Every Sunday the papers tell you what improvements add value to your house and what do not. In the case of commercial and industrial premises, separating the value of land and structures is admittedly more complicated. And there are at least three other problems:

- The formal incidence of NNDR is on occupiers, who are often tenants, of industrial and commercial premises. The formal incidence of land value tax would be on owners. In economic theory that does not matter. In practice it does, because UK commercial leases are long, with 'upwards-only' rent review provisions. A fair way for transferring the tax burden from the occupier to the owner, and adjusting leases in return, would have to be found.
- An effective land value tax should fall on all land above the exempt threshold, whether or not it has planning permission. Land on urban fringes may change hands at high prices in anticipation of a future planning permission. This feature could catch some families with paddocks on the edge of town on which they graze a horse – paddocks that are almost valueless at their current use, but which might change hands for many thousands of pounds a hectare.
- Charities are exempt from NNDR or pay it at a reduced rate on property they occupy for charitable purposes, and are exempt from stamp duty on trades of assets held for investment purposes. If those exemptions were generalised to an exemption from LVT, there

would be a huge transfer of land ownership to charities. If they were not, charities would complain about unfair tax treatment.

I do not belittle these objections to LVT. However, as everybody knows that there will be a storm about NNDR revaluation in 2005, and another one about council tax revaluation in 2007, the time to work on these tricky problems is immediately.

No existing class of taxation comes anywhere near capturing the windfall gains of which Winston Churchill spoke in 1909, nor anywhere near recouping any of them for the public sector. The Jubilee Line Extension (JLE) of the London Underground, from Green Park to Stratford, was commissioned in the early 1990s for completion in time for the opening of the Millennium Dome, at its North Greenwich station. Because it was common knowledge that government credibility depended on its opening by 1 January 2000, its costs overran hugely. Nevertheless, studies commissioned by Transport for London show that, even at those bloated costs, the Jubilee Line Extension could very easily have been financed by a land tax. Land values adjacent to its stations rose hugely above the general increase in London land values over the same period – by £2.8 bn at Southwark and Canary Wharf alone from 1992 to 2002. This compares to a total construction cost for the JLE of £3.5 bn. Even at stations not on the Extension, property values rose by more than the general rate. People living at Stanmore could travel conveniently not only to the Dome, but also to useful places such as Southwark and Canary Wharf. However, the UK government not only failed to extract any tax revenues from the uplift at Canary Wharf, it actually offered the area an undeserved and instantly capitalised tax break in the shape of stamp duty exemption for sales of commercial properties in 'deprived wards' (McLean and McMillan 2003b).

Transport improvements cost money. The commonest source of land value gain, however, costs nothing except staff wages: namely, planning permissions for changes from a low-yield land use such as agriculture to a high-yield use such as shops. Here, the economic rent is created because planning law, for basically benign reasons, deliberately creates a scarcity. Left to themselves, market forces might produce a suburban Britain that looks like suburban America. Almost nobody at any point of the political spectrum wants that. Therefore, since 1947, there have been tight zoning restrictions on land-use planning in the UK. However, there has been too much sentiment and too little hard-headedness about the economic and social issues involved in the 1947 regime, which is still in place. It privileges farming over other land uses, which was appropriate after the blockades and food shortages of both World Wars, but no longer is. It produced socially desirable policies such as Green Belts by command-and-control, not by price signals. And, although nobody wants an unregulated market in land use, a regulated market would so far outperform the present command-and-control regime that protection of scenically valuable land could be financed as an almost incidental benefit, out of the small change.

The UK has a raft of bad land taxes. They include Council Tax; NNDR; Stamp Duty Land Tax; inheritance tax (IHT) and capital gains tax (CGT) to the extent that they catch increases in land values (which is not much, as those who benefit can pay for sophisticated tax advice); and, probably worst of all, Section 106 Agreements.[12] The last are agreements between a developer and a local authority whereby the developer agrees to contribute to some socially desired outcome (such as subsidising social housing or urban transport) in return for the grant of planning permission. Section 106 agreements are the worst sort of disguised taxation. They are extremely costly to both developers and local authorities; and the gains they produce are in no way commensurate to the cost. A simple auction of planning permissions would do far better. A tax levied on land value (and not on transactions, like IHT, CGT, Stamp Duty, and the abortive earlier land taxes) would be better yet.

In the meantime, it is obvious that Council Tax must be rebanded to become more progressive. Both the top band (Band H) and the bottom band (Band A) must be split in order to be fair to households at both ends of the property value distribution. That is a necessary reform for reasons given by Muellbauer (2004; see also McLean and McMillan 2003b), but an insufficient one. It would not address the spatial inequity of council tax – the property that it bears more heavily on households in poor parts of England than in rich parts. In fact, rebanding on its own might make that inequity worse. That defies all conceptions of equity and efficiency.

In this chapter we have shown that the spatial distribution around England of both local taxation and local public expenditure is hard to defend. In the next chapter we attempt to bring together the conclusions of the last five in order to look at the big picture of the distribution of fiscal flows around the United Kingdom.

8
The Whys and Wherefores of Fiscal Flows

Summary: the position so far

As previous chapters have shown, the distribution of UK revenue to the regional and territorial governments, health authorities, and local authorities which spend the money is a based on a hotch-potch of badly designed formulae. The Barnett formula, which allocates money to the devolved territories, has been attacked from all sides; its progenitor Lord Barnett now disowns it. The mechanism by which resources were distributed to local authorities within the English regions was changed in 2002, but the current system has not wholly escaped the faults of its predecessor.

Recall that the Scottish Office dates back to 1885; the Northern Ireland executive to 1921. As previous chapters have shown, there is therefore over a century of friction between the UK government (represented principally by the Treasury) and the Ulster and Scots administrations over the terms of their block grants from the centre. This controversy long predates political devolution, and has continued when Northern Ireland has had no devolved government. By contrast, the creation of the Welsh Office was an absent-minded commitment of the incoming government in 1964. Wales never had devolved government until 1998. A student of lobbying and entrenchment would therefore predict that Scotland would do best, Northern Ireland next best, and Wales worst out of these arrangements. The strength of distributional coalitions (cf. Olson 1982) is a function of the length of time since their establishment. So it has proved (Tables 1.1, 8.2, 8.3), although Northern Ireland's historical spending advantage on domestic programmes has eroded rapidly under the Labour government's Comprehensive Spending Review regime.

The financial arrangements for devolution derailed the Home Rule Bill of 1886. The Goschen formula, or proportion, was introduced in 1888 and its shadow persisted until the Barnett Formula was introduced in 1978. The Barnett Formula has only since 1998 started to achieve what its originators wanted it to. As and when it does, the results would be very unfair at least to Wales and perhaps to all three devolved territories. Wales has already been a victim, not a beneficiary, of Barnett. According to the Office of the First Minister and Deputy First Minister in Northern Ireland, it too was due to drop from 'winner' to 'loser' during the lifetime of the 2002 Spending Review, i.e. by the end of financial year 2005–6 (*source*: NI Civil Service seminar presentation in Belfast, 2003, but see also House of Lords 2002, Evidence of Dr Andrew McCormick and Mr Victor Hewitt, pp. 331–5). Northern Irish civil servants are maintaining the 'needs' database use by the Treasury and the territorial departments to compile the notorious Needs Assessment of 1979 (HM Treasury 1979). They concede that, before the Spending review regime, Northern Ireland was assigned a block for public expenditure that was higher than her relative needs. However, by the end of the 2002 spending review regime in 2006, they maintain that Northern Ireland's block grant will have dropped below her relative needs. One Treasury riposte is buried in the Spending Review 2004: 'A major programme of reform to modernise water, rating, and public administration will be introduced in Northern Ireland' (HM Treasury 2004c, 23.18). Decoded, this means 'While Northern Ireland remains under direct rule, the UK government will force it to increase its tax effort by raising domestic rates, which remain the basis for property taxation in Ulster'.

Meanwhile the allocation of grant to the regions of England has been governed by a completely different set of formulae, under two main government departments. Whereas HM Treasury has always been the custodian of Goschen and Barnett, the Department of Health is the custodian of the formula that assigns grant to health authorities, and the Office of the Deputy Prime Minister (ODPM) of the regression-based formula, currently called Local Government Finance Formula Grant Distribution, that assigns grant to the local authorities. As examined in Chapters 6 and 7, the health formulae work relatively well; the local government finance formulae work relatively badly. I speculated in Chapter 7 that this outcome may, perversely, reflect the fact that health authorities are not elected, whereas local authorities are elected.

This chapter proceeds as follows. A section on the private world of Area Cost Adjustment attempts to justify the claim that the allocation of expenditure among unelected authorities may actually be fairer than its allocation among elected authorities. Then I temporarily retire from democratic politics in order to give a first sketch of how a benevolent dictator might assign public expenditure fairly across the nations and regions of the UK. This sketch deliberately ignores two things for simplicity. One is the tax side of the question, and the other is distributive politics. I return to those matters in the concluding chapters, after the examination in Chapters 9 and 10 of the two best comparator systems for

- devolved taxes;
- expenditure allocation from the centre by formula-based block grant,
- and two tiers of democratic government.

These comparators are the Commonwealth of Australia and (what used to be called) the Dominion of Canada.[1]

The private government of Area Cost Adjustment

A landmark study of the politics of public finance in the UK was entitled *The private government of public money* (Heclo and Wildavsky 1974). At the time of their research, the government of public money was truly private. Only a few mandarins and few (if any) Ministers understood it. Most of the mandarins were in the Treasury; a few were in the local government department (successively, in that era, the Ministry of Housing and Local Government and the Department of the Environment); a few more were in Scotland and Northern Ireland. Most politicians and almost all academics were utterly ignorant of it. So aloof was the public reputation of the Treasury of the time (cf. e.g. Sampson 1962) that British academics and journalists seem to have been scared even to ask permission to penetrate the fortress of public finance. It took two brash Americans to make the breach.

In general, things have changed remarkably since then. In recent years, the Treasury has been very welcoming to outside academic observers, and so have the devolved administrations. But one sub-world seems to be as private as in Heclo and Wildavsky's day. It is the world of Area Cost Adjustment. How should the funding formulae be adjusted for the fact that it may cost more to deliver public services in some parts of the UK than in others?

At first sight, this is a tractable problem, more so in the UK than in countries with wider variations in wage costs. Even after devolution, Britain has a unified civil service, and pay and conditions for central government employees are therefore uniform throughout Britain. Servants of the Scottish Executive and the National Assembly for Wales continue therefore to be employed on the same terms and conditions as civil servants working for UK government departments. The Northern Ireland Civil Service is a separate body, but with similar pay and conditions to the UK Civil Service.

Local government and health service employees are mostly members of strong trade unions, which negotiate national wage agreements for all the main groups of staff. This includes not only local government 'civil servants' – i.e. administrative staff – but all the people who deliver services – e.g. teachers, police officers, and fire officers on the local government side; all the professional groups in the NHS on the health side.

All of these wage scales include 'London weighting'. In all public sector occupations, pay in London is higher than outside London, in recognition of the higher cost of living in London. In some groups, London weighting is split into a (higher) inner London and (lower) outer London rate. In some groups, there are higher rates of pay for other high-cost regions of the UK outside London. London weighting is often of the order of 5 per cent of basic pay.

The first approximation to estimating the cost of delivering public services in different parts of the UK would therefore be simply to look at the actual pay scales of public service employees – or, better, if the data are available, the actual wage bill. Lobbyists in high-cost regions insist that this is not enough to give a full picture. Academic observers agree, for a number of reasons. The most important of these is that the wage bill does not control for the level of skills and experience of public servants in different areas. Differences in the cost of living are greater than the differences in public sector wage scales. Some areas of the country are unpleasant to work in and you have to pay a premium to get employees to work there. Conversely some areas are very attractive and you could pay less and people would still want to work there. For these reasons, the actual pay costs faced by local authorities may be an inadequate guide to the true costs of doing business.

Area Cost Adjustment was first introduced to the local government revenue support formula (the predecessor of SSA) in 1977/8, using data from available social surveys about the level of pay for each group of occupations in each region of the UK. Until 1997, ACA was payable only to authorities in London and the south-east. This led to disquiet in many other parts of England, most acutely in counties that lay just outside the South-East standard region but claimed plausibly to have high wage costs. Swindon (South-west) and Cambridge (East of England) were prominent examples. But everybody knew that the game was zero-sum. As government used the aggregate of SSA for England as a control total, and in the mid-1990s was capping local authorities that spent more than their SSA said they should spend, any change in the formula to benefit one class of authorities was bound to harm all the other classes.

In 1995, the local government minister David Curry commissioned a review of ACA. It was a sign of the universally acknowledged zero-sum nature of the problem that two of the three people he asked to conduct the review (Elliott 1996) were in Scotland – a labour economist and the former secretary of the Scottish local authority association. Presumably any English-based expert would have been accused of vested interest by the losers from its recommendations.

The Elliott review steered a middle course. It reported that ACA (or more pedantically, LCA, labour cost adjustment, which has always been by far the most important component of ACA because labour is the most important component of local authority costs) was calculated by an elaboration of the method introduced in 1977/8. Regional wage relativities were calculated from sample surveys of the workforce after controlling for variations in the skill and age mix of the workforce in different parts of England. It recommended that a regression-based method should continue to be used, but that it should be extended from the south-east to the whole of England. This should be done by taking the lowest-wage county in England (which turned out to be Cornwall) as a baseline, and then setting an LCA for each county, and for the three London zones Outer, Inner, and City of London as a multiplier of the wage costs for Cornwall. There should be special arrangements for the two island counties (Scilly and Wight) to reflect their higher non-labour costs. A table of exemplifications (Elliott 1996, Table 6.2) showed how each authority would do if the review's recommendations were accepted.

This middle course lay between two extremes, which would have had different distributional consequences. One was the real data approach of looking at the actual wage bills and pay rates in different parts of the country. Proponents of this view complained that the regression methodology 'shows an over-compensation of the order of 60 per cent for teachers and fire-fighters and of 40 per cent for police officers' (Elliott 1996, 4.2.18). Teachers, fire-fighters and police officers are by far the three largest single groups of local authority workers – adding up to about half of the total. Their wages are set nationally. Unlike some other public service workers (e.g. care assistants, solicitors, computer specialists), they do not move very often into or out of the private sector. If, therefore, LCA was giving London and south-eastern authorities more than the actual excess of their wage costs per teacher (etc.), it was over-compensating them. The proponents of this view are not identified, but it is easy to guess that they did not come from the south-east.

The third approach starts from the same fact that the three biggest groups of local government employees do not tend to move to and from the private sector, but gives it an opposite twist. This approach accepts the Department's (and Elliott's) basic methodology of a deriving LCA from a regression analysis of survey data on pay, controlling for confounding factors such as skill level, gender, and age. But it claims that the right-hand side of the regression equation[2] should contain data for private sector pay only. That should improve the prediction because 'market forces are more easily identified in the private sector' (Elliott 1996, 4.3.4). Also, public-sector pay is centrally determined and governments always try to hold it down. To put data on it into the regression equation is statistically bad practice because it sets up a vicious circle. Public-sector pay appears on both the left- and the right-hand side of the regression equation. Area labour costs for the public sector would be determined by a number of factors, one of which would be .... area labour costs for the public sector.

This view is closely associated with the Warwick economist Andrew Oswald, who took part in three of the four research studies commissioned by the Elliott review:

> The Cabinet meeting room should have a large sign hung on the wall: *we cannot force people to take public-sector jobs in the South-East.....*
> But exactly how much more should public-sector workers earn in the expensive parts of the country? The right approach is to match the pay differentials, area by area, in the private sector. This does not mean matching the salary levels; it means matching the percentage differentials between the different regions. So if private-sector workers earn 29 per cent more in an expensive region like Surrey than in a cheap one like Humberside, then so should public-sector workers.

When a proper statistical analysis is done, here is what is found, for a worker with standardised qualifications, from one region to another. These figures draw on a sample of 200,000 randomly sampled private-sector workers across the country.

In Central and Inner London, private-sector workers earn 54% more than in Tyne and Wear.

Outer London workers earn 24% more than those in Tyne and Wear.

Rest-of- the-South-East workers earn 13% more than those in Tyne and Wear. (Oswald 2002).

This view, too, has strong distributional implications, which go in the opposite direction to the 'real costs' approach. Because Oswald makes the comparator the private sector (only), his method would open an even larger gap than do the other two approaches between the high-cost and the low-cost parts of England, such as Tyne and Wear which by 2002 had supplanted Cornwall as the lowest-wage county. No government has considered paying public sector workers in central and inner London 54 per cent more than those in Tyne & Wear doing the same job.

Nothing came of this work immediately. Ministers looked at the zero-sum distributional implications of Elliott (his Table 6.2) and put it hastily back on the shelf. After the change in government in 1997, an MP for a Cambridgeshire constituency secured an adjournment debate to complain about the non-implementation of Elliott's recommendations. His local authorities would be among the most obvious gainers from a formula that assigned some ACA to every authority except the cheapest. The Minister, Nick Raynsford, explained that

> [a]ll four local authority associations asked that the review's recommendations should not be implemented for 1997–98 SSAs.... [T]he review did not convince critics that the system recommended by the review team would not overcompensate some authorities ..... [G]iven the zero sum process, it is understandable that those concerns must be given serious weight (*Hansard* 18.07.1997, col. 669).

The current situation (2004) is about half way to Elliott. In a 2002 consultation paper, the Department proposed to apply ACA to every authority other than the cheapest (DTLR 2002) – in other words, the Elliott methodology. This generated predictable zero-sum lobbying. The outcome in 2004 is that ACA applies to a range of authorities wider than London and the South-East region but narrower than the whole of England (Table 8.1).

Table 8.1   Area Cost Adjustment factors for English local authorities, 2004–05

	Education	PSS children & younger adults	PSS older people	Police	Fire	Highways	EPCS
ACA areas							
Common Council of the City of London	1.4697	1.4534	1.5026	1.532		1.442	1.4462
Inner London	1.2681	1.2503	1.2799			1.2329	1.2343
West, North West and South West Outer London	1.1518	1.1407	1.1575			1.1312	1.132
Rest of Outer London	1.0927	1.0853	1.0947			1.0832	1.084
Berkshire, Surrey and West Sussex Fringe	1.1401	1.135	1.1494	1.1588	1.1615	1.1326	1.1339
Hertfordshire and Buckinghamshire Fringe							1.1096
Kent and Essex Fringe	1.0807	1.0793	1.0862			1.0843	1.0856
Bedfordshire and Hertfordshire Non-Fringe	1.0529	1.0488	1.0541	1.0573	1.0583	1.0477	1.0482
Berkshire Non-Fringe	1.1323	1.1232	1.1385			1.1122	1.1127
Buckinghamshire Non-Fringe	1.0885	1.0822	1.0919			1.0766	1.0771
Essex Non-Fringe	1.0119	1.0104	1.0106			1.0144	1.0149
Kent Non-Fringe	1.0177	1.0158	1.0167			1.0191	1.0196
West Sussex Non-Fringe							1.0308
Avon	1.031	1.0306	1.0336		1.0373	1.0313	1.0317
Cambridgeshire	1.0465	1.0451	1.05	1.0529	1.0537	1.0438	1.0442
Cheshire	1.0212	1.0204	1.0225	1.0242	1.0247	1.0204	1.0206
East Sussex	1.0096	1.0082	1.0081		1.0123	1.0125	1.013
Gloucestershire	1.0197	1.02	1.0216	1.0245	1.0253	1.0221	1.0225
Greater Manchester	1.0184	1.0178	1.0195	1.0212	1.0217	1.0181	1.0183
Hampshire and Isle of Wight	1.0433	1.0398	1.0439	1.0471	1.0481	1.0399	1.0404
Merseyside	1.0078	1.0078	1.0082	1.0099	1.0104	1.0096	1.0098
Northamptonshire	1.0265	1.0264	1.0288	1.0317	1.0325	1.0276	1.028
Oxfordshire	1.0863	1.0801	1.0896		1.0938	1.0748	1.0753
Warwickshire	1.0339	1.0333	1.0367	1.0396	1.0404	1.0337	1.0341
West Midlands	1.0258	1.0257	1.0281	1.031	1.0318	1.027	1.0274
West Yorkshire	1.0094	1.0094	1.01	1.0117	1.0122	1.0109	1.0111
Wiltshire	1.0303	1.03	1.0329	1.0358	1.0366	1.0307	1.0311

Table 8.1 Area Cost Adjustment factors for English local authorities, 2004–05 – continued

	Education	PSS children & younger adults	PSS older people	Police	Fire	Highways	EPCS
Authorities which cut across ACA areas							
Buckinghamshire County Council	1.0953	1.09	1.1			1.0866	1.0874
Essex County Council	1.0346	1.0331	1.0356			1.0374	1.0382
Hertfordshire County Council	1.0993	1.0959	1.1055		1.1161	1.0967	1.0979
Kent County Council	1.0268	1.0251	1.0268			1.0286	1.0292
West Sussex County Council	1.0458	1.0427	1.0469		1.0522	1.0438	1.0444
Council of the Isles of Scilly	1.5	1.5	1.5		1	1	1.5
Avon & Somerset Police Authority				1.0242			
Essex Police Authority				1.0431			
Hertfordshire Police Authority				1.1137			
Kent Police Authority				1.0292			
Sussex Police Authority				1.0313			
Thames Valley Police Authority				1.1176			
Greater London Authority				1.1867	1.189		
Berkshire Combined Fire Authority					1.1511		
Buckinghamshire Combined Fire Authority					1.1035		
Essex Combined Fire Authority					1.0446		
Kent Combined Fire Authority					1.0304		

Notes:
1. The area cost adjustment factors for all other English authorities are 1.
2. EPCS: Environmental, Protective, and Cultural Services.
Source: ODPM, at http://www.local.odpm.gov.uk/finance/0405/lgfrs/annexh.pdf, accessed 02.09.04. Crown copyright.

This story shows several things. One is that it is harder to measure local authorities' spending needs than health authorities'. Another is that there is no agreement, even among the few experts, as to the best way to do it. Third and most important, the process is intensely political. It is much more political than the process of setting grant to health authorities, because local authorities are elected and health authorities are not. Governments want to reward their favourite local authorities or their favourite voters. If they are unsophisticated governments, they favour the people most likely to vote for them. If they are more sophisticated, they favour the median voter, or the authorities where the median voter is likeliest to be found. If they were ultra-sophisticated and fully informed, therefore, Labour and Conservative governments would load grant on to the identical place – the home of the median voter. They are sophisticated, but not ultra-sophisticated; well-informed, but not fully informed. Everybody in the game knows that increasing ACA will tend to favour the south (Conservative voting) and London (multi-party but since 1997 distinctly more Labour-voting than before then). Reducing ACA will tend to favour the North of England (Labour voting). ACA was introduced and reviewed under the Conservatives. The new Labour government initially refused to introduce the graded ACA recommended by Elliott, but by 2004–5 was operating a truncated version of it. The full-blooded Oswald alternative would transfer substantially more resources to the south of England than does the modified Elliott version in operation.

In the light of this, the next section of this chapter introduces a fantasy figure, the benevolent dictator. The benevolent dictator is concerned only to maximise social welfare. As she is a dictator, she does not face re-election, but she is aware that the constitution she creates will be operated by elected politicians. The purpose of this device is to outline the characteristics of an ideal system. The following two chapters then describe real-world systems. Armed with some knowledge of these, we can then return in Chapter 11 to designing a system for the UK to be created by political agents rather than benevolent dictators.

What a benevolent dictator might do

The elected authorities in the Barnett territories and London have the legitimacy of two election cycles under their belts (albeit that the Northern Ireland Assembly elected in November 2003 remains suspended at the time of writing). They will not be abolished. Even the Conservatives, who bitterly opposed the creation of the Scottish and

Welsh assemblies, accept their legitimacy, not least because their proportional electoral systems give the Conservatives a block of seats in
those assemblies which has no counterpart in the House of Commons.
The Conservatives hold no seats in Wales and only one in Scotland in
the Parliament of 2001. After the 2003–4 cycle of elections in the territories, Scotland is governed (as in the previous cycle) by a Labour-
Liberal Democrat coalition; Wales by a minority Labour administration
(during part of the first cycle it, too, was a Lab-Lib coalition); and
London by the prodigal Labour son Ken Livingstone, who was readmit-
ted to the Labour Party in time for the 2004 mayoral election. In the
first cycle he ran as an independent. Unlike most opposition parties,
the Conservative have only once (in September 2000) led Labour in the
polls since Labour rule began in 1997. At the time of writing, therefore,
Labour looks like a hegemonic party in the UK and in three of the four
territories with devolved government. Many commentators have noted
(overseas ones with wonder) that Labour has hardly used the formal
procedures for resolving devolution disputes since 1999. It has relied
on intra-Labour discussions between the Labour government and the
sort-of-Labour devolved administrations. That is unsustainable. Labour
will not be in power for ever (probably). Even if parties with the same
label govern the centre and the periphery, experience in mature federal
systems suggests that they will develop in different ways. In Canada,
for instance, parties with the same or similar titles fight federal and
provincial elections, but they are different parties. The Liberal administration of Ontario neither controls nor is it controlled by the federal
Liberal Party, nor by Liberal members from Ontario of the Ottawa
House of Commons. The Québec sovereigntist party in Québec provincial election is the Parti Québécois. In federal elections it is a different
party, the Bloc Québécois.

In the generic politics of devolution, it is predictable that all parties
in the Territories other than that controlling the UK government will
blame the UK government for starving their territory of money. In
Wales, and increasingly in Northern Ireland, that complaint will be
justified. The UK government will deny that it has starved them of
money. But the Barnett Squeeze is real, so it will find that denial
difficult. Meanwhile it will find it difficult to address any apparent
overspend on 'devolved' services in London, given Ken Livingstone's
successful defiance of his once and future party in 2000.

Meanwhile, the English regions that seem to do poorly out of the
grant distributions are becoming vocal for the first time since 1977.
Urged on by the Government's apparent commitment to regionalism

in England, the regions have each formed a Campaign for the (North East/North West/Yorkshire/West Midlands etc), typically headed by a local bishop. Each complains about its region's share of public spending. The painful juxtaposition of Alnwick and Duns is becoming difficult to ignore and was aired in regional media after the Spending Review 2002 (e.g. Linford 2002; Warner 2002). Until summer 2004, when he departed to become prospective Labour candidate for a safe seat in Yorkshire, Chancellor Brown's right-hand man Ed Balls was the most powerful voice in government for the English regions, jointly with Deputy Prime Minister John Prescott. They did not have a smooth ride in all respects. Prescott's ambition for elected regional assemblies had by then boiled down to a referendum in just one region, the North-East, which everybody expected to be the region most favourable to an elected assembly just because it is the regional whose territorial grievances have been aired most articulately. The 2004 Spending Review contained some dollops for northern England under Balls's influence, showing particular favour to a new creation called the Northern Way, which unites the development agencies of the three northern English regions.

None of this squabbling surprises a political scientist. The game of distributive politics is essentially zero-sum and politicians will fight for their districts. However, a disinterested finance minister (hereafter DFM) might try to convince a Cabinet of territorial representatives with the following memorandum.

1. *Why replace the Barnett mechanism?* Because it has come under fierce criticism for two opposite reasons. In England it is widely perceived, in Joel Barnett's words, as 'terribly unfair' especially because of the relativities between the poorer English regions on one hand, and Scotland (and sometimes London) on the other. In the territories especially Scotland it is perceived as a 'Barnett squeeze' which will, at least in the long run, cut the allocation of spending to the territories to a point below their needs – in Wales it probably has done so. Also, a formula that makes change in identifiable spending on the territories a function of change in identifiable spending on England is incompatible with devolution, properly understood.

2. *Why not just allow these arguments to cancel out?* They won't. Both of the main arguments will become more strident. Inter-region discrepancies will be more widely noticed even if convergence makes them less extreme. Meanwhile the accelerating

convergence accentuates the 'Barnett squeeze' argument, and may force a territory's spending allocations down too far.

3. **Why act now?** When public expenditure is going up sharply, no region need suffer an absolute loss from one year to another after a revision of the formula. As redistributive politics are zero-sum, there are bound to be agonised squeals from the losers (whoever they are) at any other time. The suggested replacement of the Barnett and English formula funding mechanisms would:

- be more transparent;
- give better accountability of politicians to those who elect them;
- increase fiscal responsibility;
- clarify the constitutional relationship between the UK Government and the devolved administrations;
- improve the performance of the UK economy by removing perverse incentives to be 'needy' and substitute incentives, or at least help, for a territory to become less needy.

4. In the following proposals, the whole of England could be one unit. Or each Government Office Region of England could be one unit. Each unit must be represented in negotiations by a minister (or functional equivalent) – from the government of England (as distinct from the UK) or the Assembly of each region as the case may be. This memorandum assumes that devolution will necessitate new arrangements for the government of England in any case.

5. Two models are suggested below. In Model A, there is a new Territorial Grants Commission, a non-departmental public body staffed by public servants who could be secondees from HM Treasury, the Office for National Statistics, ODPM, or the territorial administrations. The Commissioners would be appointed after consultation among the finance ministers of the UK and all the territories, but would not be territorial representatives. Its constitutional status would be the same as that of the Electoral Commission, so that its operations and recommendations are insulated from partisan political interference. This commission would make an annual report on territorial 'equalisation' and 'needs' (these terms are defined at paragraph 8) to a joint ministerial council of the UK and territorial governments.

6. In Model B, there is either no commission at all, or a slim commission that determines an equalisation formula but not a needs formula. The model for the equalisation formula would be that

operated in Canada by the Privy Council Office (PCO) and Finance Canada (Chapter 10). 'Needs' would be directly negotiated at the joint ministerial meeting.

7. Both models would share two essential, and complementary, features:

   - any decision by the joint ministerial council must be unanimous, with each territory having one vote;
   - in the event of failure to produce a unanimous decision, incremental grants for the next time period would be allocated by predetermined multiplier. We propose that this default multiplier be (UK GDP/head)/(territory i GDP/head) for all i. The mean amount available per head for equalisation would be multiplied, for each region, by this number, which is, of course, greater than 1 in poor territories and less than 1 in rich territories. This formula is called 'inverse GDP' below.

8. Model A is based on the widely admired (and copied) Commonwealth Grants Commission of Australia (Chapter 9). The UK Commission would apply an 'equalisation' formula, modified for 'needs', using an algorithm similar to the CGC's. 'Equalisation' means 'placing each territory in a position to offer the same mean level of provision of each service, should it choose to do so'. 'Needs' means 'factors that raise the cost of delivering a service and that are beyond the capacity of governments to alter'. Cold weather, mountainous or indented terrain, and high wages in occupations which are alternatives to the public service are examples of 'needs'. Health status (and *a fortiori* current health spending), congestion, and housing costs would not count as 'needs', because

   - governments can, and should try to, ameliorate them;
   - factors such as congestion and housing costs will already be embodied in wages, so it would be double-counting to include them.

9. An objection to Model A is that needs are what philosophers call 'essentially contested', such that no agreement on what constitutes a need is possible. The history of HM Treasury's 1979 Needs Assessment lends credence to this objection.

10. In Model B, all the work of the 'needs' component of Model A would fall to the joint ministerial council, and, if they fail to agree,

would default on to inverse GDP. Inverse GDP is not a bad surrogate for (an incentive-compatible definition of) needs.

11. An alternative default that has been suggested is social security
spending per head (Bell and Christie 2001, p. 142). However:

- using an indicator that itself derives from a government programme (albeit a non-devolved one) risks circularity, with elements of the same programme appearing on both sides of the
regression equation. This is a similar objection to that encoun-
tered in the previous section on ACA.
- GDP per head is not the direct result of government policy,
although it is highly correlated with things that governments
must try to improve, such as human capital and health status.
- GDP per head is measured by an independent non-partisan
agency (ONS), not by any party to the proposed negotiations.
- There would not, as now, be perverse incentives to become and
remain 'needy'. A good example of the current perverse incentives lies in the argument about EU Objective One status in
Wales. Wales gained from being 'needy', and it will lose at a
marginal tax rate of at least 100 per cent when West Wales and
the Valleys (see Chapter 5) cease to be 'needy', which pre-
dictably will occur in 2006, when the next round of EU regional
programmes begins. By contrast, if a territory's government im-
proves its GDP per head, then income/head must rise by more
than grant/head would fall on an inverse GDP formula, as government spending is less than 100 per cent of GDP. Therefore
the marginal tax rate on success would always be less than 100
per cent.

12. The proposal for a unanimity rule combined with an inverse
GDP default derives from game theory and a study of UK political history. In (re)distributive politics, actors with a credible
threat do better than those without. In normal times, the territories which pose a credible threat to the Union, or the interests
of the governing party, are (in descending order) Northern Ireland, then Scotland, then London, then Wales. No other English
region normally poses a credible threat. February 1977, when
a North-east lobby defeated the Scotland and Wales Bill, is an
exception. Not coincidentally, the four regions with a credible
threat are the four regions with devolved government, which in
turn increases their threat potential. A unanimity rule gives each

territory an equally credible threat, and is therefore the only fair rule.

13. However, a unanimity rule on its own gives each and every territory a veto over change. Any territory that stands to lose from a change from the status quo would veto it. Therefore there must be a default option, and it must be common knowledge among the players before the game starts what the default option is. If there is a Pareto-superior allocation to inverse GDP, rational bargainers will find it. If not, inverse GDP satisfies rough justice and is cheap to calculate.

The analytic properties of inverse GDP

Table 8.2 develops Table 1.4 by showing how much the UK government would have distributed per head for devolved services in each region of the UK if it had used the inverse GDP formula just suggested[3] rather than the combination of Barnett and SSA that was actually used.

The rightmost column of Table 8.2 shows the residuals for each region: that is, the difference between actual public spending per head and the public spending per head that an inverse GDP formula would have delivered. These range from +£1145 for London to –£823 for the North East Region. In other words, London received £1145 per head more, and the North East Region £823 per head less, than they would have received under an inverse GDP scheme.

Some of these differences may be for good reasons – such as, perhaps, that it costs more (even with efficient local authorities) to provide a given level of service in London than in the North. Others may be for bad reasons – such as, perhaps, that London contains more marginal seats, or presents a more credible threat to the Union, than the North, or that the SSA has given too much weight to inefficient high-spending authorities or to former Conservative flagship authorities, or both.

The issue of the different cost of goods and services across regions can be addressed by adjusting the measure of GDP with a price deflator. Using ONS estimates of regional price differentials (Baran and O'Donoghue, 2002) to adjust the figures in Table 8.2 allows a simulation of regional government expediture at purchasing-power parity (PPP).[4] Table 8.3 and Figure 8.1 compare the unadjusted and adjusted figures. The analysis suggests that the positive residual associated with government expenditure in London is reduced from £1145 to £990 per head when the regional price level is incorporated in the analysis, and the negative residual for the North East changes from –£823 to an

Table 8.2 Public spending under an inverse GDP formula (12 regions/territories)

Region	Actual Public expenditure/ head (A)	Index public expenditure/ head	GDP/head	Index GDP/head	InvGDP public expenditure/ head (B)	Residual (column A–column B)
South-east	2,550	86	15,098	116	2,553	–3
East	2,624	88	15,094	116	2,553	71
Greater London	3,431	115	16,859	130	2,286	1145
South West	2,654	89	11,782	91	3,271	–617
West Midlands	2,736	92	11,900	92	3,239	–503
East Midlands	2,632	89	12,146	94	3,173	–541
Yorkshire and Humberside	2,905	98	11,404	88	3,379	–474
North West	2,928	99	11,273	87	3,419	–491
North East	3,022	102	10,024	77	3,845	–823
Wales	3,289	111	10,449	81	3,688	–399
Scotland	3,638	122	12,512	96	3,080	558
NI	4,347	146	10,050	77	3,835	512
UK	2,971	100	12,972	100	2,971	0

Table 8.3 Public spending under an inverse GDP formula, adjusted for regional price differentials (12 regions/territories)

Region	Price index compared to UK average[a]	GDP/head at PPP	Index GDP/ head	Index GDP/ head at PPP	InvGDP public expenditure/ head	InvGDP public expenditure/ head at PPP	Unadjusted Residual (from Table 8.1)	Residual at PPP
South-east	3.1	14,730	116	114	2,553	2,408	-3	-66
East	1.5	14,871	116	115	2,553	2,385	71	32
Greater London	6.8	15,786	130	122	2,286	2,242	1145	990
South West	-0.7	11,865	91	91	3,271	2,985	-617	-594
West Midlands	-1.2	12,045	92	93	3,239	2,945	-503	-464
East Midlands	-1.7	12,356	94	95	3,173	2,882	-541	-487
Yorkshire and Humberside	-3.4	11,805	88	91	3,379	3,006	-474	-360
North West	-2.2	11,527	87	89	3,419	3,070	-491	-416
North East	-4.7	10,518	77	81	3,845	3,381	-823	-642
Wales	-3.8	10,862	81	84	3,688	3,282	-399	-259
Scotland	-0.9	12,626	96	97	3,080	2,813	558	585
Northern Ireland	-0.2	10,070	77	78	3,835	3,506	512	520
UK		12,972	100	100	2,971	2,729	0	0

Notes: [a] Data for all units except Northern Ireland are inclusive of housing rents. For NI, relative housing rents are not available, so data are presented exclusive of housing rents. The effect of this is probably to exaggerate the positive residual for NI.
Source: HM Treasury, *Public Spending Statistical Analysis 2002–3*, derived from Tables 8.6b and 8.12b. Office for National Statistics, *Regional GDP 1999*, summary table. Crown copyright. Price figures from Baran and O'Donoghue 2002: Table 2.

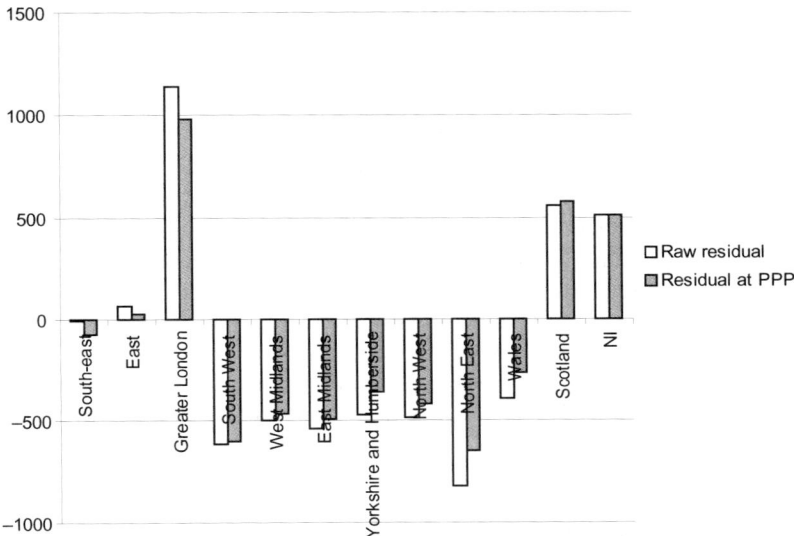

Figure 8.1   Raw and PPP-adjusted residuals: actual regional government expenditure per head minus simulated expenditure under inverse GDP formula, £
Source: PESA, various years; our calculations.

adjusted figure of –£642. The relatively low level of prices in Scotland and Northern Ireland mean that the estimated residual of spending over inverse-GDP projection is even larger when a price adjustment is included in the simulation.

The only way to meet Lord Barnett's complaint that the present arrangements are 'terribly unfair' is to use the same formulae to distribute grant to both the devolved and the non-devolved territories of the UK. If grant to the English regions, which at present have no elected governments, is set by formula, then those parts of it that go to local authorities should be determined after the regional total has been set. Grant to the devolved territories will, of course, continue to be assigned without strings.

There is no easy alternative to a regression-based formula. The preceding analysis shows what traps any new formula must avoid. Above all, it must not use the units to which grant is distributed as the units from which data as to need are collected. That way lie circularity, inefficiency, and ecological fallacy. If the data are collected either at a level below or at a level above that of the local authority, at least the worst problems will be avoided.

However, if it is to be used for the devolved authorities, a regression-based formula cannot simply be imposed. The specification of the formula would be up to the territorial grants board. But it has to be agreed, and as argued above, it ought to be agreed unanimously, by a joint ministerial council of all the governments affected. A government of England, or governments of the devolved regions of England, must exist for this purpose. In the scheme just suggested, 'inverse GDP' is a default to which the increment in grant will revert for the next period if the joint ministerial council fails to agree either the formula or the outcomes of the formula by the due date.

Like Barnett, inverse GDP would operate on increments of grant, not total grant, and for the same reason. There are 120 years of rent-seeking built into the present allocations (cf. Olson 1982). To move direct to inverse GDP would cause unacceptable disruption. An incremental, convergent, formula would avoid this. There is nothing wrong with convergence, so long as it is convergence on the right thing. Barnett converges on the wrong thing, namely population ratios. If Barnett is allowed to run until full convergence is achieved, then public expenditure per head will be too low in all three Barnett territories. A formula which converges on need, where need is defined in a politician-proof way, is superior in both equity and efficiency.

The English local government white paper (DTLR 2001; Cm 5237) lays great stress on efficiency measures, and on giving local authorities incentives to become 'best value councils'. These are praiseworthy, but efficiency criteria can operate only at the margin. They cannot distribute core grant because inefficient councils are likely to be in poor areas. The formula for core grant must be an equity formula that is consistent with efficiency. It cannot be a pure efficiency formula. Also, given devolution, neither the UK Government nor the joint ministerial council can apply efficiency conditions to the devolved territories. These matters are for their governments and parliaments alone.

The arrangements just proposed involve persuading politicians to give up power. Ministers and their advisers would no longer have the power to set grant allocation formulae for either health or local government, nor for deciding when to observe and when to bypass Barnett. Persuading politicians to give up power is difficult. But they have three material interests in putting formulae beyond manipulation:

1. Removing a formula from political manipulation prevents a future government from manipulating it against you. The evidence that SSA was coloured by the Conservative governments' 1990 priorities

for years afterwards might suggest to Labour politicians that it is a dangerous power.

2. It prevents people from blaming you. Compare the voluntary surrender of levers of macroeconomic policy by Margaret Thatcher (who gave up the traditional macro levers of economic management) and Gordon Brown (who gave the central bank the sole right to fix interest rates, see McLean 2001b, chapter 8).

3. yet more profoundly, a government is more credible the less it has power to manipulate levers for partisan advantage. Credible commitments not to manipulate economic instruments can improve welfare. For illustrations, see North and Weingast (1989) on 18th century Britain; McLean (2001b, pp. 229–30) on Bank independence and the 'golden rule' since 1997. Regional economies might be stronger if investors did not think that investment and spending decisions were dependent on the machinations of electoral politics. Local governments who did not think that spending levels were dependent on lobbying ministers might concentrate their attention on better provision of services. The general flow of resources could be towards the areas in which it had most effect on the improvement of public service provision and the equitable economic development of the UK.

By using these arguments, our hypothesised disinterested finance minister might even convince a cabinet of territorial representatives to give up the power of vertical distribution. After reviewing Australia and Canada, we will revert in Chapter 11 to this model, adding more political realism to it.

9
The Australian Model

Introduction

Australia displays high vertical fiscal imbalance (VFI) for historical and constitutional reasons. It also attempts to achieve the highest degree of horizontal fiscal equalisation (HFE) to be found in any democratic federation. The Commonwealth Grants Commission (CGC), a non-partisan body at arms length from politicians, oversees the regime. A report published shortly before I visited Australia in September 2002 to study the model (Garnaut and FitzGerald 2001, 2002) claims that equity, efficiency, and transparency would all improve if the regime were abolished. Such a change was politically unachievable, but it raised interesting issues in public finance and public administration, which carry over to other federations and union states, such as the United Kingdom.

An economically efficient system would: minimise perverse incentives, especially incentives to seek rent; encourage states to grow; discourage suboptimal location decisions; minimise transaction costs. An equitable system would maximise equity between relevantly similar individuals. This chapter explains how the arrangements for fiscal federalism – that is, for revenue sharing between the Commonwealth and the States – came into being in the Commonwealth of Australia; evaluates current criticisms of the regime; and assesses how far these arrangements could serve as a model for a country such as the UK. Aspects of the Australian system that should be copied include the non-partisan agency and the target of HFE between component parts of the country. Aspects that should be discussed and perhaps copied include the very extensive equalisation, including the feature of equalising away the effects of grants for special purposes. Aspects that should probably not be copied include the cumbersome formulae, and some of the perverse methods of calculating for 'needs'.

History

The Commonwealth of Australia came into existence in 1901 as the result of conventions and referendums in the six ratifying colonies. In 1933, the Commonwealth created a mechanism for distributing grant from the Commonwealth to the States, which has been widely admired. Several writers including myself (e.g. Heald and Geaughan 1996; McLean and McMillan 2003a; Péloquin and Chong 2002) have already recommended that it be copied elsewhere.

The units of Australian federalism remain the same six colonies, now the States, plus the two self-governing Territories (ACT and NT – see Glossary). The units are extremely heterogeneous by population and land area, but the most homogeneous of any democratic federation by GDP per head. Although most people think that NT is extremely poor, and it certainly contains a massive proportion of extremely poor Indigenous people, yet its GDP per head on the output measure is the second highest in Australia, because of its substantial mineral output. Table 9.1 contains the basic details.

Before Federation, the colonies got most of their revenue from customs and excise – 76 per cent in 1896–7. A purpose of Federation was to reduce barriers to trade such as State tariffs and railway changes of gauge at State borders (the latter not yet achieved). What the states lost in revenue from tariffs against each other, they must regain either

Table 9.1   The units of Australian federalism

Unit	Population, 000	Land area, km^2	GDP/head, AUD
NSW	6,643	800,640	35,021
Vic	4,854	227,420	33,882
Qld	3,670	1,730,650	28,790
WA	1,919	2,529,880	36,828
SA	1,519	983,480	27,639
Tas	473	68,400	24,062
ACT	323	2,360	40,808
NT	200	1,349,130	38,397
Australia	19,604	7,692,030	33,037

Source: Australian Bureau of Statistics website, www.abs.gov.au, various tables, consulted 2.10.02. GDP data (known in Australia as GSP, gross State product) for June 2002. Population for 31.12.2001.

in common Australian tariffs against the rest of the world, or from some other tax base. As in other federations, the States were divided in their relative exposure to the world economy, and hence in their median voter preference over tariff policy. The Constitution failed to carry in referendum in NSW. In subsequent bargaining, the Premiers of NSW and Victoria persuaded the other states to insert a clause (now s. 96 of the Australian Constitution) empowering the Commonwealth to make grants to the States. All the action in Australian fiscal federalism now takes place under this clause.

The first Commonwealth party labels were Protection and Free Trade. The free-trading outliers were Western Australia and Tasmania. As remote primary producers with little import-substituting domestic industry, they lost out twice over from the switch from State to Australia-wide tariffs. They faced tariffs on their inputs and did not benefit from tariff protection for their outputs. The Great Depression exacerbated WA's position, and in a 1933 referendum its voters voted by a margin of 2 to 1 to secede from the Commonwealth. This induced Prime Minister Joseph Lyons (to date the only Tasmanian to hold that post) to legislate for a statutory commission to report on any application from a State for financial assistance under s. 96 of the Constitution. The CGC was accordingly constituted in the same year under L.F. Giblin, a Tasmanian statistician who took an egalitarian view of the CGC's mandate in the face of objections from his chairman, who believed that this was to expand the CGC's role beyond its statutory duty to report on claims by States in difficulty. The two conceptions of the CGC's role both appeared in early statements, allowing modern commentators to pick an 'ideology' of the CGC to suit their present-day argument.

The CGC's First Report stated that 'It seems, therefore, to be unavoidable to use as some measure of disability the financial position of a State'. Successive statisticians, the most important being Giblin himself and R.L. Mathews, who became a Commissioner in 1972, elaborated formulae for evaluating 'disabilities'. By Mathews' time it had become explicit that a State suffered a disability (which could be negative) if its revenue capacity differed from the mean of the States. It also suffered a disability (again, possibly negative) if the cost of delivering services differed from the mean, for reasons such as remoteness, congestion, or differential prices of wages or supplies. This approach implied that revenue and expenditure relativities must be measured across all States.

The CGC's Second Report, however, stated that 'the only ground for ... assistance is the inability to carry on without it.... Some States are certainly in serious financial difficulties. It must be made possible for them to function as States of the Commonwealth at some minimum standard of efficiency' (quoted in CGC 1983, p. 36). On this conception the CGC should enquire explicitly only into conditions in claimant States, although implicitly even this necessarily involves comparison with the rest; and any special grant available only to claimants means by definition less grant available to non-claimants.

The Giblin/Mathews interpretation seems to have prevailed. The CGC has adopted successive, quite egalitarian, statements of the principle of horizontal fiscal equalisation (HFE). The most recent version runs:

> each State should be given the capacity to provide the average standard of State-type public services, assuming it does so at an average level of operational efficiency and makes an average effort to raise revenue from its own sources. (*Source*: www.cgc.gov.au, consulted 02.10.2002)

Critics allege that the CGC has been surreptitiously making the formula more egalitarian over the years without statutory warrant. Its defenders reply that the CGC is entirely open about its formula, and that it would be open to States at any Premiers' Conference, or at the Intergovernmental Conference specially convened to discuss fiscal federalism in 1999, to raise the issue.

VFI and HFE in Australia

From the outset, Australia has had a substantial vertical fiscal imbalance (VFI). The States have always had more line responsibilities than the Commonwealth, but the Commonwealth has always controlled more of the tax base. In the beginning, the States handed control of customs and excise, then the principal tax base, to the Commonwealth. This followed from the framers' conception of Australia as an internal free trade area surrounded by a common external tariff. Both limbs of this policy required the Commonwealth to be the taxing authority. However, the States did not concede to the Commonwealth the domestic policy areas that they had already, as colonies, been running for decades. The Australian Constitution is difficult to amend, requiring high multiple thresholds. The financial clauses have never been amended, and therefore they remain the framework into which all VFI (and HFE) arrangements must fit.

There therefore had to be a transfer mechanism. Tax receipts were transferred in *ad hoc* ways until the creation of the CGC. Although the CGC (and its critics) have always seen its role as one of securing a greater or lesser degree of HFE, the purchase for that role, and the need for some body such as the Commission, both arose from VFI. Wherever VFI exists, there must be a body or mechanism to make the required transfers. That body may or may not also attempt to achieve HFE. VFI, measured as the States' ratio of Commonwealth grant revenue to total revenue, was just below 0.4 at Federation. It declined to a little above 0.1 in 1939, soared during the Second World War and the foundation of the welfare state, peaking at 0.6 in 1959. It declined unsteadily to below 0.4 in 1999 but is now rising again due to new arrangements for revenue sharing.

The Commonwealth took over income tax from the States in 1942. The switch was supposed to be for the duration of the war only, but it has proved permanent. In the bipartisan welfarist climate of the 1950s and 1960s, nobody except the State governments opposed the income tax power staying at Commonwealth level. When States tried to re-assert their power to tax, the Commonwealth legislated to reduce its grants dollar for dollar to any State that did so. The High Court has upheld the constitutionality of the *de facto* Commonwealth monopoly of the income tax base. In practice this does not displease State Premiers, as they can spend more than they tax – a position all politicians would like to be in, but not all can.

In 1997 the High Court outlawed State 'franchise fees'. It held that they were an excise tax and hence constitutionally the province of the Commonwealth only. The Commonwealth agreed to increase its excise taxes and return the proceeds to the States, thus necessarily increasing VFI. It introduced a goods and services tax (GST, functionally equivalent to a VAT) in 1999. Australia was thus one of the last mature democracies to introduce a broad-based expenditure tax. The Commonwealth agreed that the whole proceeds of GST, net of the cost of collection, would be remitted to the States. GST is a more robust tax base than those it replaced, and its yield is expected to grow in real terms in line with the growth of GDP. The Commonwealth makes transitional grants (shown as 'budget balancing assistance' in Table 9.2) to ensure that no State is worse off than under the previous arrangements.

As of May 2004 the Australian political landscape is as follows. The Liberal-National coalition has controlled the Commonwealth government since 1996, and the Australian Labor Party has controlled all eight States and territories since 2001 (though it lacks a majority in ACT). Government could hardly be more divided than that. But GST has largely removed debate about the size of the untied assistance from the system. States can increase their untied grants only by reducing those of other States and the zero-sum nature of the game has become explicit. But State politicians can plausibly say, *It is our money, raised from our taxpayers. We want our money back* – either in the form of a distribution according to the amount of GST raised, or an equal per capita (EPC) distribution. The CGC does neither. Because of its strong version of HFE, it returns GST proceeds in such a way as to ensure that *gross* Commonwealth grants to the States (i.e. the sum of tied and untied grant) satisfy its HFE criteria.

As the welfare state developed, the Commonwealth wished more and more to intervene in policy areas that were constitutionally reserved to the states. The scope to do so by constitutional amendment being extremely restricted, it did so by tied grants, known in Australia as special purpose payments (SPPs). An SPP offers a grant to a State in a policy area that is constitutionally in the State's domain, but with Commonwealth conditions attached. By financial year 2002/3, SPPs constituted AUD22bn of the total AUD54bn (i.e. 40 per cent) of the volume of Commonwealth grants (Table 9.2).

In pursuit of Giblin's Tasmanian conception of HFE, the Grants Commission equalises both revenue capacity and expenditure disabilities. Péloquin and Chong (2002) show (Table 9.3) that Australia has the most egalitarian equalisation regime of any democratic federation. The column entries in Table 9.3 are population-weighted standard

Table 9.2   Commonwealth payments to State and local government, 2002–03

	AUDm
GST payments	29,380
Budget balancing assistance	1,741
Other untied grants	755
Subtotal: untied grants	*31,876*
SPPs to States	15,827
SPPs 'through' States to other bodies (e.g., private schools)	5,491
SPPs to local government	332
Subtotal: tied grants	*21,650*
Grand total	**53,526**

Source: Adapted from Garnaut and FitzGerald (2002), Table 3.1.

Table 9.3   Overall magnitude of revenue capacity and expenditure need disparities in selected federations, population-weighted standard deviations, $US per capita at PPP

Federation and year		Pre-equalisation	Post-equalisation
Australia 2000–01 (excl. local govt)	Revenue	$136	$0
	Expenditure need	$303	$0
Germany 1999 (incl. local govt)	Revenue	$463	$142
USA 1996 (incl. local govt)	Revenue	$392	$392
	Expenditure need	$482	$482
Canada, 2001–02 (incl. local govt)	Revenue	$1020	$640
Switzerland, 1999 (incl. local government)	Revenue	$1510	$1175

Source: Derived from Péloquin and Chong (2002), Table 2.

deviations of fiscal disparities measured in $US per capita at purchasing power parity. The exclusion of Australian local government does not seriously degrade their data because it is small and weak ('roads, rates, and rubbish').

Table 9.3 shows that only Australia attempts to equalise for expenditure need, although it has the smallest disparities before equalisation. The next most egalitarian federation is Germany. The USA, which does not attempt to equalise, nevertheless has smaller population-weighted standard deviations than Canada, even after the Canadian equalisation process.

Table 9.4 introduces the CGC's mode of operation. It should be read first across and then down. Row *a* shows the mean per capita amount available from GST, net of costs of collection. Row *b* is the CGC's calculation of the states' revenue disabilities. A positive sign implies a positive disability. As expected, two of the three donor states have negative signs (NSW because of a buoyant housing market and WA because of mineral wealth). The high positive disability of the ACT, a high-income area, arises because under the Constitution (s. 114), the States and the Commonwealth may not tax one another's property. As the largest employer and property-holder in ACT is the Commonwealth, the territory's payroll and property tax base is to that extent disabled.

Table 9.4 Contributions of needs to grant shares, 2002–03 (all entries in Rows a–f are AUD per capita)

		NSW	Vic	Qld	WA	SA	Tas	ACT	NT
Per Cap share of GST pool	a	1,848	1,848	1,848	1,848	1,848	1,848	1,848	1,848
Needs adjustments:									
Revenue	b	-156	69	63	-225	336	579	272	148
Expenditure	c	-48	-338	-69	357	29	457	340	6,320
SPPs	d	33	27	29	-176	-4	-10	-20	-465
Total	$e = b + c + d$	-172	-242	23	-43	361	1,026	283	6,003
Grant entitlement	$f = a + e$	1,676	1,606	1,871	1,805	2,209	2,875	2,131	7,851
Relativity	$g = f/a$	**0.906**	**0.868**	**1.012**	**0.976**	**1.194**	**1.554**	**1.152**	**4.245**

Source: Garnaut & FitzGerald (2002), Table 4.1 Cf. also CGC (2001), Table 1, (2002a) Table A–10.

Row *c* of Table 9.4 results from an extremely detailed examination of the cost of delivering public services, and the services required to enable each State citizen to enjoy public services to the level of the average of similarly placed citizens in all States. In all states the quality of public services enjoyed by remote rural dwellers is below that enjoyed by city dwellers. The comparability exercise is designed to ensure that a rural citizen of NT has comparable outcomes to a rural citizen of NSW, and an urban citizen of NT to an urban citizen of NSW. This row gives huge per capita weighting to NT, and shows significant positive disabilities in WA (remote) and Tas (small and poor).

Row *d* compensates for the effects of SPPs. A negative sign means that the State receives above average SPP payments per capita; a positive sign means that it receives below average SPP payments per capita. Row *e* is simply the sum of the three above, and it gives the net difference for each State from an EPC distribution. This generates the absolute (row *f*) and relative (row *g*) per capita payments to each State.

The outcome is not well aligned with GDP per head, but it is not designed to be. Critics object to the high net grant per head to the high income ACT. The CGC retorts that the grant reflects what actually affects the financial capacities of State governments, given the services States in general provide and the revenues they raise. GDP or household income per head do not themselves affect State budgets.

SPPs are fully equalised away. This prompts a number of questions, such as: in that case why does the Commonwealth bother to make them? And why do States bother to accept them?

(Mostly) Australian criticisms of the system

Changes to the regime are a zero-sum game. It is fiercely criticised by people in donor states, but it continues without substantial change. The three donor States, namely NSW, Vic., and WA, commissioned the Review (Garnaut and FitzGerald 2001, 2002; Dixon *et al.* 2002; Harding *et al.* 2002), whose data are used copiously in this chapter. Garnaut and FitzGerald fault the system on three grounds: equity, efficiency, and transparency. I group their and my criticisms under these headings.

Equity

The primary test of equity is the vertical distribution of income. A government's policies are equitable to the extent that income per head is more equal after government intervention than before it. Therefore, in any democracy including Australia, the primary engines of equity are the personal taxation and social security systems.

A secondary test is horizontal equity; but should that be equity among States or equity among individuals? In their Executive Summary, Garnaut and FitzGerald say baldly: '[T]he concept of equity among States has no meaning; equity must relate to outcomes for individuals and households'. In their detailed discussion they are more nuanced:

> In the early decades of the 20th century when … secession was considered a realistic alternative to continued membership of the Federation in some States at some times, intrinsic horizontal equity among States was probably seen as more important than it is today. Other conceptions of horizontal equity, in terms of similar treatment of individuals and households in similar circumstances wherever they live in Australia, have become relatively more important more recently (Garnaut and FitzGerald 2002 pp. 2, 123).

Whether or not intrinsic horizontal equity among the nations and regions of the UK has meaning, or is an appropriate policy target, is considered below.

Harding *et al.* (2002) modelled the vertical equity effects of moving from the current CGC regime either to one in which GST proceeds were distributed on an EPC basis, or to one in which they were returned to states in the proportions in which they were originally raised. Their negative results are interesting (Table 9.5). The data in Table 9.5 are for households. If calculated for individuals, the pattern is exactly similar.

A Gini coefficient of 1 denotes perfect inequality; one of 0, perfect equality (of post-transfer income, in this case). The first row of Table 9.5 measures the inequality of private household income, before

Table 9.5 Gini coefficients for equivalent household income measures under the current system, EPC, and State of origin scenarios, 2000–01

	Current system	Equal per capita	State of origin
Equivalent private income	0.520	0.520	0.520
Equivalent Federal income	0.297	0.297	0.297
Equivalent SPP income	0.271	0.271	0.271
Equivalent final income	0.252	0.251	0.252

Source: Adapted from Garnaut and FitzGerald 2002, Table 9.1.

tax and transfers. The second row measures the inequality of private household income, after adding 'Commonwealth own-purpose expenditures with personal benefits attributable to households, minus the imputed value of Commonwealth taxes paid'. The third row shows the effect of adding the 'imputed value of all SPPs delivered to and through the States and all other revenue assistance, but excluding GST-financed revenue assistance, which is allocated by the ... CGC'. The purpose of this is to try to isolate the 'CGC effect', which appears in the fourth row.

Accordingly, the first three rows of Table 9.5 are invariant. They show that personal taxation and transfers do the heavy lifting of vertical equity, and that services provided via SPPs add a modest amount more. The payload comes in the fourth row. This gives the Gini co-efficients for all income sources measured in the study, namely those counted in the first three rows plus the CGC distribution of untied grant. Even though the CGC uses strong criteria of HFE, the fourth row of Table 9.5 shows that inequality as measured by the Gini coefficient would not increase if GST revenue were distributed on either the EPC or the State of origin bases.

This is striking and counter-intuitive; how can it be? The Gini coefficient is measured across all pairs of Australians in the survey. It cannot capture the specific State effects. If, as Garnaut and FitzGerald argue, equity is wholly an interpersonal and not at all an interstate concept, this is appropriate. But this begs the question. Either of the two changes would have severe adverse consequences for the people in two small states, Tas and NT. Switching to an EPC basis, for instance (which Garnaut and FitzGerald recommend), would cost each Tasmanian about AUD 900 p.a and each Northern Territorian about AUD 5000 p.a. The latter number is of the order of 13 per cent of GDP per head in NT. Switching to a State of origin basis would cost each Tasmanian about AUD 1500 p.a. and each Northern Territorian about AUD 5700 p.a. (Harding 2002, Fig. 3). That these dramatic numbers do not raise the overall Gini coefficient reflects the small size of these two states. The exercise shows that whether a State as such is an appropriate target of horizontal equity is a vital policy decision. If not, the CGC regime is inappropriate; if so, it may be appropriate.

Garnaut and FitzGerald also complain that the Commonwealth cannot make the States spend money on those services which have given rise to their needs assessments. It is frequently alleged that, although the NT gets huge weighting in its assessed expenditure needs for its high rural Indigenous population, it spends most of its untied grant in Darwin. In the UK, Scotland, Wales, and Northern Ireland will continue to be financed by untied block grant as long as they remain devolved authorities (and *a fortiori* if the UK becomes a federation). Loss of control by the centre of the subunits' spending is a necessary and intended consequence of either devolution or federalism. However, the effect of this on HFE is indeterminate. If the upper level made smaller grants to the lower level, there is no *a priori* reason to suppose that the retaining authority would spend it in either a more egalitarian or a less egalitarian way than the devolved authority.

Efficiency

A regime such as the CGC's might be economically inefficient because:

- grants which compensate for high costs of providing services in remote (or, conversely, congested) areas encourage factors of production to stay in, or move to, such areas, when it would be more efficient if they moved to, or stayed in, cheaper areas (Scott 1952);
- of deadweight administrative costs in managing the system of fiscal transfers;
- the system encourages actors to seek rents rather than to seek efficiency;
- it may discourage efficiency-seeking agents in the States who realise that State gains from efficiency will be taxed or equalised away from them; and
- it encourages an excessively large public sector in recipient states – this last being known in the literature as the 'flypaper effect'.

Dixon *et al.* (2002, p. 1) estimate that

A move from the present system of Commonwealth grants to an equal-per-capita basis would be likely to increase Australian welfare by between $150 million and $250 million a year.... A move to a State-of-origin basis for Commonwealth grants would generate a welfare gain of about $280 million a year.... The main mechanism underlying our results is the idea that the governments of States that are heavily subsidized under the present system (the Northern Territory, Tasmania and South Australia) make spending and tax decisions that are not closely in line with the preferences of their households. This is an example of the well-known flypaper effect.... The evidence that the flypaper effect is at work is that the heavily subsidized States have high per capita expenditures on State government services.

However, Dixon *et al.* beg the question. They *assume* a flypaper effect, and hence input to their model an assumption that State governments in claimant states are too large. This generates as output the proposition that savings could be made from moving to an EPC distribution. This move would force State governments to curtail their activities (severely in Tas and NT). But they do not *prove* a flypaper effect. If the size of government in the claimant States actually accords with their citizens' preferences, then the input disappears, and the result with it. There is no *a priori* reason why poor (or small) States should offer more inefficient subsidies to their people than rich (or large) States.

Dixon *et al.* both confuse different definitions of efficiency and fail to distinguish between a 'reform' and a 'design' perspective (Brennan and Pincus 2002). A reform perspective studies an existing set of arrangements; a design perspective attempts to design arrangements from the ground up. The former is appropriate to policy discussion in Australia; the latter in the UK. The existing strong protection of small states is built into the Australian constitution. Without this protection, there would have been no Federation of the form that exists at present. The definition of 'efficiency' under which Dixon *et al.*'s efficiency gains could be realised is not the standard welfare-economic definition of a Pareto improvement (maybe after compensation). Rather, it implies that Tasmanians and NT citizens would each lose welfare substantially, while Victorians and NSW citizens would in aggregate gain more than the losers would lose. It does not ask what price the losers would demand for moving to Sydney or Melbourne.

The dynamic efficiency disadvantages of the CGC regime are impossible to quantify since they depend on unmeasurable counterfactuals. Some submissions to the Garnaut-FitzGerald review (notably Court 2002; Tasman Economics 2002) complain that the regime inhibits States from promoting economic development (or, more generally, growth-friendly policies), if they rationally anticipate that the proceeds of such development will be equalised away from them. It is easier for State officials to seek rents than to seek growth. An obvious form of rent-seeking is to exaggerate one's disabilities. It is a piece of CGC lore that States never invite the Commission to visit their prosperous communities.

The point cannot be quantified but it is extremely important for institutional designers. Fundamentally, it concerns the marginal tax rates faced by subnational politicians. If the marginal tax rate is 100 per cent or higher, the arguments of Court and Tasman Economics have force. If it is below 100 per cent, then a State is in the same position as an income tax payer who faces a positive marginal tax rate greater than zero but below 100 per cent. Some but not all of the possible growth-promoting things a State may do will be done. Any State growth of this sort faces a high marginal tax rate. But that is a consequence of VFI rather than of HFE. As a State contains, at maximum, 33 per cent of Australia's population, it cannot rationally expect more than its population share of any returns from growth.

This criticism implies that the CGC regime may be too egalitarian for economic efficiency. On the revenue side, it equalises fully for States' disabilities. Recall that these may be negative. If the effect of WA's increasing mining production (assuming, for the sake of argument, that this increase was due to the policies of the WA government) is to broaden its tax base, but this then attracts a pro rata decrease in the State's disabilities, then indeed it faces a marginal tax rate of 100 per cent.

A related issue concerns the CGC's practice of fully equalising away the effects of SPPs (see Table 9.4, row *d*). Why then does the Commonwealth offer them? And why do States accept them if they come with attached conditions that may displease the State? The answers seem to involve:

- the five-year rolling average used by the CGC;
- time horizons;
- the political incentives facing politicians and line-department bureaucrats; and
- inadequate information.

As the CGC operates on a rolling average of five years' data, each year determining a new relativity (i.e. a new value for the vector of weightings in Table 9.4, row *g*), there is a lag in the equalising away of SPPs. The full five-year lag is always longer than the time to the next Commonwealth election *and* the next State election. Commonwealth elections must be at most three years apart (Constitution, s. 28) and State elections may never be further than four years apart. Therefore, even if politicians understand the CGC's equalising-away procedures, they may rationally support SPPs.

SPPs may be good for credit claiming. The same sum of money can be claimed twice, by Commonwealth and by State politicians. As State elections cannot coincide with Commonwealth elections, the public may not detect the double counting. An SPP may also represent a coalition between the line departments of the Commonwealth and the State(s) that oversee the function in question. Both gain from earmarking the grant to their function against their respective Treasuries who may wish more flexibility.

Finally, few politicians in Australia appear to know how the CGC regime works. In Australia, as in other bicameral systems, politicians who wield vetoes over policy, especially in the Senate, can block government action unless they get a pay-off for their State. Politicians would not do this energetically if they realised that any pork they get by this means can be equalised away by the CGC regime over a maximum of five years. Whether as a consequence of this or not, the Australian Senate is much less of a pork-barrelling assembly than its US counterpart.

Transparency

Critics complain that the CGC regime is both data-heavy and opaque. The CGC retorts that it is utterly open about its methods, putting thousands of pages of documents on the Web and publishing over 2000 pages of hard copy data every year. But some of its data manipulation remains opaque. To assess expenditure need for every service in every State demands voluminous data from the Australian Bureau of Statistics. It also involves numerous judgment calls.

The proportion of Indigenous people in the population is a powerful driver of needs assessments. It is well known that Indigenous people suffer poor health, poor education, and dramatically lower life expectancy than non-Indigenous. Accordingly, all needs formulae have a heavy weighting for Indigeneity. *But who is Indigenous?* The data source is the Census, where Indigeneity is self-reported. Self-reporting exaggerates the Indigenous share of the population in Tas (where at 3.7 per cent it is the second-highest of any State), and depresses it in NT. The reasons for the first are unknown. The reason for the second is the difficulty of finding the entire population in remote areas, where some of them may be away from their settlements for long periods of time. But there is no realistic alternative to self-reporting. Attempts by the official peak organisation of Indigenous people, ATSIC, to determine authoritatively who is and who is not Indigenous have ended in tears and the courts. So a powerful driver of need in each state is an unreliable number.

Secondly, how do you determine objectively the expenditure need for schools? The school-age population in each State, the proportion of them who stay on beyond the minimum school-leaving age, and the proportion who attend private schools, are all known. Australia makes SPPs 'through' States to private schools. If a State has an above-average proportion of students who leave at the first opportunity, do you raise its grant to enable it to improve its human capital, or reduce its grant because it incurs lower costs? If a State has an above-average proportion of students in private schools, do you raise its grant because they incur higher costs per head, or reduce its grant because the State is not educating them? The CGC formulae reduce grant in the first case and raise it in the second, but in each case a good argument from equity, efficiency, or both, could be made for doing the opposite.

Finally, the not-quite-regression procedures of the CGC are opaque. Its needs factors are a mixture of demographic and other drivers. Demographic features include age, sex, prevalence of low income, of rurality, of Indigeneity and of non-Anglophone families. Other features include scale economies, dispersion, wage costs (when not directly affected by government policy), and cross-border spillovers (the last relatively minor in Australia with its huge distances and small population). The CGC empirically determines the size and direction of the effects. Note that if (e.g.) low income reduces demand for a service, the CGC assesses that as a lowering of need for that service. This of course has the effect that if low-income Australians use a particular service least, the grants mechanism gives most money to those States with the fewest low-income citizens. The CGC's methodology implies that the higher the per capita income in a State, the more it 'needs' funding for its opera house.

Poverty and Indigeneity increase both demand for, and per capita cost of, health and welfare services. Poverty and Indigeneity are strongly correlated. The standard method of dealing with this problem in regression analysis is to enter both of the two predictors *and their interaction* into the model, with the intention of measuring the interaction effects as well as the direct effects. As the CGC eschews regression, it is forced to take elaborate, unreliable, and awkward steps to avoid double counting (Péloquin 2002).

But why not simply use a regression model, in which the problem of interactions would be much more tractable? One objection would be that a regression model with only eight cases would be unstable. The same objection is made by those who wish to fend off alternatives to the Barnett Formula (Midwinter 2000, 2002). The CGC's own objection is different. It is that it does not wish its model to be an impenetrable 'black box'. It believes that to use a regression model would reduce its transparency. It does use regression models as a check on the outcomes of its expenditure formulae. The UK travails with regression models described in previous chapters suggest that the CGC approach has unsuspected merits.

One problem common to the CGC regime and the English Standard Spending Assessment (SSA) regime is how to avoid perverse incentives for units to become, or remain, inefficient. If the cost of providing a service is estimated from the costs that the existing States (respectively, local authorities) have incurred in providing it, the perverse incentives are obvious. This is the problem of regression against past spending. The CGC is also sensitive to the issue, as it tries to weight for only those costs which governments cannot change – e.g. those deriving from climate or sparsity of population. But in any regime it is difficult to segregate those drivers of costs that governments can do nothing at all about. Governments can affect even sparsity of population.

Lessons

This book has detailed many defects of the UK system:

- Completely different regimes cover Scotland, Wales, and Northern Ireland (the DAs) on the one hand and the English regions on the other.
- The Barnett formula can be expected to converge on EPC, which is inappropriate for the DAs, all of which have above-average expenditure needs.
- The Barnett regime makes incremental block grant to each DA a function of incremental expenditure in England, a number over which it has no control. Furthermore, if the current offer of elected assemblies for (some) Government Office regions of England is taken up, the starting-point for Barnett calculations, namely an 'England' spending total, erodes (Heald and Short 2002).
- Conversely, the Barnett regime allows DAs to vire between capital and current spending at will, with possible consequences for HM Treasury's Golden Rule over which the Treasury has no control.
- Over the 12 standard regions of the UK, public expenditure per head has a zero statistical relationship with GDP per head, rather than the expected statistically significant inverse relationship (McLean and McMillan 2003).
- There is a particularly painful juxtaposition between Scotland and the North-east region of England. Scotland has substantially higher GDP per head but also substantially higher public expenditure per

head. Lord Barnett has repeatedly called this juxtaposition 'terribly unfair' (e.g. Barnett 2001, col. 226).

Does the CGC regime, then, have any relevant lessons for the UK?

Features to copy

The CGC is a non-partisan agency immune from political manipulation. Although it reports to the Commonwealth Department of Finance, it is independent of both that and the Commonwealth Treasury. By contrast, the UK arrangements for addressing VFI and HFE are too close to the centre of UK government, being integral functions of HM Treasury (for the DAs) and the Office of the Deputy Prime Minister (for England). As financing the DAs is an intergovernmental concern, it should be a function of an intergovernmental body. The UK Territorial Grants Commission should be a non-departmental public body, not under the line management of any UK or DA department. The UK Government, the DAs, and the English regional chambers or assemblies should jointly appoint its Commissioners. Its staff could be seconded from the Treasury, ODPM, the Office for National Statistics, the DAs, universities, and other appropriate organisations (both public and private sector).

To dislodge the CGC regime would require the unanimous support of all eight Australian States and Territories. A comparable body in the UK should also be constitutionally embedded as deeply as possible. If it distributes untied grant, the source of grant should be exogenous: i.e. it should comprise the product of a robust tax base such as VAT, not be determined endogenously by any of the parties to the bargaining.

Features to discuss

Is equity between states an appropriate policy aim? In British terminology: should policymakers care about equity among the four units of the United Kingdom? Should they care about equity among the 12 standard NUTS1 statistical units (i.e. the three DAs and the nine Government Office regions of England)? One powerful reason is that the people care (some of them, at least), and the people elect the UK government. Even Garnaut and FitzGerald (2002) concede that equity among States is policy-relevant when there is talk of secession. There has been talk of secession by Northern Ireland since it was created, and by Scotland since the 1960s. The greater transparency of UK fiscal federalism since devolution has meant that more people have noticed apparent inequity. With Joel Barnett's contributions, amongst others, public debate now commonly recognises that Scotland has higher GDP per head than six of the English regions, and yet it also enjoys higher public spending per head than any of the six. The Barnett genie is out of the bottle.

Another reason, at least for a government of the (centre-)left, is that equity between regions may be a precondition for horizontal equity between people. It is reasonable to ask that the quality of treatment a citizen gets from a public service should not be significantly worse in one standard region than another. That is why the most egalitarian of Labour's great politicians, Aneurin Bevan, was the most bitterly opposed to devolution. Devolution is a fact. The challenge to policymakers is therefore to placate the shadow of Nye Bevan without dismantling devolution. This implies ensuring equity among the four units. In any case, even granted that horizontal equity is mostly a matter of equity between persons, it is between persons as consumers of private *and* public goods. Therefore there is a case in equity for ensuring that States or territories have a comparable capacity to provide public goods.

Although the regions of England do not (yet) have elected governments, the argument for equity among all 12 units is almost as strong as the argument for equity among 4. Both the 'popular demand' and the 'equal quality of service' arguments have some force here. This implies that it is reasonable for the UK to consider a strong HFE regime like the CGC's, which coexists with Australian federalism.

Should a UK grants commission go as far as the CGC does in equalising away the effects of payments for special purposes? The largest special purpose payment to the UK regions and nations is agricultural support under the Common Agricultural Policy. There are good efficiency and equity grounds for equalising that away. Other, one-off, examples include the additional support to Wales in respect of EU Objective One, and various peace-related programmes in Northern Ireland. There is a good public finance argument in favour of equalising these away; but it would be politically unpopular. It would reignite a 25-year-old controversy between the UK government and the European Union as to whether the former annuls the regional policy of the latter by cutting its own support to the regions. If it were done, any equalising away should be over a period of years, as it is in Australia.

Features to avoid

Both the CGC regime and the English health and SSA regimes strive to condition grant on regressors whose values the beneficiaries cannot control, so as to avoid creating perverse incentives. Both have limited success.

The CGC's desire to be policy neutral takes it too far for the UK situation. In Australia, public funding of private (mostly religious) schools is embedded in the past politics of church and state there. Policy neutrality implies that the CGC can take no position on whether the States, or the Commonwealth, should subsidise private schools. Commonwealth grants to them are passed 'through' the States without stopping there. If (as is currently the case) it costs more to educate a pupil at a private than at a State school, then, *ceteris paribus*, the *fewer* pupils in a State are in its schools, the *more* it receives in grant from the CGC. This is unlikely to be acceptable in the UK, where details would in any case differ because some religious schools are fully state-funded and others are largely state-funded.

The call for a territorial grants board in the UK is gaining strength. This chapter has shown that the UK should not copy the CGC arrangements wholesale. It should adopt some with enthusiasm, think hard about some, and definitely reject others. The independence of the CGC is deeply embedded in the Australian constitution for reasons that go back to the creation of the Commonwealth. Although the Diceyan tradition of parliamentary sovereignty, allied to lofty disdain for a written constitution, are both in well-deserved decay in the UK, it is not certain whether politicians would agree to embed a non-partisan grant-making body in a place they cannot reach. But if they would, the welfare of the citizens of the UK would increase.

10
The Canadian Model

This chapter describes the system of fiscal federalism operating in Canada; compares it with that in Australia (Chapter 9); and, as with Chapter 9, discusses how far the Canadian arrangements could be the model for a revised intergovernmental financial arrangement in the UK.

Geography and history

Canada is the second-largest country, by area, in the world. It is normally regarded as comprising five regions:

- The Atlantic region (Newfoundland, Prince Edward Island, Nova Scotia, and New Brunswick)
- The central region (Québec and Ontario)
- The prairies (Manitoba, Saskatchewan, Alberta)
- The Pacific coastal region (BC)
- The sparsely inhabited north

Most of the population inhabit a narrow strip relatively close to the US border. It is hard to imagine Canada being governed in any other way than as a federation. The basic units of Canadian federalism are its ten provinces and three territories. Summary statistics are in Table 10.1.

The two largest provinces, Ontario and Québec, contain more than half of Canada's population between them. The four small Atlantic provinces (and the three territories) together contain fewer people than each of the four largest provinces. The three territories are vast in extent but tiny in population.

Table 10.1 The units of Canadian federalism, 2002

	Nfld	PEI	NS	NB	Québec	Ont	Manitoba	Sask	Alta	BC	Yukon	NWT	Nunavut
Population, 000s (2002)	532	140	945	757	7,455	12,068	1,151	1,012	3,114	4,141	30	41	29
% of total	1.7	0.5	3.1	2.5	24.1	37.8	3.7	3.4	9.7	13.2	0.1	0.1	0.1
Area, km² × 1000	405.2	5.7	55.3	72.9	1542.1	1076.4	647.8	651.0	661.8	944.7	482.4	1 346.1	2 093.2
% of total	4.1	0.1	0.6	0.7	15.4	10.8	6.5	6.5	6.6	9.5	4.8	13.5	21.0
GDP per head, $Can	22,384	21,696	23,863	24,390	27,767	34,451	27,117	29,379	39,537	29,489	34,839	52,854	27,074
Index GDP/head (Canada=100)	71.3	69.1	76.0	77.6	88.4	109.7	86.3	93.5	125.9	93.9	110.9	168.2	86.2
Party control of provincial govt, Jun 2003	Liberal	PC	PC*	PC	Liberal	PC	NDP	NDP**	PC	Liberal	Yukon Party	Non-party	Non-party
Date of joining Confederation	1949	1873	1867	1867	1867	1867	1870	1905	1905	1871	1898	1870	1999

Notes:
* Re-elected but without an overall majority in August 2003.
** Holds exactly half of the seats in the legislative assembly.
Sources: Statistics Canada; National Library of Canada; websites of each provincial and territorial government.

The spread of GDP per head between the richest and the poorest provinces is wider than in Australia (Table 9.1) or the UK. Table 10.2 compares the three countries.

Canadian regional GDP per head is highly skewed. In this it resembles the UK more than Australia. Only two provinces – Ontario and Alberta – have GDP per head above the all-Canada average. The three tiny-population territories have quite high GDP per head, two of them being above the Canada average. However, a great deal of that GDP accrues to capital rather than labour, being derived from resource exploitation. And a disproportionate amount of their labour GDP accrues to government employees – government being the largest employer in the territories. The GDP of government employees is, by convention, set to equal their pay. Otherwise, these territories tend to contain the poorest people in Canada. Their situation is obviously similar to that of the Northern Territory in Australia, which likewise has both high GDP per head on the output measure, substantial resource exploitation, and very poor indigenous people.

Constitutional issues

The British North America Act (Constitution Act) 1867[1] is silent on intergovernmental fiscal matters, except that ss. 114–117 set out the liabilities of Canada and the provinces for their public debts at Confederation. Section 118 provided for grants in aid from Canada to the provincial governments. These grants were amended under the Constitution (originally British North America) Act 1907, 7 Edw. VII, c. 11, which was likewise a UK statute applying to Canada. However, the 1907 statute merely substituted a new list of fixed grants and per capita additions. Like the 1867 list it was not dynamic, and it was intended only 'for its local purposes and the support of its Government and Legislature'. By s. 92 of the 1867 Act, which enumerated provincial powers, the provinces had the power over the Management and Sale of the Public Lands belonging to the Province and of the Timber and Wood thereon.

Only in 1982 was this broadened to a wider authority over natural resources, by the addition of a s. 92A to the 1867 Act which states in part:

> In each province, the legislature may make laws in relation to the raising of money by any mode or system of taxation in respect of
>> (a) non-renewable natural resources and forestry resources in the province and the primary production therefrom, and

Table 10.2 The dispersion of regional GDP per head: Canada, Australia, and the UK

Canada

Provincial GDP per head 2001 (Canada = 100)	Nfld	PEI	NS	NB	Qu	Ont	Man	Sask	Alta	BC	Yukon	NWT	Nunavut
	71.3	69.1	76.0	77.6	88.4	109.7	86.3	93.5	125.9	93.9	110.9	168.2	86.2

Australia

Gross State product per head 2001 (Australia = 100)	NSW	Vic	Qld	SA	WA	Tas	NT	ACT
	104.2	102.8	87.6	84.1	111.4	70.7	125.3	120.9

UK

Regional GDP per head 1999 (UK excl Extra Regio = 100)	NE	NW	YH	EM	WM	EE	L	SE	SW	Scot	Wales	NI
	77.3	86.9	87.9	93.6	91.7	116.4	130	116.4	90.8	96.5	80.5	77.5

Sources: Author's calculations, based on data from Statistics Canada; Australian Bureau of Statistics; Office for National Statistics, Crown copyright. For the full names of the English regions, see Figure 5.1, p. 85

(b) sites and facilities in the province for the generation of electrical energy and the production therefrom,

whether or not such production is exported in whole or in part from the province....

The Canadian Constitution (Constitution Act 1982) states at s. 36:

(1) Without altering the legislative authority of Parliament or of the provincial legislatures, or the rights of any of them with respect to the exercise of their legislative authority, Parliament and the legislatures, together with the government of Canada and the provincial governments, are committed to
  (a) promoting equal opportunities for the well-being of Canadians;
  (b) furthering economic development to reduce disparity in opportunities; and
  (c) providing essential public services of reasonable quality to all Canadians.
(2) Parliament and the government of Canada are committed to the principle of making equalization payments to ensure that provincial governments have sufficient revenues to provide reasonably comparable levels of public services at reasonably comparable levels of taxation.

The language of s. 36 is strikingly non-committal. 'Parliament and the legislatures, together with the government of Canada and the provincial governments, are committed to....' does not in fact commit anybody to anything enforceable. Thus, intergovernmental fiscal arrangements in Canada depend on convention and mutual convenience more than they do on statute.

The original federation of Canada comprised Ontario, Québec, New Brunswick, and Nova Scotia, which joined with various degrees of enthusiasm. Manitoba joined in 1870; British Columbia in 1871; Prince Edward Island in 1873; Alberta and Saskatchewan as they became fully-fledged provinces in 1905. Newfoundland did not join until as recently as 1949. Before that it was a Dominion in its own right, but its government had gone bankrupt and it was incorporated into Canada with the active (some Newfoundlanders say over-active) collaboration of the UK government, which would not have been happy with the alternatives of Newfoundland remaining independent but bankrupt, or joining the USA.

For most of the life of the Dominion of Canada, Ontario and Québec have been the richest, as well as the most populous, provinces. Since the discovery of onshore oil reserves in Alberta in 1947, Alberta has become much the richest province. The current ranking of provinces by GDP per head (Table 10.1) seems stable. Alberta and Ontario are the only two donor provinces. They do not donate money directly to the other provinces, but money is fungible and they do not receive the equalisation grants that all other provinces do. Of the recipient provinces, BC and Québec have diversified economies. Manitoba, Saskatchewan, and the four Atlantic provinces are all primary producers, all of whose products except oil have hit hard times.

A natural question for a political scientist is: how does a federation with such disparate components cohere? As is well known, the overt threats of secession come not from the richest, nor from the poorest, but from the most culturally distinctive province, namely Québec. Twice, in 1980 and in 1995, the government of Québec promoted referendums on loosening the association with Canada to what they called 'sovereignty-association' and Anglophones tended to call secession. On both occasions the proposal was narrowly defeated. After the second defeat, the federal government made a reference to the Supreme Court to clarify the conditions under which a province could secede, and later enacted the Clarity Act 2000 ('An Act to give effect to the requirement for clarity as set out in the opinion of the Supreme Court of Canada in the Quebec Secession Reference'). The preamble of the Clarity Act begins uncompromisingly:

> WHEREAS the Supreme Court of Canada has confirmed that there is no right, under international law or under the Constitution of Canada, for the National Assembly, legislature or government of Quebec to effect the secession of Quebec from Canada unilaterally

The Act proceeds to lay down demanding conditions for any future secession referendum to meet those requirements. The effect is to raise the threshold that a separatist movement in Québec (or Newfoundland, or Alberta, or any other province) must meet.

Nevertheless, Québec always poses a credible threat, comparable to that posed by secessionist movements in other nation-states. Probably the two most disaffected provinces outside Québec are the richest and the second-poorest, viz., Alberta and Newfoundland. But even before the Clarity Act, these two provinces posed no credible threat to the federation.

The reasons are constitutional and political. Constitutionally, a nation forged in reaction to the Union victory in the American Civil War and to a perceived threat of southern invasion was never going to make secession easy. The Clarity Act has made it yet harder. Politically, Canada shares two features with India, both explicable in terms of their British origins: a plurality electoral system in the lower house, and a weak upper house. This combination has distinctive implications.

Duverger's Law (Duverger 1954, p. 217) states in part (the valid part): 'The simple-majority single-ballot system favours the two-party system'. The intuition behind Duverger's Law is that in the long run everyone can see that in each district ('riding' in Canada) there can only be one credible challenger to the incumbent. Any party that comes third or lower in a riding might as well give up, and its supporters may as well (and, in the long run, will) transfer their allegiance to another party. However, Duverger's Law implies that in equilibrium, only two parties can credibly compete in each riding. It does not imply that only two parties can credibly compete in the nation. The pattern of two-party competition may differ radically in different parts of the country. In Canada, it does, and the effect has been for long spells (as also in India) to produce just one hegemonic party – currently the Liberal Party – and a disparate group of regional challengers.

Until 1993, there were two parties with the capacity to form a single-party government in Canada: the Liberals and the Progressive Conservatives. But in that year's federal election, the Progressive Conservatives suffered the most dramatic instance ever of the fate of a declining national party with evenly distributed support in a plurality electoral system. The governing party was reduced to two seats, not including its leader's. Two regional parties, namely the Bloc Québécois and the western party the Alliance, vied from 1993 to 2003 for the status of official opposition. In 2003 the Alliance and the Progressive Conservatives merged to form the Conservative Party of Canada. In the General Election in June 2004, the Liberals lost their overall majority (Table 10.3) But the opposition remains fragmented. The Conservatives are dominant in the West, and the BQ in Québec (Table 10.4). The final column of Table 10.4 shows that Duverger's Law operates in Canada to make almost every province safe for one party, in terms of seats. Only a big swing from Liberal to Conservative in Ontario could foreseeably upset the Liberal hegemony – even though the Liberals lack a majority of seats.

The Canadian Senate, unlike its counterparts in Australia or the USA, is not a house of the territories. Senators are appointed to retirement by the

Table 10.3   The Canadian House of Commons, June 2003 and June 2004

Party	2003		2004	
	N. of seats	% of seats	N. of seats	% of seats
Liberal	169	56.15	135	43.83
Alliance (formerly Reform)	63	20.93	–	
Bloc Québecois	34	11.3	54	17.53
PC (2004: Conservative)	15	4.98	99	32.14
NDP	14	4.65	19	6.17
Independent	4	1.33	1	0.32
Vacant	2	0.66		
Total	301	100	308	100

Source: www.parl.gc.ca, consulted June 2003 and June 2004; author's calculations.

Table 10.4   The Canadian House of Commons, by party and province, June 2004

Province	Lib	Cons	BQ	NDP	Ind	Total	% of province seats held by largest party
Alberta	2	26				28	92.86
BC	8	22		5	1	36	61.11
Manitoba	3	7		4		14	50.00
NB	7	2		1		10	70.00
Nfld/Labrador	5	2				7	71.43
NWT	1					1	100.00
NS	6	3		3		11	54.55
Nunavut	1					1	100.00
Ontario	75	24		7		106	70.75
PEI	4					4	100.00
Québec	21		54			75	72.00
Sask	1	13		2	1	14	92.86
Yukon	1					1	100.00
Total	135	99	54	22	2	308	

Source: www.parl.gc.ca, consulted June 2004; author's calculations.

Governor-General on the advice of the Prime Minister. The Senate therefore naturally mimics the party composition of the House of Commons with a time-lag. Because they are wholly appointed, the Canadian Senate has been even less prone than the UK House of Lords to sustain a challenge to the elected house, as its legitimacy would be very quickly queried (see further Russell 2000). As in the UK, the government of the day usually has an interest in keeping the upper house quiescent. Therefore, moves by Alberta and others to increase the powers and the legitimacy of the Senate, by making it an explicitly territorial house elected directly or indirectly, have no foreseeable chance of success.

It follows that disaffected provinces have no political tool with which to challenge the power of the dominant party. In India the equivalent situation has sometimes led to violence. In Canada it has not. But it means that provincial grievance has to be channelled to a large extent through the intergovernmental fiscal arrangements: and that in a state in which neither the richest nor the poorest provinces can credibly threaten to secede if they do not get their way.

Equalisation arrangements

Canada has an elaborate horizontal fiscal equalisation (HFE) programme. As in other federations, this programme aims to compensate for the lower tax capacity of the poorer provinces: in the language of s. 36 of the Constitution, to making 'equalization payments to ensure that provincial governments have sufficient revenues to provide reasonably comparable levels of public services at reasonably comparable levels of taxation'. Note that this is equalisation for unequal resources only: Canada does not attempt to equalise for differential needs for, or cost of providing, public services in the ten provinces. (It does, however, make a needs-based grant to each of the three territories). To this extent, Canada's HFE arrangements are much more restricted than Australia's, which are perhaps the most elaborate and egalitarian in the world on the needs side. On the resources side, however, Canada's procedures are elaborate and distinctive.

Canada makes two main transfers from Ottawa to the provinces. One is called CHST (Canada Health and Social Transfer), to be split in 2004–5 into two transfers, one for health and the other for other social programmes (which in Canada are deemed to include post-secondary education). These transfers reflect the fact that Canadians see health as overwhelmingly the most important political issue for them; that there seems to be a cross-Canada commitment to nationally uniform (or at least comparable) standards and a commitment to uniform rights for all Canadians. Health is a provincial responsibility, and the federal transfer to the provinces is without strings except that the federal government requires the provinces to adhere to the 'five principles of the Canada Health Act'. These principles are:

1. Public administration (health care insurance plans to be administered and operated on a non-profit basis by a public authority);

2. Comprehensiveness (of provincial health care insurance plans);
3. Universality (all residents of a province or territory to be entitled to medically necessary health care services);
4. Portability (of cover for all Canadians anywhere in Canada); and
5. Accessibility (all Canadians to have access to insured health care services, without any barriers – particularly financial barriers). See http://web1.liberal.ca/lpc/news.aspx?site=news&news=331

This list serves the political need for the federal government to be seen to be guaranteeing health standards while not entrenching on the provinces' jurisdiction. Québec states that it does not accept the federal government's right to enforce the five principles, but that it accepts the principles themselves.

The transfer has in principle an equal per capita value for all provinces (thus there is no allowance for health costs to differ systematically from one province to another). It has, however, a small HFE component in that part of what the federal government describes as its transfer is a transfer of tax points to the provinces. This is explained below. The HFE effect is that it leads the cash transfer per head to be smaller in the two richest provinces, Ontario and Alberta. In 2001–02 the CHST amounted to Can$1 102 per head in total, or Can$ 622 per head in cash in most provinces. Of the Can$46 bn of transfers to provinces and territories, CHST accounted in 2001–02 for $33 bn, about $3/4$ (Canadian High Commission 2002, p. 403[2]).

The second main transfer is the federal equalisation programme, worth $11.7 bn (about 1/4 of all transfers) in 2001–02. In Canada this predates its constitutionalisation in 1982, although it does not date as far back as in Australia, where the equivalent programme began in 1933 (Chapter 9). The federal Department of Finance examines each tax base, estimates the average per capita yield of the tax, and compensates those provinces where the per capita yield is below average. It does not explicitly withdraw funding from provinces where the per capita yield is above average (although, since money is fungible, there must be an implicit withdrawal from them). Some of the detail, however complex, must be grasped, especially:

• the exclusion of outliers when calculating a 'standard';
• the concept, and the implications, of 'transferring tax points'.

From 1957 to 1962, equalisation payments applied only to three tax bases, the two main ones being personal and corporate income tax. All provinces which received less per capita from these taxes than the then-richest (Ontario and Québec) received federal equalisation. Since then, the number of provinces taken as the standard has fluctuated, while the number of tax bases to which equalisation has applied has risen steadily.

The federal Department of Finance defines the fiscal capacity of a province as its ability to raise revenues from the aggregate of 33 revenue sources – including personal income tax, corporate income tax, sales taxes, property tax, and other sources – assuming that province has average tax rates. The average fiscal capacity per head of the five 'middle income' provinces – Quebec, Ontario, Manitoba, Saskatchewan and British Columbia – is $5924 for 2003–04 (*source*: Department of Finance website at http://www.fin.gc.ca/FEDPROV/ eqpe.html). The calculations exclude the richest province (Alberta) and the four poorest (the four Atlantic provinces) from the calculation of the standard. The amounts, and amount per head, of equalisation payments that go to each recipient province are shown in Table 10.5.

Some of the 33 tax bases that are used in the calculations are confined to one or a few provinces. The effects of excluding the outliers from the calculation of the standard are therefore complex. So are some related endogeneity issues. At the top end, Alberta is not in the standard. Two of the bottom four provinces (NL and NS) have significant oil royalties, as does Alberta (outside at the top) and Saskatchewan (inside the 5-province standard). The effects of an increase in either the tax base or the tax take on one of the 33 taxes that is restricted to any of those three sets of provinces are different. Consider for simplicity a tax base that is confined to a single province. If that province is inside the 5-province standard and it increases its revenue from the tax, the standard income for that tax will go up, and the province's equalisation receipts will go down, but by less than 100 per cent. But if the province is outside the 5-province standard and it increases its revenue from the tax, the standard income for that tax remains at $0, and the province's equalisation entitlement goes down

Table 10.5   Equalisation entitlements, 2003–04

	NL	PEI	NS	NB	QC	MB	SK	BC	**Total**
$m	866	240	1,209	1,184	4,543	1,239	355	862	**10,499**
$ per capita	1627.82	1714.29	1279.37	1564.07	609.39	1076.46	350.79	208.16	

Source: Department of Finance Canada; author's calculations.

by 100 per cent, dollar for dollar. As four of the five provinces outside the standard are poor, this is perverse. The formula contains a patch known as 'the Generic Solution' (an odd name as it seems to be a very specific solution) which ensures that in those circumstances a province's receipts taper off at a maximum of 70c in the $ (http://www.fin.gc.ca/FEDPROV/eqgse.html). The Department of Finance states that 'Newfoundland (offshore revenues), Nova Scotia (offshore revenues), Québec (asbestos), and Saskatchewan (potash) have all benefited from the generic solution'. A more truly generic solution would be to calculate the standard revenue for all tax bases over all ten provinces. As the effect of that would probably be to increase equalisation payments, it is predictably advocated by poor provinces and resisted by rich ones.

Tax points are another curiosity. They are used in the CHST calculation, not the Equalisation calculation, but their effect is of a slightly disguised equalisation. The tax points transfer that goes into the calculation of what is now CHST was part of a federal-provincial arrangement that took effect in 1977. The federal government then transferred 13.5 percentage points of its personal income tax and one percentage point of its corporate income tax to the provinces and territories.

This transfer of tax points is a neat solution to vertical fiscal imbalance, where even in 1977 and still more today it was evident that the federal government had substantial excess tax capacity and the provinces had substantial excess spending demand, especially in health. But it has two opaque consequences: the double-counting of expenditure when politicians are claiming credit, and its disguised equalisation implications.

As to double-counting, the Federal government counts the tax points transferred in 1977 as part of its CHST contribution to the provinces in all its documents. If the transferred tax points are treated as a federal transfer to the provinces, then the federal claim that VFI in Canada as a whole is close to zero is bolstered. Federal politicians claim extra credit for the amount they say they are transferring to the provinces every year, and can reiterate the five health principles on every occasion they choose to do so.

Provincial governments dissent. They argue that the points transferred in 1977 stay transferred, and that it is double counting for the federal government to count them anew every year. This enables the provinces to say that the federal government is transferring far too little to match their growing need to spend money on health.

The disguised equalisation implications have already been mentioned. As the Department of Finance explains, 'Since tax points are worth more in some provinces than others, the federal government agreed [in 1977] to equalise the tax points on an on-going basis' (http://www.fin.gc.ca/FEDPROV/aseqe.html).

Dispersed powers to tax imply dispersed tax collection. Here Canada is intermediate between the USA and the UK. Federalism in the USA entails completely separate arrangements for assessment and collection at federal and state, and sometimes municipal, levels. While this of course allows each tier of government to choose its own rates and schedules it incurs very high transaction costs, some of which fall on the taxpayer, as anyone who has wrestled with federal and state income tax returns can testify. The UK, on the other hand, is so centralised that the only tax not collected by a national agency is Council Tax. In many parts of the UK, more than one authority has the right to collect tax from householders – there may be two-tier local government, or a fire or police authority with the right to 'precept': that is, dictate to the collecting authority that it must collect such and such amount on behalf of the precepting authority. Because almost nobody in the UK is aware which authority provides which service, precepting fatally blurs accountability and responsibility for expenditure.

Multiple collection with high transaction costs is obviously bad. Precepting is obviously bad because of its anti-democratic and anti-efficiency effects. Has Canada found a happy medium? Most of the provinces have entered an agreement with the federal government to levy and collect income tax jointly. This sharply reduces transaction costs, both for government and for the taxpayer, compared with the USA. But it does deprive provinces of the flexibility to set their own reliefs, exemptions, and thresholds. It probably does not obscure citizens' knowledge of which government delivers which service, because in a federal system citizens are likely to have a much better idea who does what than in a unitary system in any case. Québec does not participate in the joint collection of income tax, but it does collect GST (=VAT) for both itself and the federal government.

Tax competition is always an issue in fiscal federalism. There is limited tax competition between the Canadian provinces. Some tax bases, such as real estate and natural resources, are where they are and cannot be shifted. The most mobile tax base is the corporation. All interviewees concurred that it is hard for corporations to shop for a jurisdiction within Canada. Corporations are taxed by the location of their activities and no order of government has an incentive to collude with a corporation to pretend that its activities are elsewhere than they truly are.

As regards competition over income tax, there is some movement of Anglophone Canadians to Alberta, the province with the lowest personal taxation. There appears to be little tax migration of francophones, although Québec has traditionally been one of the highest taxing and spending provinces. Language may explain this limited movement.

As regards sales taxes, Canada, like Australia, has a small number of geographically large jurisdictions. Unlike the USA and even more unlike the UK, there are few conurbations that straddle jurisdictional lines such that it would be worth shopping around for lower sales (or property) taxes. The only Canadian conurbation that crosses a provincial boundary is Ottawa-Hull. There are sharp differences between property tax rates in the two cities – they are much higher in Hull (which is in Quebec) than in Ottawa. However, all witnesses concur that this effect is fully capitalised into house prices. The drop in house prices as one goes from Ottawa to Hull reflects the higher level of property taxation in Hull.

North-south tax competition may be a more serious issue than east-west competition. Most provinces have more north-south than east-west trade. They always have done, and the North American Free Trade Agreement accentuates this. The economy of the Atlantic provinces is linked to New England, of central Ontario to Detroit and Chicago, of the Canadian prairies to the US prairies, and of the Canadian Pacific region to the US Pacific North-West. Canada is a relatively high-tax country and the USA a relatively low-tax country. As a proportion of GDP, the overall tax burden in Canada in 1999 was 38.2 per cent and in the USA 28.9 per cent (Séguin 2002, chart 23; *source*: OECD). This limits the scope for HFE in Canada compared with (for instance) Australia or the UK.

On the expenditure side, it is important to note that Canada has relatively few direct federal employees. Only the post office and the Royal Canadian Mounted Police (who supply police services under contract to some provinces) employ substantial numbers. There is no unified public sector pay bargaining in Canada. Each province negotiates its own pay arrangements with its employees. Federal pay rates are equal throughout Canada, but that has limited knock-on effects given that, typically, federal and provincial employees are in different trade unions. Consequently, provincial pay rates and hence the cost of delivering public services are lower in poor provinces than in rich ones. This seems to be one reason for the surprisingly small role of 'needs' claims in Canadian intergovernmentalism.

The special problem of natural resources

In Canada (like Australia but unlike the UK), natural resources are taxable by the provinces. Beginning in 1967, provinces' natural resource tax revenues were subject to 100 per cent equalisation. This soon led to complaints that they were over-equalised (for similar issues in Australia, see Chapter 9). In 1973 the government of Newfoundland, which had developed a very large hydro power scheme jointly with Québec and a private developer, discovered that all its resource income would be equalised away from it and it therefore threatened to expropriate the private sector partner (Feehan 2002, p. 3). The sharp rises in oil prices in the 1970s had the effect of hugely stretching the range of provinces' resource tax capacities, and consequently in the federal government's equalisation liabilities. Since 1982, the natural resource equalisation formula has operated on a five-province standard. As for other tax bases, the richest province (Alberta) and the poorest four provinces (the four Atlantic provinces) are excluded from the calculation of the standard per capita receipt. In all, 14 of the now 33 revenue sources that are equalised are natural-resource related (Feehan 2002, p. 5). But this generates perverse effects both for provinces that are in, and for provinces that are outside, the five-province standard. In general, it gives them an incentive to underprice existing natural resources and to fail to develop new sources:

> [W]henever a single jurisdiction dominates a particular tax base to such an extent that its tax rate becomes, in effect, the national tax rate … , there is no incentive for an equalization-receiving jurisdiction to extract any revenues at all from the resource and maximum incentive for it to dissipate the revenues that it could raise (e.g. … directly to consumers in the form of inexpensive hydroelectric power). (Péloquin 2003 p. 10).

All of this, with the parallel evidence from Australia (Garnaut and FitzGerald 2002), suggests that natural resource tax capacity should be equalised away at a level below 100 per cent.

Vertical imbalance and horizontal fiscal equalisation

The Québec Government recently commissioned a report (Séguin 2002; cf. also Conference Board 2002) on what it described as the 'fiscal disequilibrium' in Canada. Though commissioned by a Parti

Québécois government, it was bipartisan in Québec politics. The chairman became a minister in the succeeding Liberal provincial government in 2003. The provinces agree that fiscal disequilibrium exists but disagree as to the remedy. The federal government denies that it exists.

All ten provinces agree with the Québécois complaint that the federal government taxes more than it needs to and fails to hand the proceeds to the provinces, which expect their service delivery to continue to become more expensive, especially for health. A projection (Conference Board 2002) shows the federal government accumulating a massive surplus by 2020, while the provinces barely break even.

One might therefore expect the provinces to unite behind a demand for the federal government simply to transfer more cash to them under its equalisation programme. However, politics intervenes. Governments in Québec cannot consistently demand transfers from a federal government that they think should have no authority in Québec. They would therefore prefer a transfer of tax points (although as explained above this also implies an increase in equalisation payments).

The federal government brusquely replies, in a Web document headed 'The Fiscal Balance in Canada: the Facts' (Department of Finance Canada 2003), that the most robust tax bases are open to both orders of government (Table 10.6) and that provincial-only sources (such as natural resource royalties and gambling taxes) are more robust than federal-only sources (such as tariffs). At Confederation, the then-dominant tax base, namely customs and excise, went to the federal level. But that tax base is now small, especially since the North American Free Trade Agreement abolished tariffs against Canada's overwhelmingly dominant trade partner, the USA. In aggregate, the

Table 10.6   Revenue sources in Canada

Tax base	Available at federal level?	Available at provincial level?
Personal income tax	Y	Y
Corporate income tax	Y	Y
Sales tax	Y	Y
Payroll tax	Y	Y
Gambling tax		Y
Alcohol tax		Y
Natural resources		Y
Tariffs	Y	
Taxes on non-residents	Y	

Source: Department of Finance Canada.

vertical fiscal gap between the federal government and the provinces is small, although the gap between the federal government and any one of the poor provinces is large. In other words, so the federal argument runs, there is no structural vertical imbalance, but there is (and probably always will be) a need for horizontal equalisation. The federal government dismisses the Conference Board projections as being inconsistent with other projections by the same body, and as unrealistically assuming no changes in policy before 2020, and the use of all federal surpluses for debt reduction. Those are some, but not all, of the facts about fiscal balance in Canada.

The surprisingly limited role of needs

Consider various dates. In 1867 no politicians acknowledged that horizontal fiscal equalisation was a role of government. Therefore nothing relating to HFE appears in the original Canadian constitution. The Australian constitution of 1900, written as socialism was becoming a mass movement, is distinctly more egalitarian. In its shadow the egalitarian Australian HFE arrangements began in 1933 (Chapter 9). The most puzzling date in the series is therefore 1982. Why does Canada's current constitution, written after four decades of the Welfare State, make only the limited and non-justiciable section 36 references to equalisation quoted above?

The 1982 text had to pass the highest possible threshold – a unanimity rule. Only what each and every province could accept would be enacted, in the special circumstances of patriation of the Constitution. The failure of subsequent attempts to change the constitution by unanimity (at Meech Lake in 1987 and Charlottetown in 1992) shows what a high threshold the unanimity rule imposes. Any text empowering the federal government to make HFE payments had to satisfy the most reluctant provinces, which would probably have been Alberta (for economic reasons) and Quebec (for cultural and constitutional reasons).

Accordingly, there are needs-based payments to the three territories, which are not fully-fledged provinces, but not in any serious way to the provinces. Nor is it politically likely that the campaigns of some poor provinces for greater recognition of their needs will succeed.

The needs payments to the territories are in Table 10.7, which shows that they are so huge that they swamp CHST and equalisation payments. Territorial formula funding accounts for well over half of the territories' revenues, and 91 per cent of Nunavut's.

Table 10.7   Federal transfers to the three territories, $m, 2003–04

		Nunavut	NWT	Yukon
Canada Health and Social Transfer:				
	Cash	25	22	23
	Tax points	10	28	13
	Total	35	50	36
Health Reform Fund		1	1	1
Territorial Formula Financing		664	581	409
Total Major Transfers		700	632	446
Federal transfers as % of territory revenues		91	52	73

Source: Department of Finance Canada, Federal-Provincial Relations Division.

The formula is based on the actual expenditure in the territories in 1985, when they had much less autonomy than now, adjusted for the growth in their responsibilities and general GDP and relative population change. Thus, unlike the Australian or English regimes, it does not attempt to measure the true cost of providing public services efficiently in the territories, but is driven by the historic cost of providing them in the past.

A Martian (or Australian) would expect to find intense political pressure from the poorer provinces to be treated on a similar basis to the territories and have their higher needs acknowledged by formula. Some such pressure exists. The government of Newfoundland & Labrador wants to explore a move to a needs basis. However it is short of allies. The government of Prince Edward Island would like a recognition of the diseconomies of scale to be built into the formula, recognising the higher per capita cost of providing the full range of provincial government services in an island with a population of only 140,000. But there seems to be no chorus of demands to move to a needs-based formula.

There appear to be various reasons for this. In contrast to both Australia and the UK, the Canadian evidence on the cost of public services does not always suggest a heavy weighting for sparsity of settlement (except in the special case of the territories). All provinces except PEI have sparsely populated hinterlands. It is open to a province to reduce the cost of public services to remote areas by encouraging migration *within* the province, as might happen anyhow for economic reasons (e.g. the migration of Newfoundlanders from 'outports' to the Avalon peninsula around St. Johns). Because provincial governments control their own wage bills, these are lower in low-GDP than in high-

GDP provinces. So are accommodation costs. At the other tail of the distribution – congestion costs – Canada has only three metropolitan areas, viz., Montreal, Toronto, and Vancouver. Of these, Vancouver has a highly constricted site, Toronto has a site that is constricted on one side by Lake Ontario, and Montreal has an unconstricted site. This should lead to Vancouver, and hence BC, having the highest congestion costs, but also to its having the most robust property tax base; and to the converse on both counts for Montreal.

Another possible reason for the lack of clamour for a needs assessment lies in the special position of Québec, which we should revisit.

Credible threats in Québec and Scotland

Here is a paradox. The threat of Québec separatism to the unity of the Canadian state is obvious. It is stronger on all counts than the threat of Scottish separatism to the unity of the UK. The two Québec sovereigntist parties (the Parti Québécois, which contests provincial elections, and the Bloc Québécois, which contests federal elections) have gained a plurality of the votes and a majority of the seats in Québec in several elections to each order of government. The Scottish National Party (SNP) has never won a plurality of the Scottish vote or of seats. Two referenda on sovereignty, in 1980 and 1995, each brought the sovereigntists tantalisingly close to a majority although both failed to produce one. There has never been a referendum on Scottish independence. The proportion of the population who favour independence is higher in Québec (Blais *et al.* 2002 p. 104; Curtice 2003, Table 10.11.1). An obvious way for governments to buy off discontent is through public expenditure. As argued elsewhere in this book, a plausible explanation of the unexpectedly high public transfers per head to Scotland is that Scotland has posed a threat of sorts to the Union since 1885, and a tangible threat since the emergence of the SNP as a credible electoral force in 1967. *Why then are federal transfers per head not differentially high in Québec?*

One reason is just that Canadian fiscal federalism is not needs-based. Accordingly, it cannot be 'needs' based. Here, a need is what someone needs; a 'need' is what it is politically convenient to recognise as a need. If needs are essentially contested, there are no needs in politics, only 'needs'. Even if that is too extreme a position, 'needs' are prevalent in all democratic political systems. Of course, Quebeckers of both main parties there argue that the federal government pays too little attention to the 'needs' of Québec. But:

1. in Canada, provincial parties are organised entirely separately from federal parties, even when they have the same name. The provincial Liberals cannot directly bring pressure on the federal Liberals. The Parti Québécois is a separate organisation to the Bloc Québécois;
2. in federal politics, sovereigntists cannot argue for more redistribution of federal funds to Québec without compromising their main position. If Québec were to become a sovereign state, their primary goal, then of course it would receive no federal transfers. Liberals are also constrained, because the federal Liberal party is an all-Canada party, and voters in the rest of Canada resent any special treatment for Québec.

An alternative lever would be the balance of power in the federal legislature. However, as noted above, the Canadian Senate is not a house of the provinces, unlike its counterparts in Australia, Germany, and the USA. Therefore no province can use it to threaten the output of the House of Commons. As to the Commons, the Bloc Québécois is in the same position as the Irish Party of Parnell and his successors between 1880 and 1914. It cannot expect and does not want to form part of the government of Canada. But, as its very name implies, it reliably holds a bloc of seats in every parliament that are inaccessible to any other party.

Such a bloc is powerful when, and only when, it holds the balance of power. The Irish Party did so from November 1885 to June 1886; from 1892 to 1895; and from 1910 until 1915. Only in those periods did the governing parties consider any concessions to Irish opinion. Unluckily for the Bloc, its prospects of being pivotal are not strong. The Liberal Party is more hegemonic in Canadian party politics than the UK's most hegemonic parties (the Conservatives under Margaret Thatcher and New Labour) have ever been in modern times. The most recent academic evidence relates to the autumn 2000 election campaign. At that time, 26 per cent of Canadians, and over half of those who professed any party identification at all, identified themselves as Liberals; the next largest bloc (11%) was of identifiers with the Alliance (Blais *et al.* 2002, Fig. 8.2). Party identification does not always translate into vote, and votes do not always map to seats; but in 2000 both of these mappings worked and the Liberals secured a comfortable overall majority. Tables 10.3, 10.4, 10.8, 10.9a and 10.9b contain the details.

Table 10.8 Party shares of the vote, Canada, 1997 and 2000 federal elections

Region	Liberal		Alliance (1997: Reform)		Prog Cons		NDP		Bloc		Other	
	1997	2000	1997	2000	1997	2000	1997	2000	1997	2000	1997	2000
Atlantic	32.8	40.7	9.0	10.2	33.8	31.3	23.7	16.5			0.7	1.2
Québec	46.7	44.2	0.3	6.2	22.2	5.6	2.0	1.8	37.9	39.9	1.0	2.3
Ontario	49.5	51.5	19.1	23.6	18.8	14.4	10.7	8.3			1.8	2.2
West	27.6	25.3	43.0	49.9	10.5	10.0	16.7	12.3			2.2	2.6
Canada	38.5	40.8	19.4	25.5	18.8	12.2	11.0	8.5	10.7	10.7	1.6	2.3

Source: Elections Canada; Blais *et al.* 2002 Table 4.1.

Table 10.9a First and second preferences, Canada, excluding Québec, 2000

2nd preference	Reported vote			
	Liberal	Alliance	Prog Cons	NDP
Liberal		27	45	48
Alliance	13		17	3
Prog Cons	34	38		17
NDP	24	7	14	
Other, DK, None	29	29	25	32
Total	100	100	100	100
N	559	455	169	160

Table 10.9b First and second preferences, Québec, 2000

2nd preference	1st preference	
	Liberal	Bloc
Liberal		14
Bloc	16	
Alliance	16	16
Prog Cons	26	17
NDP	4	11
Other, DK, None	39	43
Total	100	100
N	254	280

Source: derived from Blais *et al*. 2002 Table.4.3. Columns with fewer than 50 respondents suppressed. Columns may not total 100 because of rounding.

The Anglophone opposition to the Liberals has been divided three ways: to the NDP to the Liberals' left, and two rivals (Progressive Conservative and Alliance) to their right. Accordingly, a pact on the right is a perennial Canadian talking-point. Only in 2003 did the two right-wing parties merge. Survey data for the 2004 General Election are not yet available. The aggregate data (Tables 10.3 and 10.4) show that the Alliance-Conservative merger has been more successful than the 2000 survey data would have predicted. However, it scarcely lessens the isolation of Québec.

Québec, meanwhile, gives every appearance of an electorally divided society. The supporters of the two big parties there are (unsurprisingly) unwilling to give second preferences to one another. But they are also relatively unwilling to give them to anyone else. The proportion saying 'None' in Québec is much higher than in the rest of Canada (Table 10.9b).

Of course, the plurality electoral system could sweep the Liberals out as it swept the Conservatives out in 1993. But they are more secure than were the old Progressive-Conservatives for several reasons. The Conservatives have collapsed in Québec. The chances that the leadership of the Bloc Québécois could emulate Parnell and John Redmond, in extracting concessions for their territory in a hung parliament, look remote. Even in the 2004 Parliament it would require a grand coalition of Conservatives, Bloc, and NDP to defeat the Liberals. The Conservatives and the Bloc are one seat short of a joint majority. Such a majority, on anything relating to the status or finances of Québec, is unlikely because the potential partners are on opposite sides. Quebeckers want more for Québec; westerners, where both the Conservatives and the NDP are strongest, want less. And, as described above, the reference to the Supreme Court and the Clarity Act have raised the threshold for any future referendum on sovereignty. Thus paradoxically, the strong sovereigntist movement in Québec is weak, and the weak separatist movement in Scotland is strong.

Comparisons with Australia

Canada is more diverse than Australia, politically, socially, and economically. Whereas the Australian states were all (with the partial exception of Western Australia) enthusiasts for federation, and all had signed up to the Commonwealth within a year of its creation, the Canadian provinces joined more slowly, Newfoundland not until 1949 in a narrow referendum vote. Between Québec and its neighboring provinces (and within Québec) the faultline between Anglophones and Francophones goes back to the 18th century. The range of GDP per head is considerably wider in Canada than in Australia.

The Canadian confederation was driven by defence considerations as much as by economics. The Canadian provinces decided to shelter together in the cold light of the Union victory in the American Civil War, which led Canadian politicians to fear that the resurgent US might revive earlier claims on Canada or part of it. The 1866 invasion of New Brunswick by Fenian raiders (Irish-Americans who had been Union soldiers in the Civil War) was enough to convince the dubious politicians of that province to join. By contrast, there was no external threat to Australia in the 1890s; federation was driven by a desire to make the Australian economy more efficient. The 1867 Canadian constitution predates socialism. The Australian constitution was written by politicians who already had socialist parties and a socialist vote in their states. Canada is just larger, its provinces more diverse than the Australian states, and their economies more subject to exogenous shocks (e.g. the Yukon gold rush in 1897; the discovery of oil in 1947 which turned Alberta from one of the poorest to one of the richest provinces; the collapse of the Newfoundland fisheries).

Federal finance in the two countries reflects these differences. The Australian arrangements for fiscal federalism are more egalitarian than the Canadian. The Commonwealth Grants Commission attempts to equalise fully both for differences in states' resources, and for differences in their needs, where 'needs' includes both the demand for each public service and the cost per head of providing it. Canada does not equalise for needs, except to the three territories – huge in extent but tiny in population. When equalising for resources, it uses a five province standard as a yardstick for resource equalisation, that excludes the outliers – rich Alberta and the four poor Atlantic provinces.

A feature that Canada and Australia share with each other but not with the UK is that the provinces/states have a resource tax base. In Canada this is supposed to be confined to onshore resources (Constitution Act 1982, Section 92A), but the Federal government has agreed that Newfoundland's offshore oil may be subject to provincial taxation. The resource tax base of course differs hugely between states with extensive natural resources and those with few or none. In the UK this issue was at its most prominent in the mid-1970s, when the Scottish National Party (SNP)'s demand that 'It's Scotland's Oil' secured widespread support among Scots of all political persuasions. However, the UK Government of the day was fundamentally unwilling to concede any resource tax base to Scotland, and has remained so.

Lessons for other countries

To an observer from the UK, the best feature of Canadian fiscal federalism is that VFI is so low. The federal government denies that it exists at all; the provinces insist that it does. An outsider does not need to get involved in that argument. *Ceteris paribus*, the most efficient government is one whose power to tax equals its duty to spend. When there is any VFI, there is an incentive for governments to shift blame to one another and to shirk doing things that may be economically efficient but politically unpopular. Where there is no VFI, and where (as in Canada) the electorate is relatively well informed as to which order of government does what, each order of government is answerable to its own median voter for its tax and spending decisions. Each has a maximal incentive to be fiscally responsible. Canada seems to have efficient arrangements for joint collection of taxes.

One consequence which could be carried over to the UK, even if VFI is not reduced there, is that provinces are responsible for their own debt servicing. A direct incentive towards fiscal responsibility is that their sovereign (or near-sovereign) debt is rated by the debt-rating agencies. The latest available figures are in Table 10.10.

Unless and until the UK reduces its VFI by giving more power to tax to devolved administrations, the prospective English regional assemblies, and/or local authorities, the Canadian HFE arrangements have less to teach policy makers in the UK. The Canadian arrangements are wholly designed to equalise for unequal taxable capacity, and not at all for unequal needs, nor unequal costs of providing public services. UK policymakers looking for possible models in these areas should look to Australia rather than to Canada. However, Canada provides a refreshing note of scepticism about needs. In a vast and diverse country, there is no significant lobby for special treatment on grounds of exceptional needs. Instead, there seems to be a widely accepted view that disadvantages of poor areas (poor health and educational status; remoteness) are offset by lower costs of providing public services. Such scepticism is unknown in the UK.

Table 10.10   Credit ratings of Governments in Canada (in basis points), 2002

	Spread on 10 years bond	Rate (S&P)
Federal government	–	AAA
Alberta	29	AA+
Ontario	38	AA–
BC	44	AA–
Manitoba	44	AA–
New Brunswick	47	AA–
Saskatchewan	45	A+
Québec	55	A+
Nova Scotia	59	A–
Newfoundland	60	A–

Source: Séguin 2002, Table 5.

11
Honest Centralism and Honest Localism

Government signals and government noise

'Letting local people decide'. 'Local democracy'. 'New localism'. Any phrase with 'community' in it (except 'community charge'[1]). They all sound as good as motherhood and apple pie. Therefore governments of all complexions say that they are in favour of all of those things. They would not say so if they did not expect to get plaudits from the electorate. Which they do.

'Postcode prescribing'. 'NIMBYism'. 'Petty parochialism'. They all sound as bad as a wet day in Scunthorpe. Therefore governments of all complexions say that they are against all of those things. They would not say so if they did not expect to get plaudits from the electorate. Which they do.

But of course these two sets of labels belong to the same things. If governments allow local bodies to decide on health or education policy, then inevitably some of them – covering one set of postcodes – will prioritise some policies, while others – covering other postcodes – will prioritise others. If governments let local authorities decide what can and cannot be built in their territory, then people who do not want development in their back yard will use their democratic right to object and to lobby the local authority. They have votes in the authority. The people who might benefit do not. For example, new housing benefits people who do not (yet) live in the area; new runways benefit people all over the world but harm those living in the flight paths.

It is therefore not surprising that governments say contradictory things, or say one thing and do another. They are democratically reflecting the minds of citizens, who are comfortable about holding contradictory propositions in their minds at the same time. Citizens can innocently want local democracy and uniform national standards at the same time. Citizens are not full-time politicians. Those who are, and their advisers, have to make hard choices.

Therefore governments since Layfield should not be faulted for their rhetoric. But they can, and should, be faulted for failing to make hard choices between honest centralism and honest localism. The Labour government in office at the time of writing talks the talk of new localism.

> As a government, we are seeking to decentralise the way that governance works in Britain. We want to do this because it will enhance service delivery, allowing those on the front line more freedom to decide what services to deliver, and how to do this. We also understand that a revitalisation of our democracy ... depends on building up and expanding democratic power at local and community level (Wood 2003).

But the language is carefully chosen. 'Enhancing service delivery' is another applehood concept. A government could enhance service delivery while retaining tight central control over its contents. The commitment to new localism is not necessarily a commitment to allowing elected sub-national governments more freedom to do what they want. In this chapter we explore the implications of making policy more consistently (honestly) centralist, and of making it more consistently (honestly) localist. In short, of separating noise from signal in Government messages.

There are limits to both centralism and localism. A UK government can no longer be wholly centralist because devolution is a done deal. Scotland, Wales, and London will not foreseeably cease to have elected sub-national government (unless they become entirely independent, currently conceivable only for Scotland). As and when its Legislative Assembly is restored to office, the same applies to Northern Ireland. In the run-up to devolution, soon-to-be Prime Minister Tony Blair seemed to misunderstand what it was all about. 'Sovereignty rests with me as an English MP and that's the way it will stay', he was reported as saying during the 1997 general election campaign (*Scotsman* 04.04.97, quoted by McLean, 1998, p. 166). The Scotland Act 1998 indeed contains a sovereignty clause asserting the power of the UK Parliament to enact laws for Scotland, even in devolved areas.[2] The Scottish Parliament does invite the UK Parliament to legislate in devolved matters, by means of what is known as a 'Sewel motion' (Mitchell

2004b, p. 29). But it is hard to envisage any other circumstance in which Westminster would legislate in devolved matters. All of the main domestic policy areas including health and education are devolved.

In finance, the centre retains more power over the Territories. The Treasury operations manual (HM Treasury 2004a) defines circumstances in which the UK government might act without the consent of the Territories for reasons of macroeconomic management (for instance to protect the Chancellor's self-imposed Golden Rule and Sustainable Investment Rule). And the Barnett Formula itself makes increments in spending in the Territories a function of increments in spending in England by the UK government. As argued in earlier chapters, this mutual dependency is unhealthy and unsustainable.

In the first few years of devolution, the centre has shown signs of forgetting that it does not run Scotland and Wales. This has ranged from the trivial (the English agriculture department authorising field trials of genetically modified crops in a field that turned out to be in Wales) to the potentially serious (the Higher Education White Paper and Act in 2003–04 have substantial knock-on implications for higher education in the Territories, for which see McLean 2003). But the centre is slowly learning two lessons from devolution. One is that the UK government cannot make policy for Edinburgh or Cardiff. The other is that policy coordination cannot remain a private game played within the structures of the Labour Party. The formal mechanisms to resolve devolution differences, created in 1998 and barely used, will come more and more into use as the UK becomes more and more like a normal federation of four countries.

But equally, a UK government cannot be wholly localist. At a minimum, nobody would propose localising the *Social Protection* function of government. The main element of social protection is transfer payments to needy people – pensioners, the unemployed, the sick, the handicapped. It is the *locus classicus* of the 'redistributive' function of government. Previous chapters have shown that since Edwin Chadwick policymakers have realised that needy people are more concentrated in some places than in others. Therefore transfers must be funded from the proceeds of national, not local, taxation. Also, people's entitlement to transfer payments derives either from their contribution record or from their UK citizenship itself. Therefore it must not be affected by where in the UK they live. It could be argued that transfer payments – at least those triggered by entitlement rather than contribution record – should be lower in lower cost areas (or, the same thing put more palatably, higher in higher cost areas). But that has never been UK government practice. Apart from personal social services, considered below, none of the components of social protection are devolved in the UK, nor is it foreseeable that they would be.

Thus the existence of devolution sets a limit beyond which centralism cannot go. The existence of national rates and conditions for social protection sets a limit beyond which localism cannot go. In the next three sections we return to Layfield's challenge to outline honest centralism and honest localism for the UK. In this outline, a government would be honestly centralist if it took direct control of the main domestic services other than the NHS and ran them along similar lines to the NHS. Local bodies might still be responsible for running them, but they would be responsible, like NHS bodies, to central government, not to the local electorate. Elected local government would withdraw from the 'redistributive' functions of government to concentrate on the provision of 'beneficial' local public goods – roads, street lighting and cleaning, waste disposal, land-use planning, and cultural services such as libraries and museums being the obvious candidates (see Foster *et al.* 1980 for this distinction). The balance of funding between central and local government would cease to be a problem, although a possible new problem would be that the tax base of local authorities in rich areas would be *too* generous for their remaining functions.

A less extreme, but still honest, centralism would see elected local authorities retaining some redistributive functions, but central government committing itself to funding floor standards for each service. Some tricky issues of marginal cost, marginal benefit, and gearing must then be addressed.

A government would be honestly localist if it left such redistributive services as education, police, and personal social services with elected local authorities. In that case, it must address the tangle of issues involving VFI; the balance of funding; local taxation powers; and the equalisation formula. It must have a regime for floor standards that does not create perverse incentives.

Any future government, whether centralist or localist, needs a new regime for sharing out block grant around the four countries of the UK. In an honestly centralist regime the units would be England, Scotland, Wales, and Northern Ireland. In an honestly localist regime they would be Scotland, Wales, Northern Ireland, and each of the nine standard regions of England.

Honest centralism

In the NHS, the pressure for national standards has always been there. Nye Bevan famously said that if a bedpan was dropped in Tredegar, the Minister should know. Tredegar is in Wales, so the Secretary of State for Health (currently the Member for a Scottish constituency) could not now do anything about it even if he knew. The NHS is evolving differently in the four countries of the UK, as none of the other three is eager to follow the route being set in England (Greer 2003, 2004).

Within England, however, there is no serious plan to decentralise the NHS, if decentralism means responsibility to *local* bodies. For decades, the only local accountability of the NHS was through bodies known as Community (that word again) Health Councils. But these were self-appointed bodies, made up of people who had time to complain and who all thought the NHS spent too little. Governments of both parties did not hide their impatience, and they were finally abolished in 2003 (*Source*: http://www.achcew.org.uk/, accessed 06.09.04). In its 2003 plan for NHS Foundation Hospitals, the government provided for each foundation to have its own elected governing body. But who are the electorate for a foundation hospital? It is a core part of the new NHS ideology, now shared by the post-Enthoven Conservatives and New Labour (Chapter 6), that hospitals are providers of service who compete to offer procedures to NHS purchasers who pay for them. Purchasers (currently Primary Care Trusts) therefore cover mutually exclusive and jointly exhaustive space. Providers do not. So the very idea of a democratically elected hospital board is undefined. Who are its *demos*? The more specialised a hospital, the more intractable this problem. The UCLH group (University College, London Hospital and its associated hospitals) gained NHS Foundation status in 2004. It has a 33-member partly-elected Members' Council, including three 'local residents' and fourteen 'patients' (*source*: http://www.uclh.nhs.uk/services/foundation/your_members_council.shtml, accessed 06.09.04). But it is impossible to define who is a local resident because anyone, from anywhere in England, might be treated in the UCLH group if they have a rare disease. For instance, one hospital in the group is the National Hospital for Neurology and Neurosurgery, which as its name implies attracts patients from all over England. Equally, it is possible to say who *has been* a patient, but not who might become one. Even if the *demos* for the UCLH group is regarded as its local population, that is in the millions, not the thousands. One study (Klein 2004) found that the Bradford Teaching Hospitals foundation trust sent out only

1143 ballots to its 'members'. Five hundred and fifty-one were return-ed. The 2001 population of Bradford was 467,665. Democratic gov-ernance of a foundation hospital seems to be a practical impossibility. Democratic governance of primary care trusts is perfectly possible, but politically inconceivable.

The NHS therefore remains a command-and-control service, as it was in Bevan's day. There are important differences as to who commands and controls. Compared with 1948, Ministers are much more remote from the process, while auditors, healthcare commissioners, primary care trusts and (since 2004) foundation hospital executives are much closer. But command and control achieve at least rough geographical justice within England (Chapter 6), although not among the four countries of the UK (Chapter 4). So the English NHS could be a model for honest centralism within the rest of the public service.

In descending order of cost, the locally-run redistributive services that an honest centralist might wish to transfer openly (as opposed to surreptitiously) from local to central control are: *school education*; *personal social services (PSS)*; *police*; and *fire*. There are respectable theoreti-cal arguments for transferring education and PSS, and respectable practical arguments for transferring all except, possibly, personal social services. If little is heard about nationalising PSS, the reason may be that national politicians do not want to take the blame the next, and utterly predictable, time there is a scandal about child abuse or the management of paedophiles.

The respectable theoretical argument is that education and personal social services are primarily redistributive goods. A government may reasonably want to spend more per head on them in poor areas than in rich ones. Therefore they should be financed out of national rather than local taxation. Therefore, he who pays the piper (namely a central government department acting as the agent of the UK taxpayer) is enti-tled to call the tune.

This argument applies less to police and not at all to fire. These two services provide local public goods. There are only limited reasons for the police, and no reasons at all for the fire service, to concentrate spending in the poorest regions of the country. But the argument for nationalisation is less theoretical than practical. These two services have only a pretence of local accountability at present. Police and fire authorities are elected only indirectly and in part. Their areas are usually larger than those of local authorities, but their 'elected' members are nominated by the constituent authority or authorities, not directly elected. They precept upon local authorities – that is, they simply issue a demand that the local authority must collect a certain amount per head in Council Tax from each household in their patch. In November 2003, the Chief Constable of Devon and Cornwall warned of the problems of public order likely to arise from popular resistance to high increases in Council Tax in those two counties. At the same time, his authority precepted the councils for an increase of almost 40 per cent – one of the highest percentage increases in Council Tax of any authority in the UK (*Cornish Guardian* 2003). Police and fire pay and conditions are negotiated nationally. Although the Government pretends not to intervene, the pretence is often incredible, as in the long-running pay dispute in the fire service in 2003–04. In summer 2004, Home Secretary David Blunkett went to court to force Humberside Police Authority to dismiss their Chief Constable for his alleged failings in the Soham murder investigation. Honest centralism implies a national police service and a national fire service.

Underlying all of these reasons for centralism is the fundamental one, that the public expects uniform standards in all of these services. People find postcode primary schools as offensive as postcode prescribing. Yet there are huge regional and local variations in the quality of schools. The culture of government by inspection, started under the Conservatives and accelerated under Labour, means that every school in England is ranked for its performance in public exams, in standard assessment tests (SATs), and, most recently, for its 'value added' in tests. The Audit Commission (slogan: *Minimising bureaucracy, maximising impact on public services*) publishes 'comprehensive performance assessments' of entire local authorities, on a five-point scale from 'excellent' to 'poor', at http://www.audit-commission.gov.uk/cpa/index.asp?page=index.asp&area=hpcpa (accessed 06.09.04). Not content with these pressures on local authorities, however, the Labour government has introduced ring-fencing funding for schools, so that it is now only a whisker away from a National Education Service which eliminates the role of local education authorities from everything important. Reporting the Secretary of State's press conference, the *Daily Telegraph* stated that

> Local authorities are told to recast themselves as the 'commissioner and quality assurer of educational services, not the direct supplier.'
> School funding will be channelled through the local authorities, as at present, but the Government will 'ring fence' the schools budget to prevent them from diverting the money to other areas, such as social services or libraries. 'From 2006 we will provide guar-

anteed three-year budgets for every school, geared to pupil numbers, with every school also guaranteed a minimum per pupil increase every year,' it says. (Lightfoot 2004; cf. also Baldwin 2004).

That is honest centralism, brutal style.

A less brutal and more nuanced version has been in the air since Alan Day's 1976 note of dissent on the Layfield Committee. As noted earlier, Day pointed out that his colleagues over-simplified the choice between centralism and localism when they argued that accountability demanded that the power to tax must accompany the power to spend. Day argued that accountability was satisfied so long as the authority which spent the *marginal* pound also had to raise the *marginal* pound through one of the taxes it controlled.

In a Day-model world, central government would set, and pay for, floor standards for each local service. An inspectorate such as the Audit Commission would judge whether local managers had met the floor standard. If not, they would be sacked and replaced. Local government could then choose, and pay for, those extra services that local citizens most wanted, be it more bobbies on the beat, more speed cameras, or more library books. In local government services, local government would charge, and be accountable for, the marginal pound of taxation. In central services including the NHS, central government would charge, and be accountable for, the marginal pound of taxation.

There are practical complications. An obvious one is that the task of defining a floor standard for each of the dozens of local services is large. Sidney Webb did not think so, but he was wrong. Much larger is the task of judging how much it would cost an averagely competent authority to provide that standard of service, given local input costs. As noted above, the Australian Grants Commission does this; but it is dealing with eight units, whereas the Audit Commission in England deals with some 400.

Assuming that these difficulties could be overcome, there is a more profound problem. If resources per head were equal for every council in England, *and if* the total amount raised in local taxation exactly equalled the total amount that local authorities chose to spend on local public goods plus discretionary above-floor expenditure, *and if* central government refrained from attempts to control the aggregate of local taxation or local spending, then the Day model of accountability would work. But none of these three conditions is met in England. As resources per head are not equal, there has to be an equalisation formula, as we have explored. This must either take resources from rich authorities and redistribute it to poor ones (in the event that local tax receipts in aggregate equalled local public spending in aggregate), or take the form of a support grant going to all authorities, but least to the richest and most to the poorest. Realistically, only central government can administer it, and central government will never resist the temptation to attach conditions to it. In particular, central government wishes to control the aggregate of local taxation because central government is responsible for the macro-management of the economy. Since 1997 this has taken the form of two self-imposed rules, mentioned above: the 'Golden Rule' and the 'Sustainable Investment Rule'. These are defined in the Glossary. But the idea that government should control the total of local government spending was not new in 1997. It was at the heart of the struggle between Margaret Thatcher and the local authorities; in the previous decade, of the struggle between Anthony Crosland and the local authorities. Central government therefore sets a maximum amount that it is prepared for all local authorities to spend, and takes sanctions against them if they do not comply. One sanction is that the total support from central government to local government is fixed in advance. Therefore, if a local authority wishes to spend more than the Government of the day thinks it needs to, it must raise all of the extra amount itself. As it has only one tax base, namely Council Tax, and as Council Tax covers on average about 1/5 of each authority's spending, the authority faces a 5:1 'gearing'. That is: to increase spending by 1 per cent, it must increase Council Tax receipts by 5 per cent. This gearing dissuades local authorities from taking initiatives. But it also obscures accountability, failing to observe the Day principle that the spender of the marginal pound is accountable for its spending.

Could the Day principle be introduced by abolishing the present 5:1 gearing? The nationalisation of education, PSS, police, and fire (at least up to a floor standard) would nearly eliminate it in aggregate, because these services account for around 3/4 of the total spent by local government (Table 11.1).

Table 11.1 shows that social protection, education, and public order & safety (which is mostly police and fire) between them accounted for 74.78 per cent of English local authority spending in 2002–03. All other services were therefore just over 25 per cent. On the financing side, local sources accounted for about 20 per cent of money spent. If those four big services were nationalised, therefore, the vertical fiscal gap for English local government would come down from 5:1 to 25:20. Up to a point, that is good news for the Day principle. But it brings

Table 11.1   Local authority expenditure in England, 2002–03, £ million

Function	Current expenditure	Gross capital expenditure	Total expenditure	% of total local authority expenditure
General public services	2,786	565	3351	3.84
Public order and safety	10,528	521	11,049	12.65
Enterprise and economic development	254	220	474	0.54
Employment policies	53	1	54	0.06
Agriculture, fisheries and forestry	79	7	86	0.10
Transport	3,407	2,461	5,868	6.72
Environment protection	3,404	264	3,668	4.20
Housing and community amenities	1,722	4,025	5,747	6.58
Health	449		449	0.51
Recreation, culture and religion	1,812	514	2,326	2.66
Education and training	27,762	2,287	30,049	34.41
Social protection	23,994	199	24,193	27.71
Total England	**76,250**	**11,064**	**87,314**	**100.00**
of which:				
Public order + education + social protection	62,284	3,007	65,291	74.78
Other services	13,966	8,057	22,023	25.22
Financed by:				
Revenue support grant			19,931	22.83
Non-domestic rate payments			16,633	19.05
Specific and special grants			11,455	13.12
Other current grants *			1,901	2.18
Capital support *			8,323	9.53
Central government support in departmental AME *			12,337	14.1
Locally financed expenditure **			16,734	19.17

Notes:
* Data not in source table. Additional calculations kindly made by HM Treasury.
** By subtraction.
Source: HM Treasury 2004b, from Tables 6.1, 6.7, 6.8. Crown copyright.

problems in its train. One is that rich authorities would now be able to raise *more* from council tax than they needed to spend on their remaining services. Kensington & Chelsea could fund its rubbish collection out of the small change dropped on the street. Two possible implications of that should be avoided at all costs. One is that authorities in the richest areas would have the least incentive to maximise their proceeds from taxing houses – but those are, by definition, the areas in which houses are most over-priced. It cannot be good policy to reduce the tax burden on them. The other perverse implication would be that rich authorities could buy turtle soup with gold spoons for their citizens but poor ones could not. If an authority is 'out of grant', in the jargon of local government finance, then central government lacks levers to persuade it to behave responsibly.

Someone would have to police the required horizontal fiscal equalisation (HFE). Tax proceeds must be taken from Kensington & Chelsea and used in Sedgefield. Either (implausibly) local authorities would have to do it themselves, or central government would have to do it for them by taxing rich authorities and giving grant to poor ones. But in either case, the 1:1 gearing that the Day model requires would have disappeared. Even if there was 1:1 gearing for local government *in aggregate*, it would (as with the Canadian provinces – Chapter 10) never be 1:1 *for each authority*. In the end, polite honest centralism, in which local authorities may spend above the floor on the big services and be accountable to their electors for those choices, may be unachievable. Only brutal honest centralism may be a viable model – restricting elected local authorities to 'roads, rates, and rubbish', as their role is labelled in Australia.

Honest localism

It follows that honest localism entails reducing the gearing in the opposite way: not by transferring functions from local to central government, but by transferring some power to tax from central to local government. We looked at this question in Chapter 7, where we fantasised about a 'Tiebout (1956) world' in which the power to tax matched the responsibility to spend and citizens chose where to live on the basis of their favourite bundle of local taxes and services.

Even the most obvious and uncontroversial reforms of local taxes would reduce gearing a little bit. Extending the bands of council tax would bring in more revenue to local government in aggregate, although it would bring most to the authorities that least needed the money. A general power to set congestion charges would benefit urban councils throughout England (and one or two rural ones, e.g. in the Lake District, Peak District, and other places where car-borne tourists tend to destroy the beauty they come to see). But only relocalisation of business rates or something yet more radical in the nature of a land value tax would have a serious impact on gearing.

Business rates – NNDR – bring in roughly the same amount as Council Tax. But the rate in the pound (UBR) is set centrally, and governments have promised not to increase UBR by more than the rate of inflation in any year. These arrangements were to allay the objection that previously local government was milking businesses, which had no votes, in order to pay electoral bribes to groups of voters. Business rates, like the state pension, are therefore pegged to the annual increase of prices. This means that, like the state pension, their ability to meet costs declines every year. Most of local government's direct costs are for pay. Almost all of its costs are for pay, directly or indirectly. But annual earnings are rising faster than annual prices. Therefore NNDR is coming to finance less and less of the costs of local government. The objection that businesses must not be penalised disproportionately could be met by ruling that no authority may raise its business rate poundage by a higher percentage in any one year than its Council Tax rate. If NNDR returned to local authorities, the gearing ratio would move from about 5:1 to about 5:2. The dynamic effects would also be good. As described in Chapter 7, the 2001 government introduced a Local Authority Business Growth Incentive (LABGI) scheme to try to restore to authorities the incentive to increase their business rate tax base that they lost when business rates were nationalised. But LABGI is over-complex and will become self-contradictory if it stays (McLean and McMillan 2003b).

If relocalisation of business rates would have good dynamic effects, then switching from property rates to land value tax would have better ones. As rehearsed above, land value tax (LVT) would bring both macroeconomic and microeconomic benefits to the UK. As to the first, it would tend to damp property prices during booms and thus act as an automatic stabiliser (Muellbauer 2004). As to the second, it would tend to ensure that land was allocated as efficiently as possible; would force local authorities to assess the real costs and benefits of giving and withholding planning permission; and would probably be the most buoyant achievable source of local government finance.

Any government which introduced LVT would certainly promise that it would not raise more in aggregate than the taxes it replaced, which would mostly be council tax and NNDR. Therefore a move to LVT would not in itself reduce the gearing ratio below the 5:2 that a relocalisation of business rates would produce. But it would crucially give the right incentives to local government to take responsibility for the consequences of its decisions. That is the whole point of honest localism.

But a gearing of 5:2 would still leave central government in charge of a substantial amount of block grant. It would probably have to be in charge of a substantial amount, even under honest localism, because once a rich authority goes 'out of grant' it becomes much more difficult for central government to operate HFE. So we must return to the tricky and unsatisfactory question of the equalisation formulae used around the UK. This will involve revisiting Wales, Scotland, and Northern Ireland in a moment, but leaves one English point to be disposed of first.

There are simply too many local authorities in England. As of 2004, there are 34 counties (the top tier in two-tier areas); 115 unitary authorities; and 239 county districts (the lower tier in two-tier areas). Thus there are in total 388 local authorities in England. They range in population from two tiny special cases – the Isles of Scilly and the City of London – to over a million (Table 11.2).

Table 11.2 shows that three of the tiniest authorities are all-purpose unitaries. Scilly and the City of London are special cases, but Rutland, with its three secondary schools, is some sort of affectionate anomaly. There are also separate police and fire authorities which are part of neither honest centralism nor honest localism. They must be abolished in any consistent move in either direction.

A managerial literature in the 1970s attempted to define the optimal size of councils. The idea was that for large-scale services, like strategic land-use planning, or services for rare groups in the population (such as geniuses or people with rare medical conditions), you need a large authority. Local government professionals liked the idea, as pay scales were tied to the population of the authority. Unfortunately, the evidence base for this argument is weak. If you trust the Audit Commission's CPA scores, there seems to be no correlation between population size and score. Rutland, by far the smallest conventional unitary, gets the middle 'fair' grade for its services overall (one point higher than the largest unitary, Birmingham), and an above-average 4 (the same as Birmingham) for managing its three schools.

A better argument is that the deadweight costs of being in business are excessive. Each council, however small, needs its chief executive, its

Table 11.2   Population extremes for English local authorities, 2001

Name	Population	Type
Ten smallest:		
Isles of Scilly	2,153	Unitary
City of London	7,185	Unitary
Teesdale	24,457	Lower
Berwick-upon-Tweed	25,949	Lower
Alnwick	31,029	Lower
Rutland UA	34,563	Unitary
West Somerset	35,075	Lower
Oswestry	37,308	Lower
South Shropshire	40,410	Lower
Purbeck	44,416	Lower
Median:		
Broadland	118,513	Lower
Ten largest:		
West Sussex	753,614	Upper
Norfolk	796,728	Upper
Staffordshire	806,744	Upper
Birmingham	977,087	Unitary
Hertfordshire	1,033,977	Upper
Surrey	1,059,015	Upper
Lancashire	1,134,974	Upper
Hampshire	1,240,103	Upper
Essex	1,310,835	Upper
Kent	1,329,718	Upper

Source: Adapted from Census 2001, Table KS01. Crown copyright.

council chamber, and its director of human resources. Clinchingly, if central government has to decide how to allocate resources direct to 400 local bodies, it can only use the radically faulty regression methods that this book has examined.

Two-tier local government is an awkward compromise between size and localism. England has had it for a long time, although none of the other three Territories now has it. Nobody knows which council delivers which service, especially as one may appoint the other as its agent. Therefore local accountability is impossible in two-tier areas. An attempt under the Conservatives to bring about single-tier local government everywhere in England ended in tears. Labour is currently trying again, linking the issue with that of regional devolution. If one of the eight regions outside London votes for an elected assembly, it must simultaneously vote for a unitary structure of local government. The only such vote pending at the time of writing is in the North-east. In that region, there are two two-tier areas, the counties of Northumberland (2001 population 307,190) and Durham (493,470). Northumberland contains six districts, and Durham seven. Both cover wide acres but few people. If the two counties became unitary authorities, they would still be smaller than the big cities; everybody would know who delivered local services; there would be thirteen fewer directors of human resources; and it would be easier for central government to calculate grant.

A Territorial Grants Commission: politician-proof centralist and localist versions

Equalisation is the central problem. Can the UK operate an HFE system that is fair to all, and that overcomes the technical problems that have dogged all previous efforts? In Chapter 8, I sketched the constitution for a possible Territorial Grants Commission. Such a Commission can never be fair to all unless it is politician-proof. That is not a rude or cynical remark. It is simply an elementary implication of public choice theory. Politicians want to win the next election. That is what they are there for. Therefore they will try to ensure that grant goes to the median voter in the territory in which they are contesting an election. National politicians also have an interest in the integrity of the United Kingdom. Therefore they have distributed grant generously to (Northern) Ireland and Scotland. As to England, in previous chapters I have argued that grant for services provided by elected local government seems to be distributed less fairly than grant for services provided by local NHS trusts, which are not elected.

The main difference between the centralist and localist versions of the Territorial Grants Commission is very simple. The centralist version comprises four units: Scotland, Wales, Northern Ireland, and England. The localist version comprises twelve: Scotland, Wales, Northern Ireland, and the nine standard regions of England. In the centralist version the UK government, in its other capacity as the government of England, continues to assign grant to the local authorities, health authorities, and regional bodies of England. In the localist version, the Grants Commission assigns block grant to each of the UK's twelve territorial units, which distribute it to their own local and health authorities.

What about making it politician-proof? It is easy to see why; harder to see how. Even such giants of public finance as Pitt the Younger,

W.E. Gladstone, G.J. Goschen and Gordon Brown have failed to create a fair block grant regime. The unfairnesses of 1886 have congealed to produce a system where grant to the Territories satisfies neither equity nor efficiency, and that to the regions of England looks dubious. The sums at stake are huge. Of the £419 bn public expenditure in the UK in 2002–03, perhaps £236 bn (56%) would be affected by Grants Commission equalisation formula if the regime proposed by this book were in place: that is, everything except international services, defence, debt interest, central administration, and social security. How could politicians ever be persuaded to keep their hands off the assignment of 56 per cent of the UK's public expenditure?

The example of monetary policy gives the reformer some heart. Managing the macro economy used to be one of the central things that politicians did. Between 1945 and the mid-1970s they attempted to do it by Keynesian demand management. From then until 1997 they attempted to do it by managing the money supply. Now, they do neither. By granting control over the money supply to the Bank of England in 1997, politicians made themselves stronger by making themselves weaker. The UK's commitment to low inflation has become more credible because it is known to be out of the hands of politicians who might otherwise be tempted to let rip before an election. Fiscal policy is still under government control, but constrained by the golden rule and the sustainable investment rule, which are likely to survive under a government of any party. At best, this implies that government is not blamed when things go bad but gets credit when things go well – the opposite to the traditional situation. It is no longer the government that puts up interest rates. But when people feel good about the economy, they are more likely to vote for the incumbent party tan when they feel bad about it. The UK is enjoying a long period of economic growth, which Chancellor Brown naturally ascribes to the macroeconomic policy changes of 1997.

Monetary policy is not the only area from which government has withdrawn. It has also withdrawn, although somewhat less credibly, from wage negotiations. In the 1970s, UK governments tried to control the price level by controlling the wage level – directly for public-sector wages, and by means of incomes policies for private-sector pay. Those days are also gone, although central government has been taking a perhaps unhealthy interest in fire service pay and conditions, considering that fire is supposedly a local service.

Thus government has successfully withdrawn from monetary policy and labour-market policy, and bound itself to the mast in fiscal policy with the golden rules. A wise politician would see the advantage of continuing the process. Assigning block grant to the four (or 12) territories would become a technocratic process. Complaints should be addressed to the chief executive of the Grants Commission, not to a Cabinet minister.

The proposed constitution of the Grants Commission was outlined in Chapter 8. It would be a non-departmental public body. Like the Electoral Commission or, indeed, the Bank of England, it would not be subject to the control of any UK minister, although of course ministers would nominate at least one member. The constitutional rules proposed for the Grants Commission in Chapter 8 all interlock. Its staff would determine by a rolling formula how much extra grant each territory would get in the next time period. It would equalise among its territories for needs, resources, and the cost of delivering public services. The fact that the formula would be applied with time-lags is important. As in Canada, the Commission would look carefully at the tax bases and the tax effort of each territory. It would have more independence than Finance Canada, however, because it would be an independent agency, not a central (federal) department. As in Australia, when a territory improved its tax base or its tax effort, the Commission would not instantly equalise away all the territory's extra revenue. It must preserve incentives for territories to behave responsibly, and minimise moral hazard.

The professional staff of the Commission would report to their Commissioners, one Commissioner per territory and one (or perhaps two) nominated by the UK Government. The unanimity rule and the inverse GDP default proposed in Chapter 8 are an attempt to take the Commission away from sterile zero-sum politics. The unanimity rule is needed for fairness. When some territories have more bargaining power – more credible threat power – than others, the territories with a credible threat have always done better than those without. If this book has any historical moral, it is that. The unanimity rule is the only voting rule that ensures that each territory has an equally credible threat, and that no coalition can gang up on a minority of territories and simply withdraw grant from them by majority vote.

But the unanimity rule on its own gives each territory a veto. Therefore the Commission, too, needs a credible threat at its back. That is the role of the inverse GDP rule. If the Commission fails to support either the distribution of grant proposed by its professional staff, or any other distribution, by the pre-announced deadline, then the extra grant to each territory for the next time period would be an inverse function of its GDP. The poorer the territory, the more it would get. However, no territory would have an incentive to be a mendicant (as some have labelled the strategy of sitting back and collecting grants for poverty). As public expenditure per head is always below GDP per head, a government which oversees GDP growth of 1 per cent in its territory will always bring in more than a government which secures extra grant of 1 per cent.

The above presupposes an elected government of each territory with some control over tax rates, tax bases, and tax effort. Those features are a prerequisite of mature federalism. The arrangement between the UK and the three devolved administrations is one of immature federalism. It must move somewhere, as Barnett cannot last much longer. It cannot move back to a unitary state. Therefore, the moves must be in the direction of a more mature federalism.

Outside England, the territories have elected governments already, at least in principle. But what about England? Here the centralist and localist models diverge. Even in the centralist model, however, there has to be a government of England, acting separately from the government of the UK. The task of the government of England would be to run the services that, outside England, are devolved: that is, all domestic services except social security. The task of the government of the UK would be to provide UK-wide public goods by running social security, debt management, overseas departments, defence, and macroeconomic management.

A hoary objection arises at this point. *What if the Commons majority in England is of a different party to the Commons majority in the UK?* The only practicable answer is that there is nothing new about this situation, and that the UK has weathered it before (for instance, from 1892 to 1895, from 1910 to 1914, and from 1964 to 1966). As England accounts for 85 per cent of the population of the UK, it would not be practicable to create a separate government of England, sitting somewhere other than Westminster (York? Crewe?). The Ministers for England would continue to be Ministers of the UK Government, answerable to and supported by the majority in the House of Commons, as they are at present. For instance, the Secretaries of State for Health, Education, and Transport are *de facto* Ministers for England only, for all or most of their responsibilities. So is the Deputy Prime Minister in his capacity as a departmental minister.

Nevertheless, this continuing anomaly is itself an argument for more localism. The UK government is cautiously sponsoring democracy in the regions of England. London already has elected regional government. The North-east is to vote on it after this book goes to press (but before it is published). Other regions may get elected governments later. Each region already has three region-wide public bodies: a Government Office, a Regional Development Agency, and a nominated Regional Assembly. The Government Office combines the regional operations of the main UK departments operating in the English regions – for instance Home Office, Education & Skills, and Culture, Media & Sport. The Development Agency is responsible for its region's economic development, and in recent Spending Reviews the 'single pot' of public expenditure delivered direct to the RDA to use as it chooses has been substantially enlarged, although it remains a small proportion of public expenditure in the region (McLean *et al.* 2003). The Regional Assembly could be the forerunner of an elected assembly for the region.

In the localist model, each Assembly would nominate one member to the Grants Commission. In conjunction with the Government Office and RDA (which should be merged), it would also be responsible for allocating grant onwards to its constituent health authorities and local authorities. These would still be fairly numerous. For instance, in London there are 33 boroughs, including the City. In the North-east, if Northumberland and Durham become unitary authorities, there will be 11. Where the number of constituent bodies is small, the regional authority should use a direct method of evaluating needs, resources, and costs; where it is large, it will have to use a regression method. But a regression method with thirty-odd cases should produce fewer anomalies than one with 400.

The localist model also assumes that local bodies have local tax powers. Either business rates would be returned to local control, or both they and Council Tax will be replaced by land value taxation. Property is the best tax base for local government. Houses and business premises do not move from one area to another. People do; corporations do so even more freely than people. Both the localist and the centralist model assume that Scotland, Wales, and Northern Ireland will all acquire at least the tax powers that Scotland already has, and preferably more. The Scottish Variable Rate of Income Tax could only fund a trivial proportion of domestic services in Scotland. It is probably also time to drop the idea of a unified civil service. Scotland and Wales should become responsible for employing their own civil servants, on terms and conditions they decide for themselves, as Northern Ireland already does. If, as in Canada, public service pay more closely reflects local costs, the area cost adjustment required for high cost areas is easier to calculate and to interpret than at present.

The Grants Commission regime would be both fairer and more efficient than the present regime. It would be the first practical solution to Layfield's dilemma.

Concluding remarks

The United Kingdom has been pared down to its initials throughout this book. But we must open the name up again to understand fully why the United Kingdom faces a fiscal crisis. It is not very united, and it is not a kingdom.

The union of 1707 did create, precisely, a united *kingdom* – or, to be pedantic, queendom. Queen Anne had for the first time a united set of ministers, forming the executive of the United Kingdom. Monarchs have now dropped out of the picture in practical terms. But the Queen's Ministers no longer form a united executive. Her Majesty's Scottish ministers govern Scotland in her name. Her Majesty's National Assembly governs Wales in her name. In principle, Her Majesty's First Minister and Deputy First Minister, who must be from different parties, govern Northern Ireland in her name. The Government of the United Kingdom has, thus far, failed to develop a mature relationship with Her Majesty's other governments. Between 1688 and 1707, the identical situation led to full-scale constitutional crisis in England and Scotland. The non-kingdom is not yet in a constitutional crisis again, but there are huge gaps in the constitutional settlement of devolution. One is the role of MPs from the territories in the House of Commons – the West Lothian Question (Dalyell 1977; Winetrobe 1995; Lodge, Russell and Gay 2004). A second is the government of England, as opposed to the government of the UK, by UK Ministers and the UK Parliament (Hazell 2004). The third is, of course, the unsustainable fiscal relationship between the United Kingdom and its territories.

Because the relationship is unsustainable, the non-kingdom is disunited, and likely to remain so. Northern Ireland is demanding Barnett reform. Wales soon will. The Scottish Executive is left stranded as the sole defender of Barnett, and all the opposition parties there are calling for 'fiscal federalism' (McLean 2004; MacDonald and Hallwood 2004). The classic Unionist nightmare and nationalist dream, of the break-up of Britain, is not currently very likely. The Scottish National Party and Plaid Cymru are both the main opposition parties in their national assemblies. But both did worse in the second (2003) elections there than in the first (1999). Proportional representation in both assemblies guarantees that they will not form majority administrations until they get something approaching 50 per cent of the vote. The threat to the Union is more insidious than that. It is that the distributive politics of devolution, that have been a private game for a tiny community of people in the UK government and the Territories, have opened up to be a game anyone can play. No player is satisfied with the result. The three Territories all dislike Barnett, albeit for opposite reasons (Scotland because the 'squeeze' is too harsh). The English regions all think they get a raw deal and blame it on Barnett. The pedantic and correct response that grant distribution within England is nothing to do with Barnett will not stop the complaints. They will increase with any self-government that the regions of England get. And the English regime of local taxation and grant distribution is under severe strain. It is neither equitable nor efficient. That might not matter in itself, but government is squeezed between Council Tax protesters and the coming nightmare of Council Tax revaluation in 2007. The last revaluation led to the Poll Tax. The one before that led to the Layfield Report. Perhaps the next one will produce a defensible regime for taxing and spending around the UK, probably overseen by a Grants Commission on the Australian model. If and when it does, the fiscal crisis of the United Kingdom will be resolved.

Notes

Chapter 1

1 The labelling of the functions of government changed substantially in 2004, in order to align the UK with internationally accepted classifications of the functions of Government (see HM Treasury 2004a). Most data reported in this book comes from pre-2004 sources, so the old category names are used here. The category contents have changed less than their names.

Chapter 2

1 Andrew Fletcher, the leading intellectual figure in the last Scots parliament, had argued in favour of a Scottish land tax, in order to place the government of Scotland on a firmer fiscal footing (see Robertson 1997: 41), although this would have been contingent on greater autonomy over how the finances raised would be spent.
2 Scotland was not fully incorporated in the accounting system of the England and Wales government. O'Brien (1988: 3) notes that: 'The collection of taxes in Scotland remained problematical for all departments concerned with the king's revenue, throughout the period 1707–1815'. In 1752 the Lord Chancellor lamented that 'some method should be taken to make Scotland pay the taxes but could any ministry hit upon that method?' (q. O'Brien 1988: 5).

Chapter 3

1 Quotations from Gladstone's Diary and letters are given by date, rather than by page reference. All those used in this chapter are from Matthew (1990).
2 Mostly, the Diary is a bare catalogue of church services attended, hours spent in the Commons, books read, people met, train journeys undertaken, and letters written. Only on 29 December each year does it normally break out into (usually rather morbid) speculation, on Gladstone's birthday.
3 Respectively: Catholic civil rights ('emancipation') in Ireland; a grant to the Catholic seminary at Maynooth, Co. Kildare; the Repeal of the Corn Laws; and the Second Reform Act. Typically, Gladstone does not spell it out.
4 Sources for these estimates: Population 1801: Mitchell 1962, tables Population and Vital Statistics 1–2 (Ireland – nearest year available is 1791). Population 1886: Mitchell 1962, table Population and Vital Statistics 3. Revenue 1801, and proposed contribution 1886: Gladstone's speech on the First Reading, *Hansard* 08.04.86.
5 *The Times* was not sceptical enough. Reducing pensionable age from 65 to 60 would cost *more* than twice as much as reducing it from 70 to 65. All

those who survived to 65 would have previously survived to 60; and some people would survive to 60 but not live to 65.

6 After Stanford's only child, Leland Stanford Jr, died of typhoid in Italy after eating an infected ice-cream, his grief-stricken parents endowed Stanford (full title Leland Stanford Junior) University. So some of their windfall gains were recycled for the public good in the end.

Chapter 4

1 All figures in this paragraph calculated from Butler and Pinto-Duschinsky 1971, Appendix I. Swing measured as conventional 'Butler' swing: the mean of the winning party's gain in vote share and the incumbent's loss in vote share.

2 Roughly speaking, a service administered by the Scottish, Welsh or Northern Ireland Offices, 1979–99; a service provided by the Scottish Parliament, the National Assembly for Wales, or the Northern Ireland Assembly since 1999.

3 Because in the long run the successive increments come to dominate the original assignment. For the mathematics, see Bell (2001).

Chapter 5

1 A search for the string 'barnett formula' on UK newspapers in the Lexis/Nexis Professional database yielded the results shown in Table 5.2. Refining the search to 'iniquitous barnett formula' yields 24 hits for the period from 06.03.1999 to 03.08.2004. Of the 24, one each emanate from the *Guardian, Daily Telegraph*, and *Northern Echo* (Darlington); and 21 from the *Journal* (Newcastle upon Tyne).

2 In the 1994–99 and 2000–06 EU Framework Programmes for the European Regional Development Fund, the criterion for assisted status was that an area must have less than 75 per cent of the mean GDP per head of the European Union. This rule gives Member States two perverse incentives. The first is to lump together their poorest regions and claim the resulting patchwork as a 'region'. EU rules are supposed to prevent this by insisting that regions qualifying for regional aid must be contiguous. The assisted area West Wales & the Valleys breaches this rule, because it is split by the estuary of the river Dyfi. The lowest bridge over the Dyfi is in the county of Powys, which is not part of West Wales & the Valleys. The National Assembly (and before it the Welsh Office) seems to have got away with this breach, perhaps because (as Lord Salisbury once said) of the use of maps on too small a scale by EU officials. If ever rumbled, they could either add Powys to the assisted area or get the EU to pay for a new bridge over the Dyfi.

The second, and obviously related, perversity is that governments have an incentive to make some of their regions appear as poor as possible, which is not what governments should be doing. These particular perverities will disappear after 2006, as the accession of new Member States means that no part of the UK will be able to claim to have less than 75 per cent of mean EU GDP per head, however ingeniously its boundaries are drawn. But the general objection applies more widely to redistributive spatial policies.

3 The most active appear to be *The Scotsman* (Edinburgh); *Herald* (Glasgow); *Western Mail* (Cardiff); *Irish News* (Belfast); *Journal; Northern Echo;* and *Western Morning News* (Plymouth).

Chapter 6

1 That is, expenditure flowing from the department itself, rather than by block grant to local education authorities.
2 This account of the foundation of the NHS is compiled from standard sources including Eckstein (1959, 1960); Abel-Smith (1964: 'stuffed their mouths with gold' at p. 480); Pater (1981); Campbell (1987); Klein (1989).
3 One of our recommendations, which Ministers have accepted, was that in future all Departments should use the standard hierarchy of regional boundaries in England.

Chapter 7

1 It is odd (or is it?) that the two most distinguished experts in local government finance of their era, both actually serving Cabinet ministers, should equally have failed to carry the official committees on the subject of which they were members – Goschen in 1870 and Balfour of Burleigh in 1901.
2 '[T]he great majority of the functions of the old "state power" have become so simplified and can be reduced to such exceedingly simple operations of registration, filing and checking that they can be easily performed by any literate person [and] for ordinary "workmen's wages"'. Lenin 1917/1969, pp. 41 (source of quotation) and 92.
3 *Left* and *right* should not be over-interpreted. Land tax is not inherently a left-wing cause, nor is charging for beneficial services inherently a right-wing one. But the labels are correct for the politicians who have taken these two positions in the UK.
4 However Kay and King (1990, p. 139) point out that 'progressivity is best viewed as a characteristic of the tax system as a whole, rather than as a property of each individual element of it'. But even they describe the administrative problems of making poll tax work as 'somewhere between the formidable and the overwhelming' (p. 138).
5 The PESA headings *Trade, industry, energy, and employment*, and *Culture, media and sport*, which are largely spent directly by the regional arms of the UK Government, are not discussed in detail below. Between them they account for only 7.5 per cent of spending per head on 'devolved' services.
6 Westminster and Wandsworth; Kent and Lincolnshire; Solihull and Trafford.
7 A civil servant responsible for setting grant in the mid-1980s described his task to a colleague as 'getting a formula that benefited London councils that began with W and were next to the river'.
8 In this book 'billion' is used in the American sense to mean 10^9, i.e. 1000 million.

9 Estimate of the Director of Finance, Wigan Metropolitan Borough Council. In 2003 Wigan had employees domiciled in Wales and (more surprisingly) Scotland on its payroll.
10 CIPFA assumes that English local authority LIT would be chargeable on all bands of income.
11 Because of protests led by senior citizens against sharp Council Tax increases in Devon in 2003.
12 So named because the enabling statute is the Town & Country Planning Act 1990, s. 106.

Chapter 8

1 Why Canada and Australia rather than examples nearer to the UK and inside the EU, such as Belgium, Spain, and Germany – or the oldest federation of all, namely Switzerland? One answer is that Canada and Australia have given rise to extensive academic analysis in English, more easily accessible to Anglophone policymakers than most analysis of fiscal federalism in EU member states. Another is that no EU model contains particularly useful lessons for the UK. That, at any rate, was the view of their national experts in a pair of seminars (one private, one public) organised by the ESRC Devolution Programme in January 2002 and attended by UK policy makers and academics. I share that view.
2 A regression equation has the form $Y = \alpha X_1 + \beta X_2 + \ldots + \omega X_n + \varepsilon$, where Y is the vector (list) of cost adjustments for each local authority, each X is one predictor weighted by its corresponding Greek letter ('coefficient') and e is an error term, which would be zero in this case.
3 The inverse GDP formulae in Tables 8.2 and 8.3 are calculated as follows. Let:
   E = Identifiable total managed expenditure per head on 'devolved' services
   G = UK GDP per head
   e_i = managed expenditure per head on 'devolved' services, 1999–2000, region i
   $\hat{e}_i$ = managed expenditure per head on 'devolved' services, 1999–2000, region i, applying inverse GDP multiplier
   g_i = GDP per head, region i
   Multiplier equation for all i: $\hat{e}_i = \dfrac{EG}{g_i}$
   Residuals for all $i = e_i - \hat{e}_i$
4 The GDP deflator used here is intended as a robust regional correction, which is not based on local authority data or existing (or theoretical) resource allocation.

Chapter 10

1 The British North America Act was an Act of the UK Parliament. In Canada it was renamed in 1982 as the Constitution Act 1867.
2 The numbers here differ from those in the source because we assign the equalisation component of CHST (i.e. the difference between the cash

transferred and an equal per capita transfer of tax) to equalisation rather than to CHST.

Chapter 11

1 Community charge' was the Conservative government's preferred title for the poll tax. This was partly a matter of spin, as *community charge* sounds fair and *poll tax* sounds unfair; partly an intellectual reflection of the 'beneficial tax' arguments of Foster *et al.* 1980. However, when the government statisticians responsible for compiling cost-of-living indices started to say that if it was a charge, it should go into the Retail Price Index, the term *community charge* began to disappear.

2 Scotland Act 1998 c. 46, s. 28 (7): *This section does not affect the power of the Parliament of the United Kingdom to make laws for Scotland.*

References

Abel-Smith, B. (1964) *The Hospitals, 1800–1948: a study in social administration in England and Wales* (London: Heinemann).

Acheson, D. (1998) *Independent Inquiry into Inequalities of Health* (London: TSO).

Audit Commission (1993) *Passing the Bucks* (London: HMSO).

Baldwin, T. (2004) 'Ministers can't keep their hands off local services', *The Times*, 2 July 2004.

Baran, D. and O'Donoghue, J. (2002) 'Price Levels in 2000 for London and the regions compared with the national average', *Economic Trends*, January (No. 578).

Barker, K. (2003) *Review of Housing Supply: securing our future housing needs. Interim Report – Analysis* (London: HM Treasury).

Barnett, J. (2001) Speech in House of Lords introducing motion to call attention to the case for a review of the Barnett formula. 7 November 2001, available at http://www.publications.parliament.uk/pa/ld200102/ldhansrd/vo011107/text /11107–06.htm – 11107–06_head1.

Beckett, J.C. (1966) *The Making of Modern Ireland 1603–1923* (London: Faber & Faber).

Bell, D. (2001) *The Barnett Formula*. University of Stirling, Department of Economics, available at http://www.stir.ac.uk/Departments/Management/ Economics/staff/dnfb1/Barnett Formula.pdf.

Bell, D. and Christie, A. (2001) 'Finance – The Barnett formula: Nobody's child?' in A. Trench ed., *The State of the Nations 2001: the second year of devolution in the United Kingdom* (Thorverton: Imprint Academic), 135–51.

Besley, T., Preston, I. and Ridge, M. (1997) 'Fiscal anarchy in the UK: modelling poll tax non-compliance', *Journal of Public Economics* 64 (2), 137–52.

Black, D. *et al.* (1982) in P. Townsend and N. Davidson ed., *Inequalities in Health: the Black Report* (Harmondsworth: Penguin).

Blais, A., Gidengil, E., Nadeau, R. and Nevitte, N. (2002) *Anatomy of a Liberal Victory: making sense of the vote in the 2000 Canadian election* (Peterborough, Ont: Broadview Press).

British America Act (1867) c. 3.

Bolton, G.C. (1966) *The passing of the Irish Act of Union: a study in parliamentary politics* (London: Oxford University Press).

Bradley, A.W. and Christie, D.J. (1979) *The Scotland Act of 1978* (Edinburgh: W. Green & Son).

Braithwaite, W.J. (1957) *Lloyd George's Ambulance Wagon: the memoirs of W.J. Braithwaite CB*. ed. H. Bunbury and R. Titmuss (London: Methuen).

Brennan, G. and Pincus, J. (2002) 'Fiscal Equalisation Revisited: institutional design and reform', paper to Conference of Australian Economists, Adelaide, October.

Brewer, J. (1989) *The Sinews of Power: war, money and the English state, 1688–1783* (London: Unwin Hyman).

Brittan, S. (1977) *The Economic Consequences of Democracy* (London: Temple Smith).

Brown, G. (1981) *The Labour Party and Political change in Scotland 1918–1929: the politics of five elections* (Edinburgh University Ph.D thesis).

Brown, G. (2003) 'State and Market: towards a public interest test', *Political Quarterly* 74(3), 266–84.

Butler, D.E. *et al.* (various) *The British General Election of xxxx.* Published in the same year as each General Election, or the following year (London: Macmillan). Including in particular:

Butler, D.E. and Pinto-Duschinsky, M. (1971) *The British General Election of 1970.* (London: Macmillan).

Butler, D.E. and Kavanagh, D. (1988) *The British General Election of 1987* (London: Macmillan).

Butler, D.E., Adonis, A. and Travers, T. (1994) *Failure in British government: the politics of the poll tax* (Oxford: Oxford University Press).

Cameron, G., McLean, I. and Wlezien, C. (2004) 'Public Expenditure in the English Regions: Measurement Problems and (Partial) Solutions', *Political Quarterly* 75 (2), 121–31.

Cameron, G. and Muellbauer, J. (2000) 'Earnings biases in the UK regional accounts: some economic policy and research implications', *Economic Journal* 110, 412–29.

Campbell, J. (1987) *Nye Bevan and the Mirage of British Socialism* (London: Weidenfeld & Nicolson).

Canadian High Commission (2002) 'Memorandum by the Canadian High Commission', in House of Lords, Select Committee on the Constitution, *Devolution: inter-institutional arrangements in the United Kingdom: evidence complete to 10 July 2002*, HL 147, pp. 400–06 (London: TSO).

Carr-Hill, R., Rice, N. and Smith, P. (1999), 'The determinants of expenditure on children's personal social services', *British Journal of Social Work*, 29, 679–706.

Churchill, W. (1906) *Lord Randolph Churchill*, 2 vols (London: Macmillan).

Churchill, W. (1929) *The World Crisis. Vol. 5: The Aftermath* (London: Thornton Butterworth).

CIPFA (1996) *Councillors' guide to local government finance, 1996 edition* (London: CIPFA).

Commonwealth Grants Commission (1983) *Equality in Diversity: Fifty Years of the Commonwealth Grants Commission* (Canberra: Commonwealth Grants Commission).

Commonwealth Grants Commission (2001) *The Relativities: what assessments are important?* Discussion Paper CGC2001/13, available at www.cgc.gov.au.

Commonwealth Grants Commission (2002a) *Report on State Revenue Sharing Relativities: 2002 Update* (Canberra: Commonwealth Grants Commission), available at www.cgc.gov.au.

Commonwealth Grants Commission (2002b) *Guidelines for Implementing Horizontal Fiscal Equalisation.* Information Paper CGC2002/1, available at www.cgc.gov.au.

Conference Board of Canada (2002) *Vertical Fiscal Imbalance July 2002: fiscal prospects for the federal and provincial/territorial governments* (Ottawa: Conference Board).

Cornish Guardian (2003) 'Minister Raps Police Authority', November 27, p. 31.

Court, C. (2002) Submission to Review of Commonwealth-State Funding, available at www.reviewcommstatefunding.com.au.

Crossman, R.H.S. (1977) *The Diaries of a Cabinet Minister vol. 3: secretary of state for social services 1968–1970* (London: Hamish Hamilton and Jonathan Cape).

Cullen, L.M. (1968) *Anglo-Irish trade 1660–1800* (Manchester: Manchester University Press).

Curtice, J. (2003) 'Devolution meets the voters: the prospects for 2003' in R. Hazell ed., *The State of the Nations 2003* (Exeter: Imprint Academic), pp. 263–83.

Dalyell, T. (1977) *Devolution: the end of Britain?* (London: Jonathan Cape).

Davies, B. (1968) *Social Needs and Resources in Local Services: a study of variations in standards of provision of personal social services between local authority areas* (London: Michael Joseph).

Deane, P. and Cole, W.A. (1967) *British Economic Growth 1688–1959*, 2nd ed. (Cambridge: Cambridge University Press).

Department of the Environment, Transport, & the Regions (2000) *Modernising Local Government Finance: a green paper* (London: HMSO).

Department of Finance Canada (2003) *The Fiscal Balance in Canada: The facts*, available at http://www.fin.gc.ca/factsheets/fbcfacts5_e.html.

Department of Health and Social Security (1976) *Sharing Resources for Health in England: report of the resources allocation working party* (London: HMSO).

Department of Transport, Local Government & the Regions (2001) *Strong Local Leadership – Quality Public Services*, Cm 5237.

Department of Transport, Local Government & the Regions (2002) *Your Region, Your Choice: revitalising the English regions*, Cm 5511, available at http://www.odpm.gov.uk/stellent/groups/odpm_regions/documents/pdf/odpm_regions_pdf_607900.pdf.

Dickson, P.G.M. (1967) *The Financial Revolution in England: A Study in the development of public credit 1688–1756* (London: Macmillan).

Dixon, P., Picton, M. and Rimmer, M. (2002) 'Effects of changes in Commonwealth grants to the States: an applied general equilibrium analysis' (Centre of Policy Studies, Monash University), available at www.reviewcommstatefunding.com.au/library/CoPS_EfficiencyPaper.pdf.

Duverger, M. (1954) *Political Parties* translated by B. and R. North (London: Methuen).

Eckstein, H. (1959) *The English Health Service: its origins, structure, and achievements* (Cambridge, MA: Harvard University Press).

Eckstein, H. (1960) *Pressure Group Politics: the case of the British Medical Association* (London: Allen & Unwin).

Edmonds, Timothy (2001) *The Barnett Formula*, House of Commons Library Research Paper 01/108, available at http://www.parliament.uk/commons/lib/research/rp2001/rp01–108.pdf.

Elliott, R., McDonald, D. and MacIver, R. (1996) *Local Government Finance: Review of the area cost adjustment* (Aberdeen: University of Aberdeen on behalf of Department of the Environment).

Ellis, A.M. (1979) *Welsh and Breton nationalism: a comparison* (University College, Oxford: PPE thesis).

Feehan, J. (2002) 'Equality and the Provinces' Natural Resource Revenues: Partial Equalization can Work Better', TS, (St John's: Memorial University of Newfoundland).

Foster, C.D., Jackman, R. A. and Perlman, M. (1980) *Local Government Finance in a Unitary State* (London: Allen & Unwin).

Garnaut, R. and FitzGerald, V. (2001) *Background Paper: a review of the allocation of Commonwealth Grants to the States and Territories* (Melbourne: Review of Commonwealth-State Funding), available at www.reviewcommstatefunding.com.au.

Garnaut, R. and FitzGerald, V. (2002) *Review of Commonwealth-State Funding: final report* (Melbourne: Review of Commonwealth-State Funding), available at www.reviewcommstatefunding.com.au.

George, H. (1879/[1911]) *Progress and Poverty*, Everyman Edition (London: J.M. Dent).

Gibson, J. (1998) 'Political manipulation or feedback in English local authorities' standard spending assessments? the case of the abolition of the Inner London Education Authority', *Public Administration* 76, 629–647.

Gibson, J. (1999) 'Standard Spending Assessments: The "Thorough Investigation" – Issues and Potential Improvements' *Local Governance* 25 (1), 25–52.

Glennerster, H., Hills, J., Travers, T. and Hendry, R. (2000) *Paying for Health, Education and Housing: how does the centre pull the purse strings?* (Oxford: Oxford University Press).

Goschen, G.J. (1872) *Reports and Speeches on Local Taxation* (London: Macmillan).

Goschen, G.J. (Viscount) (1905) *Essays and Addresses on Economic Questions* (London: Edward Arnold).

Government of Ireland Bill (1886) cl. 14; in Great Britain, Parliamentary Papers 1886 II, 465–88.

Great Britain, Parliamentary Papers 1886 II, 465–88.

Government of Ireland Act (1920) c. 67.

Grant, J.P. (ed.) (1976) *Independence and Devolution: the legal implications for Scotland.* (Edinburgh: W. Green & Son).

Great Britain, *Parliamentary Papers.* Cited by session, volume, and page range.

Greer, S. (2003) 'Health: how far can Wales diverge from England?' in J. Osmond ed., *Second term Challenge: can the Welsh Assembly Government hold its course?* (Cardiff: IWA), pp. 52–63.

Greer, S. (2004) *Territorial Politics and Health Policy: UK Health Policy in Comparative Perspective* (Manchester: Manchester University Press).

Guthrie, R. and McLean, I. (1978) 'Another part of the periphery: reactions to devolution in an English Development Area' *Parliamentary Affairs* 31, 190–200.

Hall, F.G. (1949) *History of the Bank of Ireland* (Dublin: Hodges, Figgis).

Hansard (Parliamentary Debates) Third, Fourth, Fifth, and Sixth Series. Cited by date of speech quoted.

Harding, A. *et al.* (2002) 'The Distributional Impact of Selected Commonwealth Outlays and Taxes' (Canberra: National Centre for Social and Economic Modelling), available at www.reviewcommstatefunding.com.au/library/NATSEM_EquityPaper.pdf.

Harris, J. (1997) *William Beveridge: a biography*, 2nd ed. (Oxford: Clarendon Press).

Hazell, R. (2004) 'Conclusion: The unfinished business of devolution' in A. Trench ed., *Has Devolution Made a Difference? The state of the nations 2004* (Exeter: Imprint Academic), pp. 255–75.

Heald, D. (1980) *Territorial Equity and Public Finances: concepts and confusion,* University of Strathclyde, Centre for the Study of Public Policy, Studies in Public Policy #75.

Heald, D. (2001) *Financing UK Devolution in Practice,* Aberdeen Papers in Accountancy, Finance & Management, Working Paper 01–8.

Heald, D. and Geaughan, N. (1996) 'Financing a Scottish Parliament' in
    S. Tindale ed., *The State and the Nations: the politics of devolution* (London:
    IPPR).
Heald, D. and Short, J. (2002) 'The regional dimension of public expenditure in
    England', *Regional Studies* 36: 743–55.
Heclo, Hugh and Wildavsky, Aaron B. (1974) *The Private Government of Public
    Money: community and policy inside British politics* (London: Macmillan).
HM Treasury (1979) *Needs Assessment Study – Report* (London: HMSO).
HM Treasury (2004a) *Funding the Scottish Parliament National Assembly for Wales
    and Northern Ireland Assembly: a statement of funding policy*, 4th ed. July, avail-
    able at http://www.hm-treasury.gov.uk/media//0861C/Funding_the_Scottish_
    Parliament_National_Assembly_for_Wales(296kb).pdf.
HM Treasury (2004b) *Public Expenditure Statistical Analyses 2004* Cm 6201
    (London: HMSO).
HM Treasury (2004c) *2004 Spending Review: new public spending plans 2005–2008*,
    Cm 6237 (London: HMSO), available at http://www.hm-treasury.gov.uk/
    spending_review/spend_sr04/report/spend_sr04_repindex.cfm.
HM Treasury (2004d) *2004 Spending Review: public service agreements 2005–2008*,
    Cm 6238 (London: HMSO).
Hetherington, P. (2001) 'Scots and Welsh face subsidy axe', *The Guardian*,
    24 April.
House of Commons, Treasury Committee (1997) *The Barnett Formula*, Second
    Report, session 1997–98, HC 341 (London: HMSO).
House of Commons Select Committee (2004) *Local Government Revenue: ninth
    report of session 2003–04*, vol. 1, Report HC 402–I.
House of Lords, Select Committee on the Constitution (2002) *Devolution: inter-
    institutional relations in the United Kingdom: Evidence complete to 10 July 2002*,
    HL 197 (London: HMSO).
Jenkins, R. (1968) *Mr Balfour's Poodle*, 2nd ed (London: Collins).
Jenkins, R. (1995) *Gladstone* (London: Macmillan).
John, P. and Ward, H. (2001), 'Political manipulation in a majoritarian democ-
    racy: central government target of public funds to English subnational gov-
    ernment, in space and across time', *British Journal of Politics and International
    Relations* 3 (3), 308–39.
Johnston, T. (1952) *Memories* (London: Collins).
Johnston, E. (1963) *Great Britain and Ireland 1760–1800: a study in political
    administration* (Edinburgh: Published for the University Court of the
    University of St. Andrews [by] Oliver & Boyd).
Jones, W.D. (2001) '"Bold Adventurers" A Quantitative Analysis of the Darien
    Subscription List (1696)', *Scottish Economic and Social History*, 21 (1), 22–42.
Kay, J.A. and King, M. (1990) *The British Tax System*, 5th ed. (Oxford: Oxford
    University Press).
Keating, M. and Bleiman, D. (1979) *Labour and Scottish Nationalism* (London:
    Macmillan).
Kellas, J. (2003) 'After the Declaration of Perth: all change?' paper for British
    Academy/Royal Society of Edinburgh conference, 'Anglo-Scottish Relations
    since 1900', Edinburgh, November.
Kilbrandon (1973): *see* Royal Commission on the Constitution.
Klein, R. (1989) *The Politics of the NHS*, 2nd ed. (London: Longman).

Klein, R. (2004) 'The first wave of NHS foundation trusts: low turnout in elections sends a warning signal', *British Medical Journal* 328:1332 (5 June).

Layfield, F. (1976) (chairman) *Report of the Committee of Inquiry into Local Government Finance*, Cmnd 6453 (London: HMSO for the Department of the Environment).

Lenin, V.I. (1917/1969) *The State and Revolution: the Marxist theory of the state and the tasks of the proletariat in the revolution* (Moscow: Progress Publishers).

Lightfoot, E. (2004) 'Labour promises school choice for all', *Daily Telegraph*, 9 July.

Linford, P. (2002) 'Prescott hints at ditching Barnett', *The Journal* (Newcastle upon Tyne), 4 July, p. 2.

Lodge, G., Russell, M. and Gay, O. (2004) 'The Impact of Devolution on Westminster. If not now, when?' in A. Trench ed., *Has Devolution Made a Difference? The state of the nations 2004* (Exeter: Imprint Academic), pp. 193–216.

MacDonald, R. and Hallwood, P. (2004) *The Economic Case for Fiscal Federalism in Scotland* (Glasgow: Fraser of Allander Institute: The Allander Series).

Macinnes, A.I (1990) 'Influencing the Vote: The Scottish Estates and the Treaty of Union, 1706–1707', *History Microcomputer Review*, pp. 11–25.

Major, J. (2000) *John Major: the autobiography*, 2nd edn (London: HarperCollins).

McCavery, T. (2000) 'Politics, public finance and the British–Irish Act of Union of 1801', *Royal Historical Society Transactions*, 6: 10 (December), pp. 353–375.

McLean, I. (1970) 'The rise and fall of the Scottish National Party', *Political Studies*, 17: 357–72.

McLean, I. (1995) 'Are Scotland and Wales over-represented in the House of Commons?' *Political Quarterly*, 66: 250–68.

McLean, I. (1998) 'The Semi-Detached Election – Scotland' in A. King ed., *New Labour Triumphs: Britain at the polls* (Chatham, NJ: Chatham House Publishers), pp. 145–75.

McLean, I. (1999) *The Legend of Red Clydeside*, 2nd ed. (Edinburgh: John Donald).

McLean, I. (2000) 'A fiscal constitution for the UK' in S. Chen and T. Wright ed., *The English Question* (London: Fabian Society), pp. 80–95.

McLean, I. (2001a) 'Scotland: towards Quebec – or Slovakia?', *Regional Studies* 35, 637–44.

McLean, I. (2001b), *Rational Choice and British Politics: an analysis of rhetoric and manipulation from Peel to Blair* (Oxford: Oxford University Press).

McLean, I. (2001c) 'The National Question' in A. Seldon ed., *The Blair Effect: the Blair government 1997–2001* (London: Little Brown), pp. 429–47.

McLean, I. (2002) 'Fiscal federalism in Australia', Nuffield College Working Papers in Politics, 2002–W28, available at http://www.nuff.ox.ac.uk/Politics/papers/2002/w28/Fiscal%20Federalism%20in%20Australia.pdf.

McLean, I. (2003) 'Devolution bites', *Prospect*, March.

McLean, I. (2005) 'Scotland after Barnett' in G. Hassan ed., *Scotland 2020* (London: Demos), pp. 000–00.

McLean, I. et al. (2003) *Identifying the flow of domestic and European expenditure in the English regions* (Oxford: Nuffield College and London: ODPM), available at http://www.nuff.ox.ac.uk/projects/odpm/Identifyingtheflow.pdf and (with the Government response) at http://www.local.odpm.gov.uk/research/regeco.htm.

McLean, I. and Johnes, M. (2000) *Aberfan: government and disasters* (Cardiff: Welsh Academic Press).

McLean, I. and McMillan, A. (2003a) 'The distribution of public expenditure across the UK regions', *Fiscal Studies*, 24:1, 45–71.

McLean, I. and McMillan, A. (2003b) *New Localism, New Finance* (London: New Local Government Network).

McLean, I. and McMillan, A. (2005) *State of the Union* (Oxford: Oxford University Press).

McLean, I. and Smith, J. (1992) 'The UK poll tax and the electoral register: unintended consequences?', Warwick University, Economic Research Papers, no. 398.

McLean I. and Smith, J. (1997) 'The 1381 Peasants' Revolt: lessons for the 1990s?' *Journal of European Economic History* 26, 137–43.

Matthew, H.C.G. (ed.) (1990) *The Gladstone Diaries*, vol. XI.: 1883–1886 (Oxford: Clarendon Press).

Matthew, H.C.G. (1999) *Gladstone 1809–1898* (Oxford: Oxford University Press).

Midwinter, A. (2000) 'The Barnett Formula: why replacing it would be a mistake', *New Economy* 7(2), 72–5.

Midwinter A. (2002) 'Territorial resource allocation in the UK: A rejoinder on needs assessment', *Regional Studies* 36 (5), 563–567.

Mitchell, B.R. (1962) *Abstract of British Historical Statistics* (Cambridge: Cambridge University Press).

Mitchell, J. (2002) 'The principles and policies of devolved financial arrangements I: the United Kingdom', paper to ESRC Conference on Comparative Fiscal Federalism, Birmingham, January.

Mitchell, J. (2003) *Governing Scotland: the invention of administrative devolution* (Basingstoke: Palgrave).

Mitchell, J. (2004a) 'Financing Devolution: Stormont and the welfare state', paper to ESRC Devolution conference, Strathclyde, January.

Mitchell, J. (2004b) 'Scotland: Expectations, Policy Types and Devolution' in A. Trench ed., *Has Devolution Made a Difference? The State of the Nations 2004* (Exeter: Imprint Academic), pp. 11–41.

Mitchell, J. and Nelson, F. (2002) 'The Barnett Formula and the 2001 General Election', *British Elections and Parties Review* 12, 171–89.

Morrison, H. (Lord) (1960) *Herbert Morrison: an autobiography* (London: Odhams Press).

Muellbauer, J. (2004) 'Property and Land, Taxation and the Economy after the Barker Review', unpublished paper available at http://hicks.nuff.ox.ac.uk/users/cameron/outlook/papers/ejjuly13full.pdf.

Mueller, D.C. (2003) *Public Choice III* (Cambridge: Cambridge University Press).

Murray, B.K. (1980) *The People's Budget 1909/10: Lloyd George and Liberal politics* (Oxford: Clarendon Press).

Murray, B.K. (1987) 'Class, Politics, and Public Finance in Edwardian Britain', inaugural lecture, University of the Witwatersrand (Johannesburg: Witwatersrand University Press).

Neal, L. (1990) *The Rise of Financial Capitalism: international capital markets in the age of reason* (Cambridge: Cambridge University Press).

North, D.C. and Weingast, B.R. (1989) 'Constitutions and Commitment – the Evolution of Institutions governing Public Choice in 17th-Century England', *Journal of Economic History* 49 (4), 803–832.

Northern Region Strategy Team (1976) *Public Expenditure in the Northern Region and other British regions*, Technical Report No. 12 (Newcastle-upon-Tyne: NRST).

Oates, W.E. (1972) *Fiscal Federalism* (New York: Harcourt Brace Jovanovich).

O'Brien, Patrick, K. (1988) 'The political economy of British taxation, 1660–1815', *Economic History Review* (second series) 41(1), 1–32.

O'Connor, J. (1973) *The Fiscal Crisis of the State* (New York: St Martins Press).

Office of the Deputy Prime Minister (2002) *Consultation on the Local Government Finance Formula Grant Distribution*, available at http://www.local.dtlr.gov. uk/review/consult/.

Office of the Deputy Prime Minister (2004a) *Balance of Funding Review: Report* (London: ODPM), available at http://www.local.dtlr.gov.uk/finance/ balance.htm.

Office of the Deputy Prime Minister (2004b) *Amending Reports: local government finance reports 2003/04 and 2004/05*, available at http://www.local.dtlr.gov.uk/ finance/ssas.htm.

Office for National Statistics (2001) 'Workplace-based gross domestic product (GDP) at current basic prices' table, available at http://www.statistics.gov.uk/ StatBase/Expodata/Spreadsheets/D6051.xls.

Olson, Mancur (1982) *The Rise and Decline of Nations: economic growth, stagflation, and social rigidities* (New Haven, CT: Yale University Press).

Oswald, Andrew (2002) *London's Public Sector Workers Need to be Paid 50% More than Those in the North*, Presentation to House of Commons, March, available at http://www2.warwick.ac.uk/fac/soc/economics/staff/faculty/oswald/region- alpublicpaymarch2002.pdf.

Pater, J. (1981) *The Making of the National Health Service* (London: Kings Fund).

Péloquin, D. (2002) *Expenditure Need Assessment Under Australia's Equalisation Regime* (MS: Canberra).

Péloquin, D. (2003) 'Incentives for grant-maximization and other distortions of provincial and state policies: a comparison of equalization regimes in Canada and Australia' (TS: Canberra).

Péloquin, D. and Chong, A. (2002) 'A comparison of fiscal disparities and equal- isation regimes in selected federations', paper to Conference of Australian Economists, Adelaide, October.

Redlich, J. and Hirst, F.W. (1903) *Local Government in England*, 2 vols (London: Macmillan).

Ricardo, D. (1817) *On the Principles of Political Economy, and Taxation* (London: John Murray).

Riley, P.W.J. (1964) *The English Ministers and Scotland 1707–1727* (London: Athlone Press).

Riley, P.W.J. (1978) *The Union of England and Scotland: A study in Anglo-Scottish politics of the eighteenth century* (Manchester: Manchester University Press).

Robertson, J. (ed.) (1997) *Andrew Fletcher: Political Works* (Cambridge: Cambridge University Press).

Royal Commission on the Constitution (Chairman Kilbrandon) (1973) *Report*, Cmnd 5460 (London: HMSO).

Royal Commission on the Poor Laws (1909) *Report*; *Minority Report* (London: HMSO).

Russell, M. (2000) *Reforming the House of Lords: lessons from overseas* (Oxford: OUP).

Sampson, A. (1962) *Anatomy of Britain* (London: Hodder & Stoughton).

Saville, R. (1996) *Bank of Scotland: A history 1695–1995* (Edinburgh: Edinburgh University Press).

Schelling, T.C. (1984) *Choice and Consequence* (Cambridge, MA: Harvard University Press).

Scotland Act (1998) c. 46.

Scott, A.D. (1952) 'Federal Grants and Resource Allocation', *Journal of Political Economy* 60, 534–6.

Scott, W.R. (1911) *The Constitution and Finance of English, Scottish and Irish Joint-Stock Companies to 1720: Volume III Water Supply, Postal, Street-Lighting, Banking, Finance and Insurance Companies Also Statements Relating to the Crown Finances* (Cambridge: Cambridge University Press).

Scottish Constitutional Convention (1995) *Scotland's Parliament, Scotland's Right* (Edinburgh: Scottish Constitutional Convention).

Séguin, Y. (Chair) (2002) *A New Division of Canada's Financial Resources* (Québec: Commission sur le déséquilibre fiscal).

Shepherd, J. (2002) *George Lansbury: at the heart of Old Labour* (Oxford: Oxford University Press).

Smith, A. (1776/1976) *An Inquiry into the Nature and Causes of the Wealth of Nations*, 2 vols continuously paginated, ed. R.H. Campbell and A.S. Skinner (Oxford: Oxford University Press). Cited by section, subsection and sub-sub-section to facilitate reference to other editions.

Smith, P.C., Rice, N. and Carr-Hill, R. (2001) 'Capitation funding in the public sector', *Journal of the Royal Statistical Society A*, 164, Part 2, 217–257.

Stasavage, D. (2003) *Public Debt and the Birth of the Democratic State* (Cambridge: Cambridge University Press).

Statutes: all English, Scottish and UK Statutes are quoted from www.justis.com.

Tasman Economics (2002) Submission to Review of Commonwealth-State Funding, available at www.reviewcommstatefunding.com.au.

Tiebout, C. (1956) 'A pure theory of local expenditure' *Journal of Political Economy*, 64(5), 416–424.

The Times (1909) *The Report of the Poor Law Commission: reprinted from* The Times. (London: *The Times*).

Thomas, W.A. (1986) *The Stock Exchanges of Ireland* (Liverpool: Francis Cairns).

Travers, A. (2001) 'Local government' in A. Seldon, ed., *The Blair Effect: the Blair Government 1997–2001* (London: Little, Brown), pp. 117–37.

Tudor Hart, J. (1971) 'The Inverse Care Law', *The Lancet*, Volume 297, Issue 7696, 27 February 1971, 405–412.

Walker, G. (1988) *Thomas Johnston* (Manchester: Manchester University Press).

Ward, H. and John, P. (1999) 'Targeting benefits for electoral gain: constituency marginality and the distribution of grants to English local authorities', *Political Studies* 47(1), 32–52.

Warner, G. (2002) 'Barnett abolition: our fiscal Flodden', *Scotland on Sunday*, 7 July, p. 19.

Webb, B. (1982) *The Diary of Beatrice Webb*, ed. by N. and J. MacKenzie, 2 vols (London: Virago).

Webb, S. and B. (1963) *Statutory Authorities for Special Purposes*, new ed. by B. Keith-Lucas (London: Cass).

Wells, J. and Wills, D. (2000) 'Revolution, Restoration, and Debt Repudiation: The Jacobite Threat to England's Institutions and Economic Growth', *Journal of Economic History* 60(2), 418–41.

Whatley, C. (2001) *Bought and Sold for English gold? Explaining the Union of 1707*, 2nd ed. (East Linton: Tuckwell Press).

Winetrobe, B.K. (1995) *The West Lothian Question*, House of Commons Library Research Paper 95/58.

Wood, S. (2003) 'Foreword' in McLean, I. and McMillan, A., *New Localism, New Finance*. (London: New Local Government Network), p. 6.

Index